Judeo-Arabic Literature in Tunisia, 1850–1950

JUDEO-ARABIC LITERATURE IN TUNISIA, 1850–1950

YOSEF TOBI AND
TSIVIA TOBI

Wayne State University Press
Detroit

18 17 16 15 14 5 4 3 2 1

Library of Congress Control Number: 2014936567
ISBN 978-0-8143-2871-2 (hardcover) ISBN 978-0-8143-4046-2 (e-book)

Designed and typeset by Bryce Schimanski
Composed in Minion Pro and Scala Pro Sans

CONTENTS

Preface

The present volume contains studies on Judeo-Arabic literature in Tunisia as well as several texts that have been translated into English. All of the translated works, which are intended to represent different genres, are included in the Hebrew version of this volume, published in 2000. Two chapters, on the flowering of Judeo-Arabic literature in North Africa (Chapter 1) and on Judeo-Arabic theater in Tunisia (Chapter 7), were previously published in English in somewhat different versions. All the previously published chapters have been edited anew and were updated for the purpose of this book.

The printed production of Tunisian Judeo-Arabic literature is richer and more diversified than the literature published in any other Arabic-speaking country in modern time. This is due not only to the creative faculties of Tunisian Jews but also to two other decisive historical-cultural facts: the introduction of the press into Tunisia in the mid-nineteenth century and the French occupation of the country in 1881. As a result, the literature under discussion flourished during the hundred years from about 1850 to the mid-twentieth century, when it almost completely disappeared because of the increasing use of French by most Tunisian Jews. But unfortunately that supreme source of knowledge and research of Tunisian Jews is actually "out of area" for all scholars, save one or two, who deal with the Tunisian Jewish community, be it history, literature, language, sociology, folklore, or any other scholarly field.

My wife and I wish to acknowledge our heartfelt gratitude to the many people who helped us in collecting the material, in the labor of the research, and in preparing the book for print. Above all, our thanks go to the immigrants from Tunisia throughout Israel, from Beersheba in the south to Tiberias and Nahariya in the north, for the warm welcome they accorded us. They are too many to name here, but we cannot omit to mention the saintly Rabbi Abraham Ha-Cohen, of blessed memory, the erstwhile rabbi of Sfax and a resident of Jerusalem in his latter years; and the late folk poet Ghzāla Māzūz, who immigrated from Djerba and settled in Tiberias.

Special mention likewise goes to the booksellers in Jerusalem and Haifa who never failed to let us know of any new (old!) book in Judeo-Arabic that reached them and who treated us with kindness and friendship. Also deserving thanks is the late Robert Attal, a member of the Ben-Zvi Institute and the leading light in research on present-day Tunisian Jewry, to whom nothing of the Judeo-Arabic literature of this country is obscure. He treated us with real benevolence and kindness and did not spare any publication of his amazing collection of Tunisian Judeo-Arabic books.

Likewise, we must thank Pinḥas Cohen of Lod, Israel, the grandson through his mother of the greatest of the *ḥakhamim* of Djerba in the first half of the twentieth century, namely, Rabbi Moshe Khalfōn Ha-Cohen, one of the mainstays of the study of Hebrew and Zionism. He was ever willing to help us in the translation of Judeo-Arabic texts and in comprehending their subject matter. Finally, our thanks go to the National Library of Israel in Jerusalem, whose rich treasures afforded us enormous assistance, and especially to its librarians Zion Shorer and Esther Liebes.

In addition, we thank David Ben-Avraham, who prepared the English translation. Thanks should be given as well to Prof. Dan Ben-Amos of Penn University, who contacted Wayne State University Press on our behalf and cordially recommended the publishing of this work. We would like to express our sincere gratitude to the wonderful team at Wayne State University Press who were involved with the long process of preparing this work for publishing: Kathryn Peterson Wildfong, Kristin Harpster, and especially Mimi Braverman, who did a wonderful job editing the English version of the book. And last but not least, thanks should be given to the anonymous reviewers of the English manuscript, in particular one of them who meticulously read the whole manuscript and awarded us with scores of highly helpful comments which, so we believe, made it better.

We are very hopeful that this modest composition will be no more than one tier and the harbinger of many to follow in the research and publication of Judeo-Arabic literature from Tunisia. The subjects presented here are certainly many, and the need for their emendation, complementation, and expansion will soon become evident in light of the development of research in the field. Most things stated here are certainly not the last word, nor was our intention anything more than to open a window on a wide and rich world whose precincts only few have entered. This literature, alongside the rabbinic literature of the Jews of Tunisia, constitutes a resource of extreme value whose significance is by no means less than that of other sources, such as the various kinds of documentary archives. May scholars of Tunisian Jewry absorb this into their consciousness: this will be our reward.

1

The Flowering of Judeo-Arabic Literature in North Africa

Background for the Development of Judeo-Arabic Literature in Modern Time

Judeo-Arabic literature first appeared no later than the sixth century CE, with the poetry of the Jews of the Ḥijāz (Al-Hejaz, located in present-day Saudi Arabia), the most famous poet being Samuel ben 'Adaya. This literature blossomed after most countries where Jews dwelled were conquered by Arab Muslim tribes; Arabic became the language of speech and of intellectual and literary writing of the members of those Jewish communities. Sa'adia Gaon (882–942) greatly encouraged writing in Arabic in all fields of intellectual effort, but not in poetry and belles lettres in general. However, the Jews of the Middle Ages did not write their Arabic works in Arabic script or on the high level that characterized Muslim writers but in Hebrew script and in a linguistic register generally known as Middle Arabic. In its Jewish context this language is known as Judeo-Arabic, and its writings are called Judeo-Arabic literature.[1]

In the fourteenth century a shift began toward composition in the dialectal Arabic languages, in which, for example, the Egyptian dialect differs from the North African and the Iraqi dialect differs from the Yemeni. This was in contrast to Middle Judeo-Arabic, which was common to all the Jewish communities, just as classical Arabic was, and still is, common to all the Arab lands. This stage of linguistic change was associated with literary change too, namely, expansion of the range of writing in Arabic to cover belles lettres. As intimated, Judeo-Arabic writing in the Middle Ages encompassed all the academic and religious disciplines except belles lettres, which was written in Hebrew. Just a handful of poems or *maqāmāt* (by Judah Alḥarīzī) were written in Judeo-Arabic. This is not the place to consider the reasons for this.[2] In the fourteenth century, then, we observe Jewish authors beginning to write belles lettres in Arabic. Yet this was not classical Arabic or even the Middle Judeo-Arabic written in Hebrew script, but dialectal Arabic; each author wrote according to his place of residence and the Judeo-Arabic dialect in which he was fluent. Naturally, the script was Hebrew.

For centuries this literature remained as manuscripts, apparently because a Hebrew press in the countries of Islam did not exist before the mid-nineteenth century (the few years in which Hebrew presses existed in Fes in Morocco, Cairo, and Safed in the sixteenth century have no bearing on our subject). But this is not enough to explain the fact that Judeo-Arabic literature was not printed until the mid-nineteenth century; many Jewish sages of the East sent their manuscripts to Jewish printing houses in Europe, in such cities as Venice, Constantinople, Amsterdam, and Livorno. However, from the middle of the nineteenth century to approximately the middle of the twentieth century, when the Jewish communities in the countries of Islam had almost ceased to exist, thousands of books were printed in Judeo-Arabic. The main centers of printing were in Livorno in Italy; Fes and Casablanca in Morocco; Algiers and Oran in Algeria; Tunis, Sousse, and Djerba in Tunisia; Tripoli in Libya; Cairo and Alexandria in Egypt; Jerusalem; Aleppo in Syria; Baghdad in Iraq; Calcutta and Bombay in India; and Aden in southern Yemen.

We should emphasize that this discussion is not intended to include Arabic literature written and published by Jewish authors in the classical

Arabic register and in Arabic script. This literature is rightly perceived as a separate part, at times even the most important part, of modern Arabic literature in general. It has been recorded and researched by Shmuel Moreh and by Samīr Naqqāsh, the Israeli writer of Iraqi origin who writes in Arabic, and it is connected only loosely to Judaism and to modern Arabic literature.[3] We do not mean that Arabic literature by Jewish authors should not be included in the domain of Jewish literature, but for a variety of reasons, some of which will be clarified later, we have excluded it from consideration here.

In general, knowledge of Judeo-Arabic literature in the nineteenth and twentieth centuries is slight. Until now, this literature has not been the subject of substantial academic research. The important work in this sphere by Eusèbe Vassel, Daniel Ḥagège, and Robert Attal is mainly noted for its biographical and bibliographical records.[4] In recent years Judeo-Arabic literature has become a research subject for graduate students at universities, and these studies too are bibliographical.[5] The senior scholars who have been working on this subject for many years, the late Robert Attal (mainly bibliographical recording of books printed in North Africa) and Haim Zafrani (Judeo-Arabic literature in Morocco), have recently been joined by Yitzhak Avishur, Joseph Chetrit, Nahem Ilan, Michal Saraf, and others.[6] As stated, the establishment of Hebrew presses in the countries of Islam[7] encouraged the publication of Judeo-Arabic books and, as we will soon see, actually encouraged writing in this language. But in parallel, a sizable number of Hebrew books were written and published. It seems, therefore, that the explanation for the use of Judeo-Arabic is to be sought through a different channel, the origin of which we can discover only if we clarify the genres and content of this literature.

Modern Judeo-Arabic literature can be classified into two divisions: (1) belles lettres, as opposed to other literature, and (2) original literature, as opposed to translated works. The belles lettres division contains only a small amount of original writing; most of it is translated works. The two divisions are not parallel; the belles lettres overlap with original material and translated literature, and traditional rabbinic literature overlaps with original and translated literature. Translations of traditional rabbinic literature form a large part of Judeo-Arabic literature: the Bible, Talmud, and Midrashim, the Passover Haggadah, *piyyutim* (sacred poems), halakhic works, Bible and Talmud commentary, ethics, histories such as *Josippon*, medical books, and everything else imaginable. Original books of traditional rabbinic literature are mainly commentaries on the Bible and on the Talmud and Midrashim, works about ethics and Halakha, and histories of the sages of the local communities. On the one hand, the belles lettres include translations of classical Arabic literature (e.g., *A Thousand and One Nights*), modern Hebrew literature, and modern French literature; on the other hand, they include original writing, mostly poems of various kinds. Our concern is with the belles lettres, both translated and original.

In any event, the need for Judeo-Arabic was not essential to the literary genre. The large number of books published in that language since the mid-nineteenth century was the result of a process that had begun many centuries before: the decline in knowledge of Hebrew among the Jews of the Islamic lands. This can be seen in the many fragments of translations of Hebrew prayers found in the Cairo Geniza and also in dictionaries and translations of Maimonides' *Mishneh Torah*.[8] The establishment of printing houses only helped to satisfy the long-standing need to put traditional rabbinic literature into the almost sole linguistic vehicle of the Jewish communities in the North African countries: dialectal Judeo-Arabic. But a clear distinction has to be made between the communities of North Africa and those of the Middle East. In North Africa knowledge of Hebrew was less, so most of the Judeo-Arabic writing and printing took place there. The communities of the Middle East knew Hebrew better and therefore had relatively less need for Judeo-Arabic literature, either original or translated works.

Exposure of North African Jewish Society to Western Culture in the Second Half of the Nineteenth Century

As a result of sweeping socioeconomic global changes, especially France's political endeavors in North Africa during the nineteenth century, the Jews of North Africa began to be exposed to Western culture in the latter half of that century,[9] and, subsequently, with this exposure also came their familiarity with the Jewish Enlightenment movement of Europe (the Haskalah).[10] This exposure not only led to the creation of diversified levels and ways of European culture on the Jewish communities, but it also gave rise to the easing of strictures or offered legitimacy to the strengthening of the surrounding Arab culture within those same communities.

This connection to Arab culture is most significant as far as our study is concerned, insofar that the beginning of Judeo-Arabic literature in Tunisia, as described by Daniel Ḥagège, is related to it.[11] As is known, in 1857 the Bey Mohammad endorsed a constitution in Tunisia that guaranteed human rights for non-Muslims, including Jews; likewise, in 1864 Mawlai Mohammad in Morocco issued a similar declaration that was a human rights accord for Jewish subjects. However, there was nothing in it to delude the Jews, because they were already part of the grassroots nationalism and preferred nurturing cultural ties with Europe. What's more, these new rights did not stem from any change in values in the way the Muslim population viewed the minority Jewish population but rather was brought about by pressure from foreign powers. Indeed, in only a few years after the constitution's ratification in Tunisia and even after a few months after the accord's ratification in Morocco, the declarations by the respective rulers were canceled altogether.[12] However, these documents did spell out the force needed to undermine the traditional policy of segregation of the Jewish and Arab societies, a segregation that had existed for more than a thousand years by way of mutual interest among both Muslim and Jewish religious leaders. We should note that on a mere folk level, which happens to be the level most frequently used to express the flowering of Judeo-Arabic literature, even the religious leaders on both sides had never been able to ensure complete segregation.

At any rate, the trend of exposure to and openness toward foreign cultures, which was reinforced at the end of the nineteenth century, is reflected in the internalizing of new cultural values along three different vectors: (1) a growing awareness of the Hebrew language, both because of its connection with the Haskalah in Europe and all its associated books and journals and because of its connection with the Zionist movement; (2) a move to draw closer to the cultural habitudes of France, French language, and French literature; and (3) expansionism and diverse literary activism in the Judeo-Arabic language. The most powerful of these vectors was the third, which we treat later in this chapter, which is essentially a peer study of the Judeo-Arabic literature printed by the Hebrew publishing houses of North Africa from the mid-nineteenth century until the mid-twentieth century. However, first, let us discuss the connection of Judeo-Arabic literature with the Haskalah.

The Association with Jewish Enlightenment in Europe

One reason for the expansion of Judeo-Arabic literature was the wish to gain an education, to broaden knowledge. Profound political, social, and economic changes occurred in Jewish communities of the Islamic countries beginning in the middle of the nineteenth century, the consequences of which are important for our purposes with respect to education.[13] In every population center of the Islamic countries, large and small, circles of Jewish intellectuals established an indirect link with the Jewish Enlightenment movement (Haskalah) in Europe. In addition, direct contact with European Christian culture through the representatives of the colonial powers, particularly in North Africa and India, where European Christian communities developed, stimulated members of the local Jewish communities to acquire education and expand their knowledge. The first immediate way was to make use of the rise of Jewish presses, which usually came into being in the countries of Islam in the wake of the non-Jewish presses, to publish translations of works in various fields into the language known best, namely, Judeo-Arabic.

One of the most impressive manifestations of this quest for education was the Jewish press in North Africa, Egypt, Iraq, and India. Attal lists no fewer than 243 journals published in the four Maghrebi countries (Libya, Tunisia, Algeria, and Morocco), almost a third of them in Judeo-Arabic.[14] The Jewish journals in Baghdad and India, despite being far fewer in number than those in North Africa, were mainly in Judeo-Arabic. The Jewish press in Baghdad and India published not only local and international political news but also pieces of a distinct educational and literary kind, in the manner of the Hebrew newspapers in Jerusalem and Eastern Europe during the second half of the nineteenth century. Most of the Jewish intellectuals in these countries were subscribers to the Eastern European Jewish papers; indeed, some were their local correspondents.

The connection of the Jews of the Islamic countries to modern Hebrew literature was evident in several fields, of which two are of concern for us: original Hebrew writing and translations of Hebrew works into Judeo-Arabic. Original Hebrew writing was influenced by the Haskalah and by more ancient sources of Hebrew culture. Among writers of this kind were Isaac Morali in Algeria, David Elqā'im (the compiler of the famous collection of *baqqashot* [entreaties] *Shir yedidot*) and David Buzaglo in Morocco, and A. Sh. Nahum in Baghdad.[15] The Haskalah provided a wealth of material for translations of Hebrew works into Judeo-Arabic. Of all the writers of the Haskalah, the most popular among the Jews of the East was Abraham Mapu (1808–1867). His book *Ahavat ṣiyyon* (Love of Zion) was translated into Ladino and Judeo-Persian and twice into Judeo-Arabic.[16] These two Judeo-Arabic translations were done by Ṣemaḥ Halevi, one of the central figures of Judeo-Arabic literature in Tunisia, and Mas'ūd M'ārek. Both translations were done as early as the 1880s. But this is not all: Mapu's other two famous books, *Ashmat shomron* (The Guilt of Samaria) and *'Ayiṭ ṣavu'a* (A Colored Eagle) (the latter still a manuscript, which was found by Attal), were translated into Judeo-Arabic by Isaac Māmo, a resident of Nabeul, Tunisia (b. 1880; d. Jerusalem, 1967).[17] Another popular Haskalah author was Mayer Lehman, four of whose books, originally written in German, were translated into Judeo-Arabic from a Hebrew translation by Shelomo Twena, a Jew from Iraq who lived in Calcutta.[18] The books are *Süss Oppenheim*, *Ha-ḥilluf* [The Change], *Ḥatan ha-melekh [The King's son-in-law],* and *Ha-sar mi-couci* [The Minister from Couci] (Calcutta, 1896, 1898). Lehman's book *Bustenai* was translated into Tunisian Judeo-Arabic and published by the printing house of Makhlūf Najjār in Sousse, Tunisia, in 1943. The books of Kalman Schulman were also popular. His *Harisot betar* (The Ruins of Betar) was translated into Judeo-Arabic by Twena (Calcutta, 1896).

Lesser known books were also translated, among them books not originally written in Hebrew, although they were translated into Judeo-Arabic from a Hebrew translation. *Sefarad Vi-Yrushalayim or Ibn Ezra and Ḥulda Daughter of Yehuda Halevi, a Tale of Lovers Originating in Ancient History, Written in the Language of Ashkenaz* [German] *by Dr Philipsohn and Rendered into Hebrew by S. R. F. Dicker*, which was published in *Ha-asif* in 1887 (3: 481–564), was translated into Judeo-Arabic by Ṣemaḥ Halevi under the title *Ḥikāyat bint rabbi yehuda halevi wa-rabbi abraham ibn ezra* (Tunis, 1904). Rabbi Mqīqeṣ Hshellī, one of the sages of Djerba in the second quarter of the twentieth century, engaged in the translation of compositions of this kind. Among his translations we note *Shoshannat ha-'amaqim* (Rose of the Valleys), which was published in Hebrew in Vilna in 1888 from the translation of Zvi Hirsch Ratner, and *Ma'ase roqe'aḥ* Apothecary's Work), titled in translation *Kitāb ḥālat al-yahūd fī frankfūrṭ* (The Book of the Condition of the Jews in Frankfurt). *Kitāb* is actually a translation of *Mi-frankfurt 'ad bagdad* (From Frankfurt to Baghdad) (Jerusalem, 1924), which is an elaborated Hebrew translation by Shemu'el Refa'eli. We should also mention *Ma'ase ha-gedolim* (Tales of the Great Ones) by Solomon

Wilf, a collection of stories from the Talmud, which was translated into Judeo-Arabic by Meir Cohen (Djerba, 1945). To this example we could join tens or perhaps hundreds of Hassidic stories translated into Judeo-Arabic, mainly from printing houses in Tunisia; usually, however, the stories were appended by the rabbis and sages to books of rabbinic literature, whether in Hebrew or Judeo-Arabic, at the bottom of the page or at the end of the book.

All these books can be defined generally as historical novels, and thus the members of the Jewish communities in the Islamic countries could identify with the content and find interest in them. So far as we know, no book from the Haskalah (except for *A Colored Eagle*, which was translated but not published) that reflected the contemporary problems of Jewish society in Europe was translated into Judeo-Arabic. Nor were there in North Africa translations of modern writing in Eretz Yisrael, despite the identification of many with the Zionist enterprise, especially in Tunisia and Libya. It seems that for mass consumption readers wanted books that were based on the ancient sources and devoted to the Jewish people.

Naturally, apart from the translated literature, original books written in Judeo-Arabic were also published. For the most part these works were poems or stories written in earlier generations and preserved until their publication in manuscript form or through oral tradition. Many of these compositions were evidently linked to folk literature. But original contemporary literature existed, including songs, poems, stories of the lives and miracles of local sages, and even novels such as *Bayn ḥuyūṭ tūnis* (Within the Walls of Tunis) (Tunis, 1926), by the prolific writer Michel Uzan (see the appendix to this chapter for an excerpt). Uzan also translated this novel into French (*Entre les murs de Tunis*. Tunis, 1956).

It is true that because we are still in the early stages of research on Judeo-Arabic literature, we can say nothing substantial about the quality of the translations, which often are paraphrases, or about the affinity of the original literature in Judeo-Arabic with contemporaneous

Hebrew literature. We are still preparing an entire record and precise description of this literature; only after these tasks are completed will we be able to fully analyze and discuss specific works of Judeo-Arabic literature.

North African Printing Houses of Judeo-Arabic Literature

For generations before the middle of the nineteenth century, the Jews of North Africa would print books of liturgy, Halakha, and Midrash at Hebrew printers in Europe, particularly in Amsterdam but also in Livorno. Livorno was reasonably close to North Africa and had strong commercial ties with it. In addition, Tunis was home to a large and important community of Livornese (the Grāna).[19] The first Judeo-Arabic books, then, were published in Livorno well before the nineteenth century. However, the first book published in Judeo-Arabic with which we are acquainted (not following a thorough check) is a work for the liturgical needs of the North African Jewish community. This collection, *The Ten Commandments* (Amsterdam, 1737), contains prayers "which are recited with joy and thankfulness . . . in the glorious city of Tunis . . . in clear and eloquent language, translation and Arabic." The appearance of this book, however, was an isolated event, not part of the continuous development that later was to characterize the printing of Judeo-Arabic books in Livorno and North Africa.

Shortly after the printing of Judeo-Arabic books began in Livorno, a Hebrew press was founded in Algeria, first in Algiers (1853) and later in Oran (1856), whereas in Tunis the first Hebrew book was printed just a few years later (1860). In Morocco and Libya Hebrew presses appeared at the end of the nineteenth century (Tangier in 1891) and after World War I (Tripoli in 1917, Rabat in 1918, and Casablanca in 1919).[20] The precedence of Algeria may stem from that country's political status under French rule and to the equality of rights granted, in principle, to its Jews by the government. The major work of publishing in Tunis and elsewhere in Tunisia did not begin until the early 1890s, and it peaked only in the twentieth century, between the two world wars, with the activities of publishers in Sousse and Djerba. Compared to these two communities, the output of the publishers in Algeria, Morocco, and Tripoli was relatively small—a few dozen to 200 titles at each house—and it is not surprising that these publications have been fairly comprehensively recorded by various scholars.[21] In contrast, each of the publishers in the cities of Tunisia produced many hundreds of books, totaling several thousands, and for that reason, apart from J. Fraenkel's work on the printers of Djerba, no overall list of these publications has so far appeared.[22]

Judeo-Arabic as a Language of Mass Communication

The role of Judeo-Arabic in the literary creations of North African Jewry began to gradually diminish in the thirteenth century. Thereafter Hebrew grew in importance in elite literature, a process already discerned by scholars of secular Judeo-Arabic literature in the Middle Ages.[23] Furthermore, Middle Arabic, the standard transregional form of the language used by leading medieval Jewish writers that was common—apart from a few inconsequential linguistic details—to all the Arabic-speaking Jewish communities, was almost entirely supplanted by the local vernaculars, which differed from community to community.

In more recent times the clearest signs of the cultural changes taking place within North African Jewry beginning in the mid-nineteenth century were the growing connection with Europe and the Hebrew printing houses there and, still more, the establishment of Hebrew printers in North Africa. The industriousness of the publishers not only reflected these changes but also stimulated them. As soon as the traditional religious leaders became aware of the enormous power of printing, they sought to exploit it to actualize their national and religious outlook.

One fundamental change was the democratization of cultural activity as a result of the almost unlimited possibility of propagating the instruments of culture—that is, books, and, naturally, newspapers and other periodicals. But such widespread democratization, covering all strata of the Jewish population, also came about through the use of the simplest, most convenient, and most encompassing medium of communication, namely, Judeo-Arabic in its various dialects. We have already mentioned the greater preoccupation with Hebrew and its grammar and the effect of French culture and language since the end of the nineteenth century. These trends were limited to fairly small circles of intellectuals and religious scholars and were mainly restricted to the capitals or the northern coastal cities. By contrast, Judeo-Arabic remained the principal language of communication, covering the middle and lower strata, the modernizers no less than the conservatives, and the coastal cities and townships no less than the inland villages. Printed Judeo-Arabic literature had a sizable market because differences among the various North African dialects were not so great as to prevent understanding of a particular vernacular by one who spoke a different native tongue. In fact, three Judeo-Arabic dialects—Tunisian, Algerian, and Libyan—are almost identical, whereas the Moroccan dialect is somewhat distinct.

The closeness of printed Judeo-Arabic to spoken vernaculars also meant that its influence encompassed not only literate males who spent a good part of their time in synagogues but also women (see later discussion). In this manner, Judeo-Arabic regained its place as the principal written mode of communication among the Jews of North Africa, after its decline in the production of Judeo-Arabic works since the fourteenth century. But since the mid-nineteenth century it was no longer the medieval Middle Arabic, which once served the most important Jewish writers of the Middle Ages, but a kind of new Middle Arabic that became the common vehicle of communication for a great part of the Jewish communities in North Africa.

Genres of Literature Published in Judeo-Arabic

The traditional Judeo-Arabic literature of North African Jewry contained writings in manuscript, particularly liturgical texts: translations of the books of the Bible and poems. It also included an extensive folklore component that had been preserved orally. The first books printed in Livorno, Algiers, and Oran in the 1850s included liturgical texts that were widely used in synagogues and whose publication, it was hoped, would be financially profitable. Folk literature was not printed at first, presumably because, being noncanonical, it was less serious and prestigious.

Among the books printed in those years was *The Ten Commandments* (Livorno, 1846), which was first published in Amsterdam in 1737; it was used in the liturgy of Shavuot, when special readings of the Ten Commandments, along with translations, commentaries, and elaborate poems related to them, were recited. Other examples are *The Havdala Ceremony in Arabic* (Algiers, 1853) and *Or ne'erav* (Pleasing Light) (Livorno, 1854), which is the *sharḥ* (Arabic translation) of the Pentateuch allegedly based on Sa'adia Gaon's *tafsīr*, or Bible translation in literary Arabic, and adapted, as the publishers state, to the linguistic and exegetic tradition of the Jews of North Africa. There were liturgical collections, such as *Sova' semaḥot* (A Wealth of Joys) (Livorno, 1855), which included a number of poems in Arabic by Moroccan poets; another collection, with the same title, was intended for the Purim festival and was written in Judeo-Arabic (Oran, 1856). Also for use on Purim was *Sharḥ mi kamokha* (Livorno, 1860), a translation of a famous poem by Yehuda Halevi, customarily recited on the Sabbath preceding Purim (Shabbat Zakhor). Another (expanded) translation is *Sharḥ of the hafṭara of yom shemini shel pessaḥ (the Eighth Day of Passover)* (Livorno, 1865), which was part of the *ḍhīr* (liturgical compilation) for that day.

Nor, of course, are books of Halakha absent. *Dat yehudit bi-al-'arabī* (The Jewish Religion in Arabic) (Algiers, 1855), subtitled *The Laws of Nidda and Ḥalla and Lighting the Candles and the Laws of Meat and Milk and*

Whole Worms and Vegetables and Salting of Meat, the Laws of Seasons, was translated from Ladino.[24] A later example of halakhic publication is *Sefer menuḥa le-ḥayyim* (The Book of Repose for Life), in three parts (Livorno, 1882), which includes the order of prayers for weekdays and the Sabbath but is primarily a Judeo-Arabic summary of the laws of prayer and matters connected with the daily ritual cycle, into which various stories are interwoven.

Books containing legends and tales having to do with the Jewish festivals were also published, as were abbreviated versions or translations of well-known Hebrew books that were attempts to deepen knowledge of Jewish and world history. Among these we note *Sefer yosef ḥen*, the story of Joseph and Zulaykha, Potiphar's wife, taken "from *Sefer ha-yashar* . . . the Gemara and the Midrash" (Algiers, 1854); and *She'erit yisrael* (The Remnant of Israel), which contains stories of the River Sambaṭion, the sons of Moses, and the Ten Tribes (Algiers, 1854).

Daniel Ḥagège notes that in 1862 the first Hebrew book was published in Tunis, actually a book in Judeo-Arabic.[25] It was *Qānūn al-dawla al-tūnisiyya*, the constitution of the state of Tunisia. The publishers, Mordekhai Tabiya, Bīshī Chemama, and Eliyahu Elmāleḥ, aimed to educate the Jews of the community and to acquaint them with the general nature of the society in which they lived. The second book published in Tunis, *Ma'ase sha'ashu'im* (A Pleasant Deed) (1867), was not concerned with rabbinic matters either but was a collection of tales translated into Judeo-Arabic. Ḥagège also tells of Ḥai Ṣarfati, a citizen of Tunis and one of the most important writers of popular literature in Judeo-Arabic in Tunisia; Ṣarfati recorded stories he heard in the coffeehouse told by an Arab storyteller from Kairouan. Most of the tales were later published. Jewish sages—citing Yosef Caro's famous utterance in the *Shulḥan 'Arukh*[26] prohibiting the reading of secular literature on the Sabbath and the copying or printing of material that might stimulate "the evil inclination" even on weekdays—did not favor the expansion of the kinds of books published in Judeo-Arabic to include "tales of passion" and "stories of kings and their wars." But both the supply and the great demand for books of this genre show that they were popular enough to overcome these reservations. In 1885 Eli'ezer Farḥi, of the Grāna community of Tunis, published in Livorno a series of chivalrous Arab tales, *Al-malik sayf al-azal* (The King of the Eternal Sword), consisting of more than twenty booklets totaling more than 2,000 pages.

Of particular interest is the first Jewish journal in Judeo-Arabic, which appeared in Algiers in 1870. This was *Adziri, journal bi-al-yahūdī wa-bi-al-franṣīṣ: L'Israélite Algérien*: "Journal commercial, industriel, agricole, maritime, littéraire, scientifique, judicaire et d'annonces, paraissant le vendredi, rédigé en français et en hébreu par M. Nessim Benisti."[27] Following it, dozens of Jewish journals were published in North Africa, mostly in Tunisia; most of them lasted less than a year. Taken together, however, they provide an extremely rich and varied kaleidoscope of Jewish journalism in Judeo-Arabic, the main influence of which was to widen the knowledge and deepen the social and political involvement of their readers.[28]

Livorno and Algiers remained the centers of Judeo-Arabic book publishing until the early 1890s, when Tunis also became an important hub of Hebrew publishing. As stated, in Tunis and subsequently in Djerba and Sousse the printing trade expanded, whereas it declined in Livorno and Algiers. The new publishing houses that opened in Morocco and Tripoli produced only books of liturgy and Halakha for local needs, that is, books on the local customs in Halakha and the synagogue service. By contrast, the printers in Tunisia, especially in Djerba, became a center for Judeo-Arabic on behalf of other North African communities as well.

The books published thereafter included all imaginable areas of creativity that were acceptable in the Jewish world. Particularly noteworthy is the large number of translations of original Hebrew literature and Hebrew translations of German works from the Haskalah. Only books dealing with traditional Jewish society were translated, not those on nineteenth-century post-Enlightenment Jewry in Europe or Jewish literature produced in Eretz Yisrael in the twentieth century. In addition to Hebrew and Jewish literature, French and English works were translated that had nothing to do with Judaism, such as Alexander Dumas's *Count of Monte Cristo* and Daniel Defoe's *Robinson Crusoe*.[29] This passion for translation also gave rise to original writing in Judeo-Arabic, albeit on a small scale, such as the aforementioned *Bayn ḥuyūṭ tūnis*.

The most intensive activity was in journalism, as previously mentioned, and in the publishing of small-format booklets containing stories translated from various sources. Usually, these stories were original Arabic literature, but some were from European sources. Hundreds of stories of this kind were published from World War I to the middle of the twentieth century, mainly by Makhlūf Najjār's publishing house in Sousse but also by other publishers. The demand was enormous. The stories, which appeared week after week, some of them in reprinted editions, were read by men and women who gathered during their leisure hours on weekdays and festivals in the market or at home.

The rabbis were not pleased with this literature, the content and publication of which were not supervised in any way. As noted, they pondered the power of the printed Judeo-Arabic story and began to work systematically in the field of publication. Their educational orientation dictated that the sources and themes of the stories be from Jewish tradition in its widest sense. Not only tales from the ancient sages and the Middle Ages but also those from Hassidic literature were published in Arabic translation and in quantities so large that it seems that there was no Hassidic story that did not find its way to North Africa in Judeo-Arabic garb. This material was printed in the following format: The main composition on a religious-traditional subject was placed on the upper part of the page of the book, and the lower part contained folktales. This not only served an educational purpose but also was a means of increasing sales of booklets on religious-traditional motifs.

Apart from this method, special collections of tales about personalities and events from Jewish tradition also appeared.[30]

Mention should be made here of the great enterprise of Rabbi Yosef Ghenassia, of the Constantine community in Algeria. In the 1920s he began to publish scores of books, including the systematic translation of almost all the religious classics into the North African Judeo-Arabic vernacular. An example is *Ḥovot ha-levavot* (Duties of the Heart), itself a Hebrew translation from Arabic of the pietistic treatise by Baḥya ibn Paquda. Another is a translation of a commentary to Rashi by Rabbi Eliyahu Mizraḥi. Ghenassia translated other commentaries on the scriptures and liturgy and rendered talmudic legends (*aggadot*) and Maimonides's code (*Mishneh Torah*) into Judeo-Arabic. His work continued until the 1950s, but, from the evidence we have, it is doubtful that there was a demand for more than a few dozen of the vast number of books he produced. The physical condition of many of these books, usually found in booksellers' markets, is excellent, indicating that they have not passed through many hands. This contrasts with the condition of other books in Judeo-Arabic, particularly journals and folktale booklets, which are ragged from extensive handling.

This contrast underlines our general point that Judeo-Arabic literature was a mirror of important social and cultural changes taking place in modern times among Maghrebi Jewish communities and that it exerted a powerful influence in shaping the spiritual portrait of the North African Jew, especially in Tunisia, around the turn of the twentieth century. Further investigation of this literature is sure to provide more nuanced insights into these processes. This influence encompassed not only the dominant male population, who knew the rudiments of reading and writing and who spent a greater part of time in the synagogue, but also the female population. Anyone standing in the company of these Jewish women from North Africa could not help but be astonished by their knowledge of Jewish tradition. For most of them this knowledge did not come from reading Jewish religious classics transcribed in Hebrew but rather from listening to literature written in the Judeo-Arabic script that was being read on different social occasions.

Appendix

Within the Walls of Tunis (Bayn ḥuyūṭ tūnis) by Michel Uzan

Chapter Seven: Purim/Passover

Purim fell about three weeks after the engagement, and Paul, who was really in love with Freda, wanted to get her some jewelry as a Purim gift. The night before Purim, Paul went to his fiancée's parents' house a little earlier than usual and, having greeted everyone, he took her hand. After being with her for a while, he took a little box from his pocket and held it out to her.

"Dearest Freda, please accept this ring as a Purim present."

Freda delightedly took the box from his hand and went to show it to her mother and her family.

"God willing, you will bring better upon her with this, my son," said Freda's mother as she entered at that moment from the kitchen, where she was baking Purim cakes.

David was rather late that night, but when he got home, Freda showed him the ring.

"May it be His will that you'll give your bride a thing like this," his mother said.

"How come you're late tonight?" Paul asked David. "Tonight it doesn't matter that he's late," said Brāham,[31] "but tomorrow night," he continued, turning to his son, "don't forget to be home early, because it's Purim night."

The next day David did his father's bidding and arrived home early. They all sat around the table to listen to the reading of the book of Esther, and when they came to the phrases "Cursed be Haman!" and "Blessed be Mordekhai!" you would think that the floor tiles would break into smithereens from the sticks' stamping brought down on Haman's head by Sarah's son and his friends who were there.

On Purim morning, after he had prayed and had some of the cakes for breakfast, Brāham went to slaughter a chicken. Afterward he went back home, took a small bag filled with copper coins, and started giving them away to the poor people who came to the house and to the children clustering around with the Members' handkerchief.[32] During the day David and Meir, and Paul too, brought wine and the bits and pieces that go with it and set about getting drunk in their house. Brāham joined in the wine drinking occasionally. The children, Sarah's son and his friends, came home after running around in the street. They climbed onto the swing and shot off fireworks. Everyone was happy that day, large and small.

In the evening the table was set with every dish you could wish for, including the chicken and the jelly for the meal. This time too Sarah's boy and his friends beat Haman around the head when they came upon his and his sons' names in the reading of the book of Esther and at the words "Cursed be Haman!" David arrived early that evening also to share the meal, because he was excused from listening to the reading of the book, as he had heard it in the synagogue. He glowed with joy when Berthe[33] entered again and again to eat with them. Paul came around that evening too and sat beside his fiancée, Freda, and time after time they turned to each other, but when they tried to talk, Brāham gave them a stern look, as if to say, "That's enough. Be quiet. You mustn't talk when we're reading the book." After the reading David, Paul, and Freda sat down to enjoy themselves, and Berthe was with them also; David didn't want to miss this opportunity so he asked his sister to invite her to join them.

On the night of the new moon of the month of Nissan, Sarah went to her parents' house to spend Passover there. She so loved being in her parents' home, and she celebrated most of the festivals there. The next day Brāham came home, accompanied by a delivery man carrying a big box of matzot. After his wife took the matzot in, she made the blessing over the tithe and set aside the share for the priest as was the custom.

"Father, why have you brought the matzot so early?" Sarah asked.

"Now what's better—that I bring them in good time and have done with it, or that I leave it to the last minute and lose two days with all the crowds of people?"

"I still remember in those days," Sarah replied, "before they set up this monopoly[34] for us, when we would bake the matzot at the bakery. That was such a joy. We'd buy the kosher flour ourselves and watch over the baking at the bakery, and those who pierced and kneaded the dough took the matzot from the oven, those poor people. We'd give them something and they'd do more for us than we expected. The little children also, when they heard that the family was planning to bake the matzot—that day would turn into a holiday for them. All in all, what a shame those days are gone. Not like now, when eventually it is done with crowding and wasting time. Oh well. It's God's will that they set up the monopoly for us. If only they'd open a dozen or so warehouses to sell the matzot, so there'd be none of that crush and time wasting."

"They know what they're doing," Brāham said. "The most important thing is to end that monopoly and rid all the people of it."

"The most important thing is what good are those useless discussions to us?" said Miriam. "Don't forget to bring the whitewash home today so that we can do the house tomorrow. There's not much time left."

"I'll bring the whitewash for you this evening," Brāham replied.

That whole week was spent on spring cleaning and whitewashing the entire house of the 'Adā'inī family. David went time and again to the Ṣabḥūns, on the pretense of seeing how the Passover work was progressing. However, his real, only purpose was to see his beloved Berthe, the sight of whom brought joy to his heart. She wore an apron and house clothes, but in his eyes she was arrayed in the finest attire.

Brāham always bought in good time whatever was needed for the wonderful Passover festival, so ten to fifteen days before the feast he began making his purchases: matzot, rice, oil, charcoal, wine, arak, and sugar. He only left perishable goods until two or three days before Passover—meat and vegetables and so on. He did not rely on his wife for the festival commodities but had a list of all that was needed for the occasion; among other things, he would buy over twenty kinds of vegetables, so that on Passover he could taste all the greens of the season. For that reason his wife did not have to bother with the shopping, and she could concentrate on the household chores.

"Mother!" Sarah called, as she entered at that moment. "Ṣabḥūn's wife wants to borrow the kettle of the *hag'ala*."[35]

"I'll just finish off, and I'll give it to her," said Miriam.

When Passover was just two days away, on al-Dabbāghīn Street,[36] where many butchers shops were located, at each one there were porgers[37] and cleaners of the mutton that several Jewish families had had slaughtered for Passover. At two in the afternoon Meir Gershon entered his father-in-law's house to eat the midday meal.

"And why are you late again this time?" Sarah demanded of her husband.

"Well obviously it's an enormous pleasure to be on al-Dabbāghīn Street in the Ḥāra[38] of 'European' Tunis—everybody passing by has all the signs of the festival unfolding before their eyes. If it weren't for the shortage of apartments, I'd leave my place on Perpignan Street and rent a flat in that part, because where we live no one feels that there is any Passover or Tabernacles or 'Rabbi Shim'on,'[39] or anything."

"I ask you why you're late, and I get a whole story!"

"I told you. I said I was having a nice time watching that festive scene."

"Kosher cakes! Kosher cakes!" The voice of the "kosher cakes" seller resounded outside.

"Don't you think it's unnecessary to shout out 'kosher cakes'? He's a Jew so his cakes are bound to be kosher," Meir said to his father-in-law, Brāham.

"It just means that he's got a kashrut certificate from the Chief Rabbi to make kosher cakes [for Passover]," Brāham replied.

"Speaking of the certificate," said Meir, "a lot of vendors keep their shops open and sell their goods on Sabbath eve long after sunset. So do some groceries. How come the rabbi lets those people sell kosher cakes?"

"Perhaps the rabbi doesn't know about it. If he did, he'd take away their license to bake kosher cakes on the spot. He did it often enough with the licenses of quite a few roast meat sellers when he found out they were breaking the Sabbath."

On the night of the search[40] David and Meir got home early because Brāham had admonished them since morning not to be late and had reminded them that that night they had to search for *ḥametz* early. Brāham held an old pitcher and a knife to pry out the *ḥametz*, and after making the blessing over the search, he began moving from door to door, closely followed by David, who lit up the darkness with a wax candle. He collected the bread crumbs lurking behind each door. When Brāham had finished this task, they all sat down at the table to eat the roast meat, as was customary on the night of the search. After she had roasted the meat, Miriam roasted the sheep's fat tail and brought in the *kānūn*[41] to permeate the room with the aroma of incense.[42] Afterward they all crowded on the floor in the far corner of the house to eat supper, because the table had already been scalded and made kosher for Passover and the supper was *ḥametz*.

"Bon appétit!" Mas'ūd Ṣabḥūn called out as he entered his neighbors' home at that moment.

"Welcome Mas'ūd," Brāham replied. "Come on, sit down with us."

Mas'ūd sat down and they began chatting for some time about Passover and the enormous amount of work everyone had to do to get matzot.

"Won't Rober[43] be coming for Passover? Hasn't he got leave from the army?" Brāham asked Mas'ūd.

"No. He wrote to say that he can only get here two or three months after Passover."

"May God keep him safe," Brāham said. He turned to his daughter Sarah:

"Go, daughter, and bring him his bag of *ḥaroset.*"

"God willing, we'll enjoy a better and more successful year," said Mas'ūd, taking from Brāham the *ḥaroset* that he himself made and sharing it among his buddies and friends.

"And is Gago[44] planning to have the seder with us this year?" asked Sarah, "or will he give us a miss, like last year?"

"He'll celebrate with us," Mas'ūd replied.

The morning of the festival eve Brāham was busy straining the Passover oil and wine, and he went on with the job toward evening, putting the finishing touches on the preparations for the festival and everything needed for the seder. At seven o'clock all the men of the two families and their guests assembled in the house, as Brāham had asked. David was very happy that for two nights he would be with his beloved Berthe until about midnight. Brāham was still fussing with the seder plate, adorning it with the matzot, the bitter herbs (lettuce), the *ḥaroset*, and everything else needed. Then they went to the evening service, and on their return they all took their places around the table. Each one of them—women and men, adults and children—held a goblet of wine in their hands and they all recited the kiddush and drank the first cup leaning,[45] to signify the freedom the Jewish people won on Passover. After that they went on with the seder until they reached the passing around of the seder plate.

"Go on, Berthe, pass the plate around," said Brāham.

Berthe stood up. She took the plate in her hands and raised it high above the assembly, who bowed their heads over the table. All of them, women and men, called out in unison, "Yesterday we were slaves." When the plate had thrice gone around the table, Berthe sat down and Brāham told Freda to circle the plate over Berthe's head, also three times. They set the plate down on the table again and began chanting *Ha laḥma 'anya*, to the well-known melody. David was the happiest of all present, and the reader undoubtedly knows why.

When they came to the part of the Haggadah relating the ten plagues in detail, Miriam went and brought a bowl and a kettle. With the mention of each plague, as those present said, "May the Lord save us," Brāham let a little wine from his glass into the bowl and his wife poured water from the kettle. After the ten plagues had been recited, he rinsed the glass very well and washed his hands, and his wife went to discard the water and then returned to her place. Later Brāham began preparing the *ḥaroset* that was needed for the partaking of the bitter herb, and continued reading the Haggadah until they reached the second cup of wine and the repast. The food was served. They ate and drank their fill.

After the meal the third cup was filled, and they recited the grace after meals and drank it, leaning. Later they poured the fourth cup and read *Shefokh* and continued reciting Hallel; when it was done, they drank the fourth cup, also leaning, and began chanting the popular verses of Passover eve, which are said after the Haggadah is finished, such as "Ḥad gadya" and "Khallīnī naskar yā yahūdī"[46] and others. At about midnight they retired, content with that joyful night that they had spent together. David continued thinking about his beloved Berthe, who filled his head that night.

"Ladies and gentlemen, early tomorrow," Brāham said to Mas'ūd and the others, "because tomorrow night we shall read the Haggadah with the translation,[47] and that will keep us busy much longer than tonight."

On the first day of Passover Brāham did not leave his house, but on the second day he and David went to pay visits to their friends, who also came to call on them. The eight days of Passover were spent pleasantly in walks taken by Paul and Freda and Berthe and David.

2

The *Piyyutim* (Liturgical Poems)

Judeo-Arabic *piyyutim* (liturgical poems) have formed the most constant literary genre in North Africa, including Tunisia, since the Middle Ages. This contrasts with most other genres, including Judeo-Arabic secular poems, most of which are innovations of recent generations. In making this distinction between holy and secular poems, we follow the convention of medieval poetry scholarship that a *piyyut* is a poem written for a liturgical purpose, that is, as part of the religious rites in the synagogue, whereas a secular poem is written without such a purpose. True, we have somewhat broadened the scope of the *piyyutim* to cover social-religious events beyond the domain of the synagogue. Such are poems for the pilgrimage to the graves of holy people, in praise of synagogues, and even for the life cycle—all these were composed by the same poets, and their overall mood is religious, pious, and righteous. This mood even encompasses the national motif of exile and redemption. None of these motifs are ever featured in the secular poems, which we discuss in Chapters 3–5.

This tradition of writing Judeo-Arabic poems, which was far more limited than that of Hebrew poems, can be traced in Tunisia to at least the late sixteenth century, in the work of Rabbi Frājī Shawwāṭ.[1] However, this genre also apparently flourished in the nineteenth century (possibly because of the use of printing, which became available then), as evidenced by the preservation of the poetical works. These poems were mainly in honor of social and religious events outside the synagogue precincts. They were certainly recited on those occasions, but we have evidence that within the body of the synagogue prayers, Arabic was also used for liturgical purposes: reciting the Lamentations for 9 Av and reading the augmented translations of various Bible passages, such as the rendering of the Ten Commandments ascribed to R. Sa'adia Gaon.[2]

In the following sections we present different kinds of poems, according to our taste and our understanding. We go no earlier than the end of the eighteenth century with a poem of the *Mi kamokha* genre, which is simply a poem telling of a well-known historical episode contemporary with the poet.[3] The event and the poet were in Tripoli and not in Tunisia, but because the Tripoli dialect is close to the Tunisian dialect and because we found no other poem of its kind and its period, we saw fit to begin the series of poems in this chapter with it.

A Poem by Rabbi Isaac Luzon About Purim Burghul

From 1754 to 1793 the city of Tripoli on the eastern Mediterranean coast of Cyrenaica (Libya) was governed by 'Alī Pāshā of the Kārāmanlī dynasty. Toward the end of his rule his two sons, Aḥmad and Yūsuf, contended for their father's place, with the result that the government grew weak. Finally, in 1793 an army officer named 'Alī Burghul took power in the city. He ruled with extreme cruelty, directed especially at the Jewish community. He had the Jewish lead caster Ḥai Dodon put to death with unusual torture because he suspected him of supporting Aḥmad and Yūsuf, who were seeking to regain power. In this the two brothers were supported by Ḥamūda, the Bey of Tunisia. Two other Jews were also executed for their involvement in activities against the regime, Joseph Cohen and David Khalfōn, as were others. 'Alī Burghul also extorted the Jews' money and imposed heavy fines on the community. Relief came to the Jews only on 29 Tevet (early in 1795), when 'Alī Burghul was forced to flee the city after Aḥmad and

Yūsuf marched from Tunis against Tripoli with a large army, aided by Ḥamūda Bey. To commemorate their salvation brought about by this event, the Jews of Tripoli set that day as a festival, which they dubbed Purim Burghul, and they celebrated it annually; in this they imitated their forebears, who ninety years earlier had initiated a celebration known as Purim al-Sharīf.[4]

This event of Purim Burghul has been described by all writers of the history of Libyan Jewry in modern times. The chief sources are the works of Rabbi Abraham Khalfōn, the greatest of the rabbis of the Tripoli community in that period. The rabbi, who also served as the president (*qā'id*) of the community,[5] was personally linked to the events described, for during them his son David was put to death by fire at the hands of the ruler 'Alī Burghul. As Hirschberg notes, Rabbi Abraham recorded the event several times: in his *Seder ha-dorot*, in laments over the murder of his son, and in a poem of the *Mi kamokha* genre, which opens with the words "Azkir ma'ase adonay bi-qhal 'adato."[6] This phrase was inserted into the service of the Sabbath preceding 29 Tevet, like the custom of reciting the poem *Mi kamokha* by Yehuda Halevi on Shabbat Zakhor before Purim.

The events leading to Purim Burghul were described by Mordekhai Ha-Cohen in his work *Higgid mordekhai* and by Avraham Elmāleḥ, Nahum Slouschz, H. Z. Hirschberg, Frīja Zuareṣ, and others.[7] The poem *Mi kamokha* has been published many times, particularly in collections of prayers and poems of the Libyan custom.[8]

We have found an until now unknown poem by Isaac Luzon, who lived at the time of the events, which he describes in his poem. The poem was printed only once, at the end of Rabbi Ya'aqov Mīmūn's book *Derekh ha-ḥayyim* (Tripoli, 1795), which we bought from a bookseller in Jerusalem. Although this book is mentioned by Ḥayyim Dov Friedberg, it is quite rare and is not in the collection at the Ben-Zvi Institute in Jerusalem; it was only recently acquired by the National Library in Jerusalem.[9] *Derekh ha-ḥayyim* was published by Rabbi Ḥai Mīmūn, the son of Rabbi Ya'aqov Mīmūn, one of the rabbis of

Tripoli, in the first half of the nineteenth century[10] in a single volume together with his book *Mayim ḥayyim* (pp. 1a–10b) (Livorno, 1860). From the author's words on the title page of *Mayim ḥayyim* (1a) we learn that it is chiefly commentaries on books of the Bible that he gleaned from his father's literary notes, with additions of his own. It concludes with a passage from the *Zohar* that was customarily said by the Tripoli community on the night of a circumcision. *Derekh ha-ḥayyim*, which occupies pages 11a–79b of the volume, is the order of reading for the deceased as set down by Rabbi Ḥ. Y. D. Azulai (Ḥida) in his *Yosef tehillot.*[11] This is augmented by new material on some passages of the Talmud by Ya'aqov Raccāḥ.[12] This also is evident from the title page of *Derekh ha-ḥayyim* (11b), which was written by Ya'aqov Raccāḥ.

At the end of the volume (pp. 90a–92a) appears the poem by Isaac Luzon. As stated, it is not known from anywhere else. It is written in the Arabic dialect of the Jews of Tripoli and presumably was printed from a manuscript in the possession of Ya'aqov Raccāḥ. *Derekh ha-Ḥayyim* was never again published, not even in later collections of prayers and poems that included the *Mi kamokha* poems of Purim al-Sharīf and Purim Burghul. On this account it remained unknown to scholars.

Although the Luzon family is known among the Jews of Libya,[13] we have found no mention of the author of the poem anywhere, including lists of the rabbis of the community published by Gabriel Raccāḥ.[14] All that is known of Isaac Luzon is from the words preceding his poem: "The learned and wise Isaac Luzon, his resting place is Eden." This means that in the year when *Derekh ha-Ḥayyim* was published, Luzon was no longer alive. It is almost certain that Luzon himself witnessed the events. This also emerges from his words at the end of the poem (line 162): "What you did for us this year." On several matters, as we note in the context of the poem itself, a textual similarity is evident between the poem and the book *Higgid mordekhai* of Mordekhai Ha-Cohen, even though the texts are different. Presumably, therefore, the poem was known to Ha-Cohen, even though he does not mention it.

As for Luzon's poem, we have no evidence that it was repeated in the synagogues, in contrast to the two Hebrew *Mi kamokha* poems by Rabbi Shabbetai Ṭayyār and Rabbi Abraham Khalfōn, which without doubt it was customary to recite. Although we can assume that Isaac Luzon wrote his poem in Arabic to make it more easily accessible to the public, precisely this fact apparently kept it out of the synagogue, because the status of Arabic was extremely unstable in the liturgy.

The orthography of the poem frequently diverges from classical Arabic orthography, and it reflects the Arabic spoken by the Jews of Tripoli, as we signify in several notes to the text of the poem. Clearly, the language also differs from classical Arabic. The following are some of the general principles:

1. The absence of *alif waṣla*, chiefly in the definite article.
2. The complete disappearance of the definite article before letters with *dagesh*.
3. The absence of *alif hamza*, such as *būnā* instead of *abūnā* (l. 163), *lawwal* instead of *al-awwal* (l. 169), and *lkhūh* instead of *li-akhīh* (l. 15).
4. Substitution of *dāl* by *ḍād*, for example, *ndarhom* instead of *naḍarahum* (l. 133), and the reverse, *yaḍbir* instead of *yadbir* (l. 37).
5. Substitution of *sīn* by *ṣād*, for example, *ṣiwār* instead of *siwār* (l. 71), and the reverse, for example, *saghīr* instead of *ṣaghīr* (l. 148).
6. Substitution of *shīn* by *sīn*, for example, *assams* instead of *al-shams* (l. 130).
7. Substitution of *tā*' by *ṭā*', for example, *ṭāb* instead of *tāb* (l. 62).
8. Disappearance of interdental consonants, for example, *dnūbnā* instead of *dhunūbanā* (l. 4) and *ktīr* instead of *kathīr* (l. 5).
9. Use of the future tense of the first-person singular *naf'alū* instead of *af'al*, for example, *naqr'ū* (l. 158), *na'mlū* (l. 159).

The use of Hebrew words is relatively infrequent, but it does occur and not necessarily at the end of lines for the purpose of rhyme.

It should be noted that the printer was remiss in several matters unconnected to a particular language dialect. For example, there are many printing errors, mainly confusion of *bet* and *kaf*.[15] Nor did the printer distinguish *jīm* from *ghayn*, setting both as *gimel* with a diacritical dot above, for example, *burghul* (l. 2) and *burūj* (l. 9). For the translation of certain words, we were assisted by the late Raphael Ginnish, a native of Tripoli.

Mi kamokha in Arabic

First we shall tell you, O sons of Israel,
Of what the uncircumcised ʿAlī Burghul wrought against us.
Some he hanged, some he burned, some he slaughtered with such killing
Our sins engulfed us:

With a great host he entered the city,
Turks and Greeks, innumerable,
And he said to them, "Go in and take the people
Because God has delivered them into our hand."

They came and entered and took the towers
Then he said to them, "Not one of them will begin to pass,
But only I and the army will pass
So that we shall inherit the land for ourselves."

He entered the fortress and was lucky;[16]
Sīdī Aḥmad opened the gate and went out,
And went to his brother Yūsuf[17] and prostrated himself and bowed down
And said to him, "In what trouble are we entrapped?"

This is the day of evil on which he[18] came
And no one of the city rose against him with his musket.
From the moment he entered the sign was given on him
It is no other than God brought it upon us.
He came with Ḥai Dodon the lead caster[19]
So that he would fight with Sīdī Aḥmad and Sīdī Yūsuf and the men;
They caught him and threw him in prison.
He said to him, "You hid our lead."[20]

He increased anger and it satisfied him
And no one went to speak for him
He said to him, "The lead you hid—what will you do with it?
Will you take it to our enemies that they may fight against us?"

They sentenced him to death
Because he had harmed the rule.
He said to them, "Hang him in agony that he might die
So no one will harm us."
They took out the tormented Ḥai Dodon
And hanged him on the wall of the synagogue opposite the city wall,
And they put on him the lead just mentioned.[21]
Remember, O God, what he did to us!

He prepared schemes against the sons of Jacob
And demanded from them about sixty thousand *maḥbūb*,[22]
And every day he stole booty from them
Until nothing was left to us.

The wicked man thought about the little children,

To take them to the citadel every day,[23]
They fled to their houses and dwelling places,
And they took them out from there by force from our people.

Night and day we worked at sea[24]
And broke our backs with mortar and stones,
They stopped us offering the morning prayer and the afternoon prayer.
We beg you, O God, forgive us!

He did not wish to deal kindly with us at all
But added anger and cruelty against us.
He even took the old men before.
O God, have mercy on us!

Joseph Ha-Cōhen[25] called the gateman[26]
And said to him, "I'll give you such-and-such gold,
Open the gate for Sīdī Aḥmad and Sīdī Yūsuf,
So they can enter their city easily."

The gateman sided with the ruler,
He went to him and said, "This is what a person said to me."
But the ruler did not believe what he said.
He told him, "Bring in his handwriting to us."

That very day when the gateman came,
David Khalfōn and Ha-Cohen were comrades.[27]
He said to them, "Give me something written in your hand."
They gave him their signature as guarantee.

When the governor read the writing
He called them, and handed them over for torture.

Then after a few days he put them to the fire
For the reason that they had harmed the rule.

Relief[28] came, and he swept over the city,
And he ruled as far as Djerba with the help of the Turks and the Greeks and the army
And he took control of the towers and the walls and the people,
As if he had conquered them since the treachery.

Sīdī Aḥmad and Sīdī Yūsuf arose and fled.
It was only that the powder was finished, and they found nothing to fire with.
They reached Sfax[29] and ate and drank,
He[30] gave them victuals, and they ate in comfort.

The *qā'id*[31] made them welcome, and escorted them,
He gave each of them a suit of clothes.
He gave them as much money as they needed
To give food to their men.

Notables and personalities went with them.
There were those from Sfax and its vicinity.
They accompanied them until they reached their place,
And they went to their city with ease.

This shall be written in our hearts,
For God saved us from all trouble
And He will again be gracious with us,
And will compensate us for what we have lost.

God came and was gracious with the sons of the Fathers,
And God saved us from the decree of the rule,
The Holy One, blessed be He, will redeem us from this exile.

So, He will send the redeemer to redeem us.

The fire of the burnt ones shouted up to heaven—
Return, God, from this anger
And save Israel from this nation!
And they will say before You, "There is no one like the Lord our God."

Whoever saw that time,
When the ruler did to us what Haman did to us,
And more than the ruler Nebuchadnezzar.
Let it never again return to us!

O God, O God, forgive our sins
And see what he did to us!
Return, O God, and deal kindly with us,
And we shall thank you always in our hearts!

Ḥamūda Pāshā took counsel with his deputies
To return ʿAlī Pāshā Kārāmanlī to his city.
He sent a large army with his sons
To send them back to their city safely.

Ḥamūda Pāshā prepared the money
And sent great ships and forces.
A vast army, strong as beasts.
This was the command of the authority.

They went down to the ships and hoisted the sails and embarked,
They came to the edge of Djerba and dropped anchor.
They conquered it, and descended on it and plundered it;
Its treasures, its houses, and the city.[32]
Ḥamūda Pāshā did not rest, nor was he still
Until they sent him letters, and told him:

"We have reached Djerba and have plundered the city
and have done
Everything our hearts desired."

The Pāshā sent word to them, and told them: "It is well.
But send through all the cities of Djerba a declaration that
No man shall plunder and no man shall breach
what is whole.
This is the will of the authority."

The people sowed seed and plowed.
And the camp arose and went to the mountain and looted
And they went to Zuwāra[33] and lay there
One night restfully.

And then they came to Tripoli
And camped below the wall before the sun rose.
Of the people not half were left.[34]
They died of hunger and plague.
Burghul saw them, that they were a large multitude,
About fifteen thousand horsemen

Not counting foot soldiers and officers and donkeys.
They were innumerable for us.
Burghul heard that they had taken Manshiyya.[35]
He fled, he and his army and people, toward evening.
Sīdī Aḥmad and Sīdī Yūsuf entered at dawn,

And we thank God who delivered us.
The townsfolk begged the rulers
That the enemy would not enter to rob us.
They heard their plea, and proclaimed in the city:
"Let no one enter and plunder our people."

O, God, we thank you in every generation

And we shall prolong praises to your name
For the goodness that you have done us.
Great and small shall say: "We thank you our God!"
The Jews took counsel with their great ones.

They placed over them Raḥamim Barda as president.[36]
Even the king and his brother agreed to this.
They said to him, "Be the governor in our stead."
Aḥmad ascended the throne,
The Bedouin traded, coming and going,

The world as it was before, everything to be found.
We ask naught but life from our God.
The Lord our God saved us from him, the Bastard.
Therefore, it behooves us to read Hallel.
We shall celebrate a Purim, like the Purim
of Mordekhai and Esther,

We shall dispense gifts every year.
How great are your deeds, O our God,
What You did for us this year!
Remember to us the Binding of Isaac, our forefather
And the Torah of Moses, our master.

We shall eat and drink on that day
For God delivered us from every sorrow.
Likewise will he deliver us from Ishmael and Edom,
And our Messiah will reign over us.
You are the first of all the first,

And You are the last of all the last.
Your deeds and your wonders are marvelous,
Even more than what You showed us in the past.
Who is like You among the mighty?

You who overpower the wicked?

Not Jews and not Muslims will stand with You,
But all will say, "Who is like You among the gods, Lord?"

A Poem in Praise of the Land of Israel by Rabbi Shelomo ben Shalom Zarqā: "Ard al-quds al-ṭāhira"

Rabbi Shelomo ben Shalom Zarqā lived in the mid-nineteenth century, served on the religious court of the Tunis community, and was the author of many compositions, including *Ẓivḥe teruʿa* (Livorno, 1872) and *Shay la-mora*, an Arabic translation of the Torah that was published in several editions.[37] "Arḍ al-quds al-ṭāhira" was written as a *muwashshaḥ* (a girdle song), a fairly rare form of Hebrew poetry since the exile from Spain. As usual in many communities of the Middle East and North Africa, the poem was written to the melody of an Arabic secular poem, whose opening is set forth in the words preceding the poem; it is a drinking song. The language of the poem is remote from the spoken dialect and is evidently influenced by medieval Judeo-Arabic literature. But the orthography is wholly corrupt with respect to correct spelling of this literature, and it appears to reflect the spoken dialect. The poem is given here as it appears in the rabbi's book *Rinna vi-yshuʿa* (Livorno, 1856: 1: 144b–45b).

It is good for a man that he gives the Holy One, blessed be he, service and praises for the miracles he has wrought with us, each according to his talent granted to him by the Lord, may He be blessed for them. We have published this poem in praise of the Land of Israel.

Melody: "Send Round, Oh Comrades, the Glass of Liquor"

Pure, holy land
God desired it

Of all the lands it was chosen
He elevated and raised it
He exiled me from it against my will
After the end of the time
I shall beg your salvation, my God, have mercy on me
And send the son of David, the Messiah, and with him Elijah.

I shall request the dearest of the Fathers
I shall see you with my eyes
I shall serve there the Lord of the gods
He has no other
His praise is eternal
One and Only
He will have pity in his mercy and will grace us
And send the son of David, the Messiah, and with him Elijah.

Happy is he who sees the offering and the altar
In the Temple
And the priest sacrificing and joyful
And Israel pardoned
And the Levite with his voice praising
The Lord of the universe
But today, how the enemies curse me
And send the son of David, the Messiah, and with him Elijah.

I have longed for your marvelous fruit
There is none like it
Honey will flow, and milk
Good and sweet
How did the Cross worshippers
Enter your land?
Why have you forgotten those who love you and you go
after the enemies?
And send the son of David, the Messiah, and with him Elijah.

All creatures
In Your land will see
Cheeks of rose and jasmine
And flowers will bud
Ritual and religion for ever
The Torah of the merciful
I hope in your loving-kindness, Oh God, want me
And send the son of David, the Messiah, and with him Elijah.

Who will let me be a bird
I shall fly on wings
I shall see the Temple and the Sanctuary
My heart rejoices
I shall visit small and large
My transgressions will be forgiven
I beg the mercies of the merciful one to have compassion
on me
And send the son of David, the Messiah, and with him Elijah.

Your love, there is cure in it
For all hosts
Torah will impart strength
To all the souls
Who with your dust will be covered,
Prostrate himself and kiss
Who will let me die there, I shall be early for resurrection
And send the son of David, the Messiah, and with him Elijah.

By virtue of the good deeds of our fathers
He will build His palace
The Merciful One in our Temple
Will plant His banner
Soon He will gather in our dispersal
Will uphold His promise

I will send you Elijah the prophet[38]
And send the son of David, the Messiah, and with him Elijah.

A Poem by Rabbi Yosef ben Hayyūn: "Yā rabb khālik jamīʿ mā kān"

The writer of the poem "Yā rabb khālik jamīʿ mā kān," Rabbi Yosef ben Ḥayyūn, is not mentioned in other sources, but he was clearly a contemporary of Rabbi Shelomo ben Shalom Zarqā, the author of the previous poem; hence he lived in the nineteenth century.[39] This work, like the previous poem, is constructed as a *muwashshaḥ*. Everything stated about the previous poem regarding language and orthography holds for this one too. This poem also is written to the melody of an Arabic song, a love song. The poem here is according to the text found in Rabbi Shelomo ben Shalom Zarqā's *Rinna vi-yshuʿa* (Livorno, 1856: 1: 125b).

Yet another [poem] by my soul mate, Torah educator, our revered teacher Rabbi Yosef ben Ḥayyūn, may the Lord protect and redeem him.

Melody: "My Assurance Is in Your Greatness,
Son of the Bird"

Please, God, Creator of all
Save your servant from the hand of man
Have Grace on me, One of mighty deeds.
Your salvation I await, supreme God
Safeguard Your servant day and night.

Your loving-kindness I request, please, the Provider
Be merciful to the man of distress
I come before You by virtue of the righteous ones.
Hear my prayer in full
Safeguard Your servant day and night.

Have mercy on Your people, please, my Lord!
Send the son of David to gather in our dispersal
And build the Temple in our day.
And my heart will rejoice in the gathering of my people
Safeguard Your servant day and night.

Let Your people prevail over Ishmael
And over the oppressor, him the uncircumcised
Build us the beloved Temple.
I shall forget my adversity and all my sad events
Safeguard Your servant day and night.

A Passover Poem for the Exodus from Egypt and the Ten Plagues by Rabbi Eliyahu ben Yosef Guej: "Khallīnī naskar yā yāhūdī"

Rabbi Eliyahu ben Yosef Guej, was one of the Tunis sages of the second half of the nineteenth century.[40] The poem is written in a simple structure of the *zajal* (a kind of a girdle song). It was published in many editions of the Passover Haggadah in the Tunisian rite. The text here is according to the edition of Rabbi David Barda's *Maggid* (Tunis, n.d.: 81–83).

Melody: *Galli sod arum gat*; and in Arabic:
"Please Send the Only One"

Let me get tipsy, Oh, Jew
On Passover, the rejoicing of my fathers.

Listen to me, feasters
He was, is, and will be my Savior
With wine I shall fill my glass
And I shall bless the God of my fathers.

I shall fill my goblet and I shall get drunk
With the Song of Songs I shall offer thanks
After the splendid seder
For the rejoicing of the freeing of my fathers.

Listeners, what have they done to us!
With hard labor they enslaved us
We built cities and warehouses
All enumerated by the hand of God.

God revealed from his heaven
May He be praised for His excellence.
He said to Moses: "My children have died,
They smote them with the rod."

"Go to them and declare to them,
Inform them of My name and make them joyful.
I am the Lord, the God of Abraham
Father of the tethered, the bound."

Israel heard his word
They complained about Pharaoh and his servants
God was jealous and eliminated his oppressors
With the massive ten plagues.

He is the true God
Turned all the waters to blood
Pharaoh's people were left thirsty
Their tongue dry as wood.

He drew forth frogs from the rivers
And dispelled the rest of all the inhabitants
Not even the ovens were stopped against them
And in their beds like worms.

With lice and wild animals
He raged at them and they did not return
The Lord of Hosts added to them
Endless pestilence.

He caused boils in plenty on them
With hail and fire he agitated them
Locusts he brought down on them
He made darkness upon them and they were left paralyzed.

Their minds withered in the darkness
They had not prepared lamps
Next he struck their firstborn
They shouted and scratched their cheeks.

This plague was hard
And Pharaoh sent all of them out
They despoiled them and they left hurriedly
And their dough was in a knotted bundle.

They camped on the shore of the sea
Pharaoh reached them racing
With six hundred heroes
And countless chariots of Egypt.

While Moses stands and prays
And God above him was revealed
He struck the sea and left a host routed
On paths twelve in number.

Moses parted the sea with his staff
And through it he took across his tribes
And drowned Pharaoh and his troops
Tossed them ashore strewn about.

He closed again the waters over the Egyptians
The young men died on their horses
And Israel in great joy
Sang a song for what had happened.

Moses turned to call out
To God of mighty greatness
And he brought out Israel in its glory
From the sea and it was made frozen.

Dry was the sea and a way was formed
Like a dry land and desert
You'd say "paved with tiles"
And it deluged Pharaoh.

They praise the God of heavens
With Miriam, Moses' sister
The women go after her
With a new Hallel and songs.

So from Egypt they went forth free men
With the bitter herbs that they ate
They made their dough into matzot
On burning fire their sleep left them.

Joseph's coffin was with them
As he had commanded them
The son of Jacob, Abraham's grandson
Like him let him be glad.

In Sinai the tribes assembled
And God was revealed in truth
Then he gave us the Torah
And all creatures are witnesses.

He led us through the wilderness and He fed us
The manna and with quail he sated us
On the desert ways forty years
And then brought us into the land of my fathers.

Goodness and glory without limit
And built for us the Temple
Remove from us our transgressions
By a sacrifice and burning fire.

Have compassion on us in mercy
And restore us to our pristine glory
And forgive us for our transgressions
And may what is lost be restored and exist.

Pardon our sins, and go on
To send us the son of David
Let us live a life of contentment
And let our constricted heart expand.

Bring us all good things
And may Elijah the Prophet come to us with good tidings
And have mercy on your lowly servant
Who praises without end.

Let me get tipsy, Oh Jew
On Passover, the rejoicing of my fathers.

Poems in Honor of Rabbi Shim'on Bar Yoḥai

Arabic *Sharḥ* of Bar Yoḥai: "A'ṭiyū li-lāhinā shukra"

Many editions of the books of the liturgy and the poems in the custom of Tunisia and Tripoli contain an Arabic *sharḥ* of the well-known poem "Bar Yoḥai nimshaḥta ashrekha" by Rabbi Shim'on ben Lavi, which is one of the favorite poems of the Jews of North Africa. The verses of the *sharḥ* are interspersed with verses of the original Hebrew, from which it draws many locutions and ideas, as if it were a work of translation; but it is far from being a translation on any level. It is a completely free rendering of the Hebrew original. Presumably, precisely because of the difficult language of the Hebrew original, which includes many kabbalistic allusions comprehensible only to scholars acquainted with Jewish mysticism, the need arose to present the poem to those who were not learned, including women, who adulated the figure of Shim'on Bar Yoḥai. In that way they would understand the recited text and could fully identify with it. The proof of this is that the *sharḥ* is written in the spoken language, in contrast to the foregoing poems in this chapter, and is devoid of recondite kabbalistic allusions. Note that the women participated in throngs in the celebrations honoring the righteous, alongside the men. It was they who prepared the food, the decorations, and the candles for the festivities. We even find that a woman composed a poem for one of the pious men whose grave it was customary to visit, namely, Rabbi Yosef Ha-Ma'ravi.

The author of this *sharḥ* is unknown, but clearly he was alive in the mid-nineteenth century, as the work is found in print from that time on. Differences in the many printings are manifold, which attests to the poem's extensive use in the diverse communities. It is certain that most of the changes in the text reflect different dialects of Arabic spoken in southern and northern Tunisia and in Tripoli, so that we cannot know where the author hails from. The version given here is according to a slim volume issued by a printing house in Djerba, without a title page or indication of the year. It contains two poems in honor of Bar Yoḥai: the one given here interspersed with verses from Shim'on ben Lavi's poem, and the poem given in the next section. The poem's structure is a kind of simple *muwashshaḥ*, suitable for a folk rendering by heart. The last line in every strophe ends with the word pair *Bar Yoḥai.*

Give thanks to your God
All who live
He will save us from every sorrow
By virtue of Bar Yoḥai.

Oil of holy unction
Anointed on the day of the festival
In the building of the sanctuary
We will make a new rejoicing
A crown embroidered with flowers like lentils
On the head of the king David
Studded with stones
By virtue of Bar Yoḥai.

A seat good and choice
In our land Zion
There a cave and trees
In the place of Rabbi Shim'on
Who is like unto him in splendor
On the land of Meron
When you go out to the field
Call out: Bar Yoḥai.

Boughs of sandalwood and amber
Are placed in the House of the Lord
With pearls and marble
The Temple is raised up
By virtue of Rabbi El'azar
He will save us from evil
And will gather us with courage
By virtue of Bar Yoḥai.

And to the apple tree
You went up on that day

To pick the blossoms that budded
Secrets of the *Zohar*
How heady grew those scents
Within the courtyards
With his colleagues in the *Iddera*[41]
My master Bar Yoḥai.

You girded yourself with courage
In the depths of the *Zohar*
Like a firebrand in the desert
Burning without sparks
In your hand the sword of heroism
Happy the eye that saw
To you will come the gratitude
My master Bar Yoḥai.

The place of the pearl stones
There the Torah was given
The lion's face in the kingship
You and the colleagues
You will save us from death's mouth
And from worms and dust
You will save us from all troubles
My master Bar Yoḥai.

In the Holy of Holies
All his colleagues with him
With crowns of gold bedecked
Kingly in his attire
For those fifty days
Seven weeks
When misfortune assailed them
Bar Yoḥai redeemed them.

A small *yod* in letters
With wisdom achieved
The mighty Torah of our God
With seventy modes was interpreted
To him I shall burst out in song
And my mouth shall not be silent
And I will not be sated of the *Iddera*
Recited by Bar Yoḥai.

A sublime and high light
Strong, and before it I shall tremble
The sound of your dear voice
Happy the eye that has seen
The eye shall not be sated of seeing
Until I see the attributes
The eye will see nothing save you
My master Bar Yoḥai.

Happy is the mother
Happy are your people
Present in the session
Hearing from your mouth.
To you I shall bring the vow
And I shall call on your name
In distress and misfortune
I shall call: Bar Yoḥai.

A Poem in Honor of Rabbi Shim'on Bar Yoḥai: "Ism allah nbārek"

As stated, the figure of Shim'on Bar Yoḥai was greatly venerated by the Jews of Tunisia, particularly in the south of the country. His festival on Lag la-'Omer was celebrated by masses of people, and to this day on the island of Djerba it is an attraction for many tourists from elsewhere in Tunisia and even abroad. These festivals used to be celebrated by crowds of simple folk and women, and for them poems were composed in the spoken Arabic dialect. This poem too was published in many editions of the liturgical books of the Jews of Tunisia; the version here is according to the same booklet published in Djerba where the previous poem was found (see previous section). The order of the verses varies in the different sources; for example, our verse order is different from the verse order printed in the four-page booklet *Nava tehilla*, published by Daniel Ḥagège in Tunis (n.d.). The author of this poem is not known. The structure of the poem is simple.

We shall bless the name of the Lord for ever
O Rabbi Shim'on, peace be upon you.

On your account, our master, we shall go up to our land
The son of David will come to us, will be zealous for us
and will redeem us
He will be preceded by Elijah who will announce for us
By virtue of the *Zohar* which Bar Yoḥai read.

Hear, O Israel, these words are pearls
Moses our teacher brought down the Tablets
On one side emerald and on the other side pearls
On them the Ten Commandments written.

Hear, O Israel, this good word
Have faith, Israel, this world will pass away
The Messiah will come to us, he will display the
declaration
He will lead us to Jerusalem and we shall see every good thing.

Hear, O Israel, this great word
Believe, Israel, in the resurrection of the dead
The Messiah will come to us and will make our worries vanish

He will lead us to Jerusalem, the *samekh mim*[42] will depart.

Hear, O Israel, at the beginning of that time
He commanded Bezalel to build the tabernacle for us
A pupil of Moses our Teacher, peace be upon him
His mother Yochebed and his sister Miriam and his
father the master Aaron the priest.

Hear, O Israel, it is written in the Midrash
The Messiah will bring us and the twelve tribes
Will bring us to Jerusalem and free of money
And will gather us all in the Temple.

There we shall bless God, His grace forever
He commanded Moses our master to take us out from
Pharaoh's hands
His horses and their riders drowned in the sea
When Israel went out, trumpet blasts were heard.

Let us ask of our Lord that our desire be fulfilled
Let the Messiah come to us, let him blow the horn
Let him gather us all small and great
And David the king will reign over us.

We shall hear the horn from heaven
The mountains will dance, the trees will clap their hands
The wise men will compose poems and their voices will
cause trembling
The nations will look upon us and their hearts will be torn.

The King the true and faithful Messiah
We shall hold a feast with the Leviathan fish
All the forefathers will be at the feast
All the matriarchs will prepare it.

How pleasant is your place, Rabbi Shim'on
How pleasant is the cave of your son El'azar
We shall rejoice in your honor, all Israel
They will lead us, our transgression will be ended.

The night of the eighteenth of Iyyar
The celebration of Rabbi Shim'on will be seen
In that cave sages will sojourn and will read the *Zohar*
The candles lit and scented with amber.

We shall make a feast in the middle of the way,
O, the joy of Israel in the sons of Moses
Efraim and Menashe will overtake them
The nations will look upon us helpless.

Worship, Israel, and refine the devotion
May the built Temple come down from Heaven
May all Israel assemble in it
Let us see our enemies laid low in the streets.

Poems for the Graves of Saintly Men

A Poem in Honor of Rabbi Frājī Shawwāṭ: "Yā ilāhanā yā ilāhanā / rabbi frājī ykūn ma'ānā"

Rabbi Frājī Shawwāṭ, who lived in the late sixteenth and early seventeenth century, was one of the figures most admired by the Jews of Tunisia. He is known principally as a poet. Most of his works were collected by Efraim Ḥazan and the remainder by Michal Saraf.[43] His grave is in Testūr, a small town in northern Tunisia, about 120 km west of Tunis. It is a major pilgrimage center for the Jews of Tunisia, together with the pilgrimage to the grave of Rabbi Yosef Ha-Ma'ravi in al-Hāmma and to the grave of Rabbi Ya'aqov Salāma in Nabeul. Some of the traditions of Rabbi Shawwāṭ's marvelous life, especially the event of his burial, were absorbed into this Judeo-Arabic poem, whose author is not known and which was printed several times. One appearance is in Ḥazan's *Shire frājī shawwāṭ*, accompanied by a Hebrew translation.[44] The version given here is according to the book *Refu'a shelema* (Djerba, 1932: 95–103).[45]

Please, our God, please, our God
Let Rabbi Frājī be with us.

O people, hear what happened
With Rabbi Frājī, how he died
He sent for the treasurer[46]
And said to him, "Come to us."

Indeed the treasurer came before him
He began to ask him with signs
Who visited him and about his honored place
His sins are forgiven before our God.

He said to him, "Do come before me
And do not interrupt my words.
Here I am, my days numbered
I go to our God."

He said to him, "Rabbi, how can you leave us?
For it is you who are like our parents
God will not take you away from us
Until the dead live."

He said to him: "What shall I do, my son
My fate is not in my hands
My fate is in the hands of my God
He can now resurrect the dead."

This event was on the Sabbath
The angels were revealed to the Rabbi.

He said, "Now came the end
Today I shall close the account."

The Rabbi said the afternoon prayer
And his forefathers made a loud noise in joy
They said, "Today we shall make a rejoicing
For our son who will come before us."

When he made the Third Repast
And stood to offer the Evening service
He found the Presence in the house
And he said, "Blessed be He who enters into us."

When he stood to offer the Evening service
The angel was revealed to him
Until he completed Havdalah
And made the blessing over the myrtle.

He washed his hands and read from the *Zohar*
And made a meal of fruit
Happy is he who comes and is present
He answered Amen in his tongue.

"Please, treasurer, Hear you
What you shall do after my death
Place me in a coffin on my beast of burden
And in the place you stop, bury me."

The Rabbi rose easily
And went up to sleep on his bed
Like one who would sleep in the bed of the dead
May our death be like his death.

Then they gathered, small and great
And all came into the house

Happy is he who came and saw
The Rabbi at the time of his death.

Then they conveyed him on the beast
And all the congregation accompanied him
On to a place. They turned him back
They said, "You shall not pass from here."

Then the sentry[47] stood frozen in his place
And his hand dried on the stocking
He said, "I shall guard no more
Until our God release me."

They told the Bey[48] about him
And informed him of all that had happened
That the sentry's hands had dried
His language halted great and small.

The Bey and his council went down
And passed before the coffin
And they begged in every tongue
Each one supplicated in his tongue.

He said to him, "Excellent man, the sentries
Are mistaken and they do not know your honor
My servant will accompany you now
Until you reach the cemetery."

Then the sentry was released
And the Bey and the council departed
And the congregation's heart was joyful
For the miracle that God had wrought.

They continued on
They came to a river in full spate and mighty

They crossed it like marble
With the help of the Lord our God.

The Rabbi's beast of burden moved forward
And the entire congregation clustered around it
When it reached Testur[49] it crouched
Like a woman with child.

The treasurer said, "Can it be
That the revered beast of the Rabbi
Wishes his burial here?
May it be that his city be near to us."

The Rabbi—his city was Fes[50]
And at Bāja[51] the people did not know him
Until they heard the sermon from his mouth
And the words he spoke in our tongue.

Then they recognized the Rabbi's worth
They built a tall structure over his grave
By morning it had receded
He did not want to lord it over his brothers.

By him Rabbi Moshe[52] is buried
The two will not be separated
He who goes up to their grave will not know sorrows
With the help of the Lord our God.

Rabbi Moshe is holy
And his family from Bet Qirqūsh
The Sabbath night at the time of the Kiddush
Is the time of his death.

And the other from the great Fes
Praised in every quarter

They came to Testur the small town
And they were buried there beside us.

Those present, please ask of the Rabbi
That we shall, with God's will, be gathered up
at the time of the resurrection of the dead
And we shall be seen by our master in our eyes.

Who will know your worth, O good one
From the time you were a child
'Til you grew up and became a master
In the way of the Lord our God.

From your childhood a chosen prophet
You know what is about to happen
You study by night and by day
The Torah of the Lord our God.

You were learned, my master the Rabbi
A poet in the language of the Arabs
God graced you with poetry
The Creator of the World and its foundations.

A sublime sage and poet
Your light is in the world of *Zohar*
Whoever shall visit you will return and worship
Our Creator and our Maker.

But for you Arabic poetry would be spurned
The poet could not express himself
Your mouth speaks poetry without impediment
And rhyme and its meter succeed.

The Hebrew language too
You have love for it

It is your true mother
You compose its poetry and its prosody.

Your marvelous poems are well-known
Meter and verse and precision
And praises to God of untold number
With fervor and passion and warmth.

Beloved of God are you, my master
In your generation one and special
I entreat you to pray, O good one
For us before our God.

Before God pray for us
That he save us from all distress
Remove every obstacle from around us
And we shall always be joyful.

A Poem by Ḥayyim Fittūsī in Honor of Rabbi Yosef Ha-Ma'ravi: "Maqāmak fī al-'en yā maḥlā"

Rabbi Yosef Ha-Ma'ravi is a legendary figure among the Jews of Tunisia, yet we have no real information on his time and place. All that is known is that he hailed from Morocco (in Arabic: al-Maghreb, the West), hence the name Ma'ravi (in Hebrew: the Western), and he apparently lived in the second half of the sixteenth century. His burial place in the town of al-Ḥāmma, about 30 km west of Gābes, was the most important place of pilgrimage for the Jews of southern Tunisia.

Many tales were told about Rabbi Yosef al-Ma'ravi, and they were first collected in a Judeo-Arabic booklet titled *History of the Deeds of al-Sayyid Rabbi Yosef al-*Ma'ravi (Djerba, 1940). Next they were gathered by Ḥwātī Dimrī in a more comprehensive book of praises titled *Yosef ḥai* (Djerba, 1945), patterned on the *Shevaḥe ha-ari*. This book contains a Hebrew text printed on the upper part of its pages and a Judeo-Arabic text on the lower part.

Many poems were also written about Rabbi Yosef Ha-Ma'ravi and about the pilgrimage to his grave, all of them in Judeo-Arabic. Some of these poems were printed as individual booklets or pamphlets, and others are known only in handwritten manuscripts. One of the poems was written by a woman called Kokḥa, wife of Bebaḥ Būkhobza of Sousse, and it was also printed as a small pamphlet under the title "A *piyyuṭa* in Honor of Rabbi Yosef al-Ma'ravi." It was published by the printing house of Makhlūf Najjār in Sousse, without indication of the year; in our view it was in the 1930s. This rare feature of a poem in honor of a saintly man written by a woman attests to the active and massive participation of women in the celebrations for saintly men, as noted earlier. Michal Malakhi (Saraf), the late renowned scholar of Tunisian Jewry, published a Hebrew book titled *The Grace of Yosef: R. Yosef Ha-Ma'ravi of Tunisia, His Life History, and His Miracles* (Lod, 1998), and in it she assembled information about the rabbi as well as stories and poems, some from manuscripts, including Koka Būkhobza's *piyyut*, with a Hebrew translation. Incidentally, the common nickname of Rabbi Yosef Ha-Ma'ravi by the Jews of Tunisia is simply al-Sayyid (the master). In his honor the given name Ma'ravi is common among the Jews of southern Tunisia.

In what follows we set out one of the poems written in the 1940s concerning the pilgrimage to Rabbi Yosef Ha-Ma'ravi's grave. It is by Ḥayyim Fittūsī, of the Gābes community, and it is set to the melody of an Arabic love song. The poem was printed as a separate sheet and is not included in Michal Malakhi's book. The poem has a singular *zajal* structure. After every second line there is the refrain *Yā sayyid* (O master!), and after every fourth line is the refrain *Yā maḥlā* (How lovely!). All these factors indicate the choral performance of the poem, most probably by women present at the celebration.

In honor of Rabbi Yosef al-Ma'ravi, may his virtue stand us in good stead, Amen

Set to the melody "Your Talk by Eye"

Its composer is the youth Ḥayyim ben
Moshe Fittūsī of Gābes.

Your grave is before my eyes, how pleasant!
The pilgrimage to the grave of the master, the paragon of beauty.

How dear is your grave
I long to dwell in proximity to you, O master!
I shall be numbered among your servants
Forever present before the eye. How lovely!

Present before the eyes
Who visits you, may he be kept safe, O master!
Rabbi Shim'on
And Rabbi Meir are guarantors for him. How lovely!

Present before my eyes
Your love rests within me, O master!
Save us from every ill
And let us not be in evil. How lovely!

We will not be in distress
Save us from all sorrows, O master!
A youth with an elder
To God and to you we hope. How lovely!

We shall hope to you
My God, do not prevent joy, O master!
All who have come
And greatly desire you. How lovely!

They desire you to excess
And bring you all the vows, O master!
Like the festivals

We shall be all joyful. How lovely!

According to custom
Reading and *piyyut* and orchestra, O master!
According to custom
Let us all be well. How lovely!

All the pilgrims
Are joyful without flaw, O master!
Great with small
You will grant their wishes. How lovely!

By virtue of the Sayyid
To every childless one a son will be born, O master!
At the place of Ha-Ma'ravi he will rejoice and celebrate
Next year at that time they will come joyful. How lovely!

Satisfy the desire
With the glory of God whom they worship, O master!
All are witnesses
To your great miracles. How lovely!

Poems on the Ghrība on the Island of Djerba

The Ghrība is a renowned ancient synagogue on the island of Djerba, which according to tradition was founded by Yo'av ben Ṣeruya, who fled from King David. The legend of the synagogue's establishment was committed to print in a Hebrew booklet titled *The Story of the Ghrība of Djerba*, produced at the printing house of Mqīqeṣ Sa'dūn in Djerba in 1939 (a second edition was published by the same printing house in 1941). It is noteworthy that the Jewish community of Djerba has in recent years become the most important spiritual center of Tunisian Jewry, among other things because of the many yeshivas and Hebrew printers there, from which have emerged hundreds of books, pamphlets, and other publications of all kinds.

Over the years the Ghrība has attracted many visitors and pilgrims from all over Tunisia and the countries of North Africa and recently Tunisian emigrants in France. Many legends and wonders have been fashioned around it. The great veneration for the synagogue led to the construction of synagogues of similar design in various Israeli places where former Tunisians created communities, such as Ofakim and Acre. A similar synagogue is planned to be built in the Talpiyyot neighborhood of Jerusalem. On Lag la-'Omer each year a great celebration is held in honor of Rabbi Shim'on Bar Yoḥai, and it draws many thousands of pilgrims, including Jews and others from Europe and Israel. The high point of the celebration is the grand procession of a menorah adorned with silk cloths and myrtle. It is brought out from the synagogue, paraded through the city streets, and then afterward returned to the synagogue. Because of this procession the festival is called *ʿīd al-manāra* (the festival of the menorah).

In what follows we set out two poems in honor of this synagogue from a Hebrew booklet titled *The Ghrība of Djerba*, published by the printing house of Eliyahu Cohen (Djerba, n.d.). The first poem is constructed in simple *zajal* form.

A Poem by Ḥayyim Fittūsī:
"Ziyārat ribbī shim'on fī kull 'amāla"
Poems in honor of al-Ghrība, may its virtue stand us in good stead, Amen

Its author is the youth Ḥayyim ben Moshe Fittūsī of Gābes

To the tune of "None Is Afflicted Like Me"

The pilgrimage to Rabbi Shim'on in every place
Women and men go up to there.

O Ghrība, your love before my eyes

For you we come as pilgrims here
May it be that by your virtue all evil will go far off
Everyone of good heart and joyous, safe in God.

O Ghrība, people march on pilgrimage
Bearing with them candles and incense
For you they march and cross oceans
He who went up to you on pilgrimage once paid his vow.

O Ghrība, every year we shall go up to you on pilgrimage
And all of us will be your servant
May it be that by your virtue your oppressors will be doomed
And the star of every pilgrim to you will shine.

O Ghrība, your glory is splendid and precious
Piyyutim and orchestra and presentation
And your name reaches as far as Paris
And every city and every place.

By virtue of Rabbi Shim'on and Rabbi Meir
With God's help all your worries will be eliminated
For another year old and young will make the pilgrimage to you
Young girls and women, children along with men.

Answer Amen, all those present
Long live Abba and Natan and Khammūs Cohen
May the wishes of all the pilgrims have fulfilled
All their wishes without delay.

How pleasant to me is the pilgrimage up to it
Forever in my heart love for it will dwell
From afar it is seen, how glorious its throng

And all its visitors will give it their wealth.

No one will make the pilgrimage to you with a heavy heart
And at your place all the Jews will be happy
With piano and cymbals, drum and fiddle
With study and *piyyut* and lighted candles.

May by your virtue all is always delighted
And all who go up to you on pilgrimage will be happy
May God let you live to go on another pilgrimage
And everyone with a wish in his heart, it will come true.

Your honor, Ribbi Shim'on, is always known
And your comeliness I have seen with my eyes
May our teacher the judge Ribbi Makhlūf live
Always with everyone may he act with forbearance.

Visiting you, O Ghrība, is sweet and delicious
May by your virtue sorrow will be eliminated
Please, God, protect us during the sailing in the ship
And no hindrance will come on us.

A Poem by Zion ben Mordekhai: "Zūrūnī yā allī 'araftūnī"

Its author is Zion ben Mordekhai ben Frīja of Gābes.

To the tune of "Cure Me, You Who Have Wounded Me"

Come to me on the pilgrimage, those who know me
Every year, and come hither
I shall be glad and I will welcome you with my eyes.

Let all the people make the pilgrimage to me
My love within you will not end

Why should you delay in visiting me
And as the measure of my love for you, love me.

Visit me once every year
All sorrow will go far from you
And you will not see a turbulent life
Set your mind to it, forget me not.

How marvelous is the night of the celebration
With menorah and lighted candles
With apples of gold
Upon it, how wonderful they are to me.

They will go round it from house to house
And in their progress they will not be late
At the yeshiva they will give funds
The virtue of the public will succor me.

People come to me on the pilgrimage from all the lands
Little ones and men and women
Long live Khammūs and Abba and Natan
They are versed in my customs.

Long live all the loved ones
In every generation order and precision
They prepare glasses of arak and wine
All I request they will grant me.

Be glad, congregation of Israel
God will reveal the End
Soon the Redeemer will come to us
I shall be glad and my eyes will look upon him.

Let us supplicate from God full of mercy
That he remove from them every worry

May Ṣiyyon and Ḥayyim live
And not see any evil.

O, members of the fellowship, may you live to see the coming year
Let there be not one anxious person among you
And God save you from any harm
Make the pilgrimage to me every year.

Poems for the Life-Cycle

At the life cycle ceremonies—birth, circumcision, bar mitzvah, marriage, and death—the women would assemble and sing Judeo-Arabic songs containing many motifs from the Jewish sources. In the following sections we present several songs that were published in a book by the mohel Gaston Gez (Tunis, 1942: 36–44).

A Poem for a Mother Giving Birth: "Yā qābla yā al-sūsiyya"

"Yā qābla yā al-sūsiyya" was written to the melody of an Arabic song that begins with the same words. The word *al-sūsiyya* refers to the midwife's place of origin, but it is doubtful that this has any significance in the Judeo-Arabic poem beyond it being copied simply because the melody of the Arabic song was borrowed. The prosodic traits of the poem are clear marks of a popular poem composed essentially orally. The versions in print are not exactly the same.

To the melody "O Midwife, Woman from Sousse"

O midwife, woman from Sousse
Everything you asked [as payment] is little
I shall get up on the seventh day
And I shall take you out wrapped up.
To you the praise our God,
A male child, not a daughter.

When she was going to give birth
She placed her hand on the sideboard
She didn't send us out for a doctor
May the Lord our God save her
To you the praise our God
She gave birth and arose happy.

When she was going to give birth
She placed her hand on the wall
Her husband rejoiced in her joy
He said, "God grant that my son and my daughter live."
To you the praise Lord our God
She gave birth and rose to my room.

When she was going to give birth
On Thursday evening
And her husband rejoiced in her joy
May it be that you bring forth a hundred for me
To you the praise our God
She gave birth without any harm.

O midwife, O welcome one
O radiant face, O fortunate one
You gave me the good news, May God give you every good thing
We shall reward you and you are alive
Tomorrow I shall arise to my family
And I shall give you whatever you may desire.

O midwife, put on the gown
And say to the lad, "Blessed be the arrival."
He said, "O my dear father,
With God's will you will see tefillin[53] and the wedding canopy."
To you the praise my God

My mother gave birth without a doctor.

O midwife, put on the embroidered material
Welcome the lad as a bridegroom
He said, "O my old father,
With God's will you will see my benediction[54] and you
will drink of the Kiddush."

A Poem for a Mother Giving Birth: "Yā qābla yā qāblatnā"

The melody of the song that this poem is set to is a well-known Hebrew refrain chanted in the North African custom when the Torah scroll is taken out of the Ark. The poem's structure is not uniform throughout, which is an indication of its popular nature.

To the melody "Torat emet natan lanu / Barukh asher baḥar banu"

O midwife, our midwife
How pleasant is your entry into our threshold
The baby, we took him
May you be like this to the members of our fellowship.
Torat emet

I knew the newborn son from when I was pregnant with him
Fluttering like a butterfly
But the hovering daughter
Causes my bones to tremble.
Torat emet

O midwife, take up my train
And show this babe to me
If you say to me "A son"
I will give you an earring from my ear
If you say "A daughter"
Your head will be broken into pieces with a jar.
Torat emet

A Poem for the Circumcised Infant: "Al-ḥaḍra al-masmiyya"

From its language, the poem "Al-ḥaḍra al-masmiyya" seems to have been entirely Muslim in origin and was borrowed by the Jews with a change of the Muslim motifs to Jewish ones.

To the melody "This is circumcision and worship of God /
And he is circumcised according to the custom"

The excellent assembly
Bedecked with flowers
The birthing mother without any harm
Will raise him and will be joyful in him.
This is a circumcision

The son, may God keep his youth constant
When he grows he will go to his school
He will make friends with his comrades
A yeshiva and even a school.
This is a circumcision

The son is sweet and pleasant to the taste
How beautiful his eyebrows, suited to his eyes
Like the day of the circumcision we shall live to see the
day of the tefillin
The beloved ones will also rejoice.
This is a circumcision

The child is sweet and jolly
He will go with his father to the shop
He will buy little children's toys
His mother too will be glad.
This is a circumcision

A Poem for a Circumcision: "Eliyahu yjī yzūrhu"

The poem "Eliyahu yjī yzūrhu" is recited on the eve of the reading of the *Zohar* (*līl al-tūmār*), the eve of the circumcision ceremony.

Poems according to the custom of Nabeul
To the melody "Ribbi Shim'on Bar Yoḥai, His Virtue
Will Defend Us"

Elijah will come to visit him
Will find him reading in the book
Today we participated at his circumcision
God willing we shall participate at his tefillin.
Ribbi Shim'on

Elijah will visit him in his room
He will find him and his wife
In his hand a book of his Torah
Light of my eye my master Bar Yoḥai
Ribbi Shim'on

Elijah will visit him in his time
He will find him wearing tefillin
God willing joyful to eternity
By virtue of the righteous Bar Yoḥai
Ribbi Shim'on

Elijah will visit him at his home
He will find him with his sons
He will continue revealing to him his secrets
Secrets of my master Bar Yoḥai
Ribbi Shim'on

A Poem for the Circumcised Child: "L-emtā narjā fīk"

The poem "L-emtā narjā fīk" is written to the melody of an Arab Muslim love song.

To the melody "'Til When Shall We Await You and Your Messenger Does Not Come"

'Til when shall we await you
And the Messiah does not come
God will bring him to us
And you will not know when.

We shall say "with a good sign"
And hearts will rejoice
The father of the beloved son
By all the people.

The midwife dressed him
Handed him over to the circumciser
He is crying with his voice
The knife is ready.

On the third night
Elijah will come to us
He will heal him in his time
His joy is ready.

His joy is learning
And *Zohar* and orchestra
And a vow with added devotion
And all the people will kiss him.

A Poem for the Circumcised Child: "Eliyahu ha-navi yzūrnā"

"Eliyahu ha-navi yzūrnā" may not be a complete poem but part of a more extensive one. In any event, it describes faithfully the customs of the Jews of Tunisia at the circumcision ceremony.

Elijah the Prophet will visit us
And will take part in our rejoicing of the circumcision.

Waft incense over the circumcision chair
And spread over it the covering and the Holy Book.

And light the candle that there be light
So that Elijah the Prophet shall be with us.

Zionist Poems by Gaston Bshīrī al-'Awwād

One of the interesting phenomena attesting to the extensive use of Judeo-Arabic by the intellectuals of the Jewish community in Tunisia since the late nineteenth century is the translation of Hebrew poems into the local Arabic dialect and their setting to the melodies of well-known Arabic songs. Several examples are found in the eight-page booklet *Part One of Songs of Zion, Translated Poems*, published by Gaston Bshīrī in Tunis at the beginning of the twentieth century. The preface on the title page signifies when these translated poems were sung: "Poems through which pupils of the Jewish Alliance school are taught by the teacher, the musician Gaston Bshīrī, and they are recited every Sabbath in the New Synagogue." Bshīrī himself was a teacher at the school, known by his nickname al-'Awwād, that is, the musician. On the overleaf (p. 2) of the booklet, Bshīrī explains the reason for publishing the songs: "At the request of a group of people, that I publish for them the poems through which the pupils at the Talmud Torah learn. And I undertook to publish all the poems which appear anew in translation. And *shalom* from your brother Gaston Bshīrī al-'Awwād." At the end of the booklet (p. 8) Bshīrī promises that soon the second part of *Songs of Zion* will appear. Presumably, he himself translated the poems, although this is not stated. The translation is generally literal, sometimes slightly enlarged. In a few places the translator has added explanatory notes in parentheses.

One of the poems is "O Motherland," two strophes probably from an unidentified modern Hebrew poem from the Zionist time.

The words "A Zionist poem" precede the poem, and there is a drawing of a shield of David after it.

The poem "Ha-tikvah" was also translated into the Tunisian Judeo-Arabic dialect, and the melody of an Arabic song was adapted for it. One account states that the Jews and Arabs used to sing it in Arabic in coffeehouses. Makhlūf Najjār noted this custom in an essay about an Arab musical ensemble in Sousse called al-Sāḥiliyya (translated from Arabic): "An Arab musical ensemble made up of Muslim and Jewish elements, and it was always a pleasant joy for the citizens of Sousse when many times they heard new Arab and Jewish melodies (among them the Zionist marching song 'Ha-tikvah') and others with the utmost precision and perfection. Training was conveyed under the leadership of the conductor Mr. al-Hādī al-Sharīf'."[55]

In addition we find a Judeo-Arabic translation of some Hebrew poems included in the traditional repertoire, such as "Yah go'ali ṣarim 'alay no'adu," by Moshe al-Ashqar; "Reṣe le-shire qehal 'adathekha," by Raphael; and "Deleni mi-yad ha-zari," by David.[56] The main subject matter of all these poems is exile and redemption.

3

The *Malzūmāt* (Satirical Ballads)

The *malzūmāt* (sing. *malzūma*) are a new genre in Judeo-Arabic literature in Tunisia, written in the vernacular dialect, and they have nothing to do with the liturgical assemblages in the synagogue or the paraliturgical ones outside it. Therefore the Hebrew element in the *malzūmāt* is extremely slight. In this sense the *malzūmāt* are closer to another modern genre in Judeo-Arabic literature in Tunisia, the *qinot* (sing. *qina*) (laments), which we deal with Chapter 4.

The *malzūmāt*, together with the *qinot* were the most important genres in Judeo-Arabic literature in Tunisia in the first half of the twentieth century. So far as we can infer from present-day research on this literature, it seems that the *malzūmāt* preceded the *qinot* as a genre. *Malzūmāt* are found throughout the nineteenth century, in fact even before the development of modern Judeo-Arabic literature in Tunisia, following the profound changes in political, social, and cultural conditions in the second half of that century.

We have not determined the relevant etymology of the word *malzūma*.[1] However, we know that the term, which signifies a literary genre, exists in Muslim Arabic literature in Tunisia, although the connection between the Muslim genre and Jewish literature is still not clear.[2] In Judeo-Arabic literature a *malzūma* is a long secular poem, a sort of epic or ballad that describes certain events. In any event the *malzūma* is a poetic work with a certain plot, a description of a certain event, or a treatment of some social or political subject, not necessarily connected with religious life. Thus it contrasts with the *piyyutim* (liturgical poems) in the widest sense, as presented in Chapter 2. The *piyyut* is a genre with a hoary tradition, dating back to the Middle Ages, and *piyyutim* are distinctly linked to religious life as liturgical compositions either for the synagogue service or for social occasions of a religious nature, such as pilgrimages to the graves of saintly men or circumcision. The *malzūma* is entirely separate from these contexts. Furthermore, the different kinds of *piyyutim* always refer to the national-religious subject of exile and redemption, whereas the *malzūmāt* are indifferent to this concern. Accordingly, a *piyyut* is always written in a grave tone, whereas a *malzūma* may be droll, such as the *malzūmāt* on the preparations for Passover. Nevertheless, we cannot state categorically that the *malzūma* is a work intended to amuse.

For the time being, it seems to us correct to describe the course of formation of the modern genres in Judeo-Arabic literature in Tunisia in the following manner.[3] The ancient tradition of the *piyyut* underwent innovation in the form of *piyyutim* written for social and religious ceremonies away from the synagogue, parallel to the steady decrease in liturgical compositions for the synagogue until they all but disappeared. On the margins of this tradition, and even before the development of modern Judeo-Arabic literature in Tunisia, several poems were written and inserted at the end of the Passover Haggadah in a rather jocular spirit. These are the *malzūmāt* depicting preparations for the festival and the economic strain they caused. We believe that in the very writing and inclusion of these *malzūmāt* in the Passover Haggadah, there is evident influence of the famous *piyyutim* "Ḥad gadya" and "Eḥad mi yodea'" which were composed as early as the Middle Ages and were accepted in the custom by almost all the Jewish communities. The liberal wine drinking on Passover eve—four glasses, and drinking was not an uncommon phenomenon among the Jews of Tunisia—certainly did nothing to hinder the creation of the lighter poetic genre, the *malzūma*. Proof of this lies in the poems that open with the somewhat surprising line *khallīnī naskar yā yahūdī* (Please, Jew, let me get tipsy).[4] This befits the mood of Purim rather than Passover. Be that as it may, in this way the tight ring of the religious *piyyut* was broken in terms of both its purpose and its content. Thereafter the Jews of Tunisia could write poems whose aim was not liturgical and whose content was not connected with religious life.

However, like any other literary development, the *malzūmāt* did not stem solely from internal factors at work in one school but also from external ones. By this we mean that in the new living conditions in North Africa in the second half of the nineteenth century, a pressing need arose in the Jewish intelligentsia, who saw themselves committed to lead their communities into modern life, as described in Chapter 1, to express their views in public, continuously and effectively. We have noted that the most suitable linguistic tool, or mode of mass communication, in Jewish circles was the Arabic dialect that was in use at the time. Clearly, the rabbinic literature, which also contained fairly prolific writings by the religious sages of Tunisia—Bible commentary, *Responsa*, and books on ethics—was entirely unsuited to the intellectuals' needs. Although such were the conditions of the time, it did not prevent the intellectuals from being observant Jews, and certainly they did not speak out against the religion; some of them bore the title of rabbi or openly held religious posts. The models that they saw worthy of emulation were to be found in the various literary genres of intellectual European society. These could be from either Christian or Jewish society: the press, theater, various kinds of belles lettres, theoretical works and propaganda, and for our purposes here, the leaflet ballad or the street ballad.[5] In this chapter we follow the citations of Shlomo Yaniv, a scholar of the Hebrew ballad, who wrote on these ballads in non-Jewish European literature.[6]

> The themes of the leaflet ballads were quite varied. They told of famous wars and battles, of seafarers, their tribulations out

> on the sailing routes in storms, and of the hardships of their families left behind on land. A large group of ballads described the ruses of felons, especially highwaymen. A common subject among them was the clash of parents and their child owing to the latter's choice of partner, which they deemed to be a poor one; also their attempt to separate the couple. Usually the tale is told of parents who try to prevent their wealthy daughter's marriage to a young man of low standing. In this context many ballads relate the lovers' ordeal, hiding and disguising themselves to escape being parted. Another body of leaflet ballads, of humorous bent, tells of the failure of marriage, accompanied by betrayal. But the particular theme that typified this kind of ballad, its generic marker, is concern with everyday matters, events of the day, especially with sensational content. In this respect the leaflet ballad performed the function later to be taken up by the gutter press.[7]

Yaniv's comments about the leaflet ballad distributed in England since the sixteenth century are closer to our concern. In his second book on the ballad, Yaniv writes:

> The appearance of the leaflet ballads, which were printed on one side of a large sheet of paper (hence the name) was assisted by both the invention of the press, which made cheap printing possible, and the thirst of the target public—a class of simple urban folk. They longed for subject matter that would satisfy their curiosity about what was going on around them and all over the world. They sought material that would make them wiser and would amuse them. . . . The specific element of this kind of ballad was its dealing with matters of the day and coverage of current affairs. In their subjects, and in the manner of their presentation, the leaflet ballads heralded the entry of the cheap press, which developed in their wake. The ballad researcher A. B. Friedman

> called them "journalistic ballads." In his view, even the leaflet ballads that contained sensational descriptions were essentially political. . . .
>
> For our discussion it is important to note that the peddlers of the leaflet ballads, who generally wrote them and delivered or presented them, developed various means to market their "product." Their concern was that the ballads be snatched up at once. They addressed the public in its language register, and they matched the ballads to the crowd's level and taste, and stimulated its interest.[8]

Indeed, three literary genres—the *malzūmāt*, the *qinot*, and the *ghnāyāt* (see Chapter 5)—became vehicles of expression at the intellectuals' disposal to present their views of the world and the events of the day, usually as satire written in a constructively critical way intended to correct negative manifestations. One evident example is the *malzūma* "Qā'im wa-nā'im," published in 1914 and presented later in this chapter. Its intention was to bring about the renewal of regular and proper working of the Jewish hospital in Tunis. There is no doubt either that these three genres heralded the appearance of the Judeo-Arabic press in Tunisia and that they continued to exist as part of the bustling activity of journalism.

But already by the end of the nineteenth century the Judeo-Arabic *malzūma* began to serve as a vehicle for expressions of sorrow on the passing of personalities, such as the president of France, or of ordinary people who lost their lives to unnatural causes. In fact, these *malzūmāt* played the literary and social role of the lament, and indeed, in due course the Hebrew word *qina* (lament) became the generic marker of the *malzūma* until the latter was wholly displaced. Thereafter—and by our estimate this occurred during the 1920s, after the center of Hebrew printing moved from Tunis to Sousse, primarily to the printing house of Makhlūf Najjār—every poetic work dealing with current affairs and tending to social satire was called a *qina*.

Early-twentieth-century scholars noted that the lament genre was in fact a satire.[9]

Apart from the present study, to date no real research on these literary genres of the *malzūma* and the *qina* has been conducted; even a bibliography of works in these genres has not been compiled. All the *malzūmāt* and the *qinot* were printed on separate sheets of various size, often without indication of the author's name or the printing house; they also appeared in eight-page booklets, mainly from the 1920s on, when the form of the separate sheet disappeared entirely, or nearly so. We have in our collection almost 200 *malzūmāt* and *qinot*, some original print editions and some photocopies from diverse collections. Without doubt, we are missing many others, for example, those located in public or private collections that are unavailable to us.

The late *malzūma*, and following it the *qina*, has its own literary structure, a kind of *zajal*: eight-line strophes with interwoven rhyming. The last line of every strophe rhymes with the rhyme of the opening short strophe. The meter of every line is usually eight feet. The number of lines is very large, mostly more than twenty strophes, that is, about 170 lines. Few *malzūmāt* or *qinot* have fewer than 100 lines. The formal identity of these two genres likewise supports our finding that the *qinot* grew out of the *malzūmāt*.

Scholars of the leaflet ballad called these writings vulgar and evaluated their literary worth as slight. The same largely applies to the *malzūmāt* and the *qinot*. Our perception, however, is not elitist or comparative, treating the decreed norms as absolute and obligatory. We wish to contemplate the worth of the *malzūmāt* and the *qinot* as wholly authentic compositions that sometimes have the qualities of a folk creation in the sense that its author is anonymous and it is propagated in oral versions. We also appreciate the way that the *malzūmāt* and *qinot* introduce us to the internal world of the Jewish communities in Tunisia in the last quarter of the nineteenth century and the first half of the twentieth century. This world usually did not succeed in expressing itself in the so-called canonical literature (i.e., the rabbinic literature) or in the documentary archives. Needless to say, these works can also serve as a historical resource of great importance, sometimes even in the simple sense of chronological information.

Malzūmāt for Passover

All the popular poems composed on the subject of Passover—some printed and some remaining oral—have a common theme, namely, the great expenses for the festival and the need for everything to be right and proper. These poems tell of preparing for the celebration and the dialogue between the householder and his wife a few days before the festival.[10] All the poems contain the subject of fat sheep, spring cleaning, the purchase of new clothes for all the family, and the special kinds of foods for the Passover seder. Because of economic hardship, the Jews relied on a higher power to help them get all that they needed. The supplication before God is the refrain.

Malzūmāt al-madrūkīn (The Epic of the Hard-Pressed): "Yā ilāhanā yā ilāhanā"

The speaker in "Yā ilāhanā yā ilāhanā" is a husband who tells of the tribulations he experiences when preparing for Passover and the strain he suffers on account of his wife. The poem is the version given in the Passover Haggadah from Rabbi David Barda's *Maggid* (Tunis, n.d.: 83–86).

Please, our God! Please, our God!
Let Rabbi Nissim be with us![11]

The days of Purim have passed
The bills of debts have fallen on us
We shall continue to pay the money
The Lord knows how many!

The wife wanted the whitewash

A cover for the house and the bed
Trousers, a scarf, and a towel
She has already gone through the wardrobe.

I had only stepped out over the threshold
The wife remembered a mantle
Please, my God, what about this trouble?
Here I am, going out without appetite!

I told her: "Now woman, wait,
We'll lay our burden on Rabbi Nissim,
He'll bring us the money we need,
I know, in truth he won't forget us."

She replied: "You're right,
But I can't wait for you.
Go on, trust in your God,
With God's will, He'll be a support for you."

I'm just going innocently
And the wife catches up with me:
"Bring the shoes and the hat,
The white material and the *indiāna*."[12]

Go buy two sheep
And don't bring a crooked butcher
One *qadīd* and *mergēz*[13]
And the other to help in the cooking.

I said to her: "Wait and calm down
Selling at the market is in the morning.
I'll go and buy two of the best
And their fat tails will be full."

She said to me: "Buy cups

And buy innards for mincing
And brooms before Nisan
And bring my sister to celebrate with us."

Please, my God, the festival is ruining me
How shall I start and how finish
My heart has become like blood
Look at me, please our God!

"Hey, husband, why are you worrying?
You forgot yourself entirely today
Bring me the whitewash for painting
God willing I'll whitewash with joy."

I said to her: "Oh wife, I've grown weary with worries
How shall I begin and how shall I finish?"
She became like the black slave angry
And I didn't know what I could do.

Hey woman, I've nothing left
After the pie and the fowl
You have become a reason for me to complain
Are you sober or drunk?

Oh husband, you are alright
All this is not nice for you
Ask of God and He will provide you
For his treasures are full.

I went out to work, I forgot about the situation
I earned a little cash
Which had not crossed my mind
I said, "Hey wife, God has given us."

I bought the whitewash and I brought it quickly.

She got the basin in a hurry
She crushed it with great happiness
Alone without help.

She put on a gown and a headscarf.
When I saw her I felt concern
A gown torn to shreds
Stockings on, and she's shoeless.

All the women become swollen up
Wool and rolled laundry
With great pressure they are stressed
Only our God will relieve it.

The house is ruined by shouts
Quarrels broke out in it
Old women and young girls
Over whitewashing the house's threshold.

"Please, my Father, when will You bring
Flour and matzot, the festival approaches
Cakes strewn with raisins
Make in the bakery for me."

He brought the suits and the shoes
The tarbooshes and the ties
I went up to him like an officer
I placed them in the wardrobe.

"Bring the *zigzag* and the lace[14]
Do not leave me in distress
Tomorrow is the eve of the *bediqa*[15]
Without doubt I'll be preoccupied."

"Look, we have eaten our fill of bitterness

Before we see the matzot
I work and you are worried
And the expenses still chase after us."

He went into the house and opened the door
He brought the matzot and the wine
And countless vegetables
And a sheep tied with a rope.

He brought oil with charcoal
Spices and eggs
He concluded everything she needed
And he said, "What do you want, my beauty?"

He slaughtered the sheep and porged it
Its head and innards were burnt.
"Right now I have
To mince its intestines."

Please, God, Creator of man
I am angry and glad
No one said to me, "Hey, what's your name,
Take out a suit for you with us."

I bought the bitter herbs and the ḥaroset[16]
And I went to make the matzot
And the olives and the fish roe
And the wine in carafes.

All the children
Got washed in the evening
And their mother with great love
Dresses them and she is happy.

My body is joyful and relaxed

As I see my children dressed
And my spouse before my eyes
Like a bamboo branch.

The day of Passover, Oh learned one
Praise and exalt the Creator
And rise as the dawn rises
For the service with a joyful body.

Let us give thanks to the worshipped God
Who gave the festival to the Jews
And made us joyous after the agonies
And gave us rest after our tribulations.

Please, Creator of the world
Fulfill the entreaty of those present
Next year at that time
May our God gather in our Exile.

The feast will pass and we shall miss it
Happy is he whose belly is replete
And has left nothing of his sheep
That is what God commanded us.

I have grown tired of detailing as a fortune-teller
All the expenses in the blink of an eye
The theft of the *mergēz* has not ceased
Whoever steals, I shall shame him.

Oh our God, oh our God,
Let Rabbi Nissim be with us!

The *Malzūma* of *Manāmat al-ʿatārīsh* (The Dream of the Sheep)

This *malzūma* was published on a separate sheet (Tunis, n.d.). No author is given.

Here I am, poor, the Passover week before me
What shall I tell you, what I saw in my dream.

I dreamt that I had grown rich and possessor of a fortune
But I don't have on me even half a *riyāl*[17] to whitewash my house.

I dream, and I am standing bewitched in the sheep square
Twenty sheep are my honest property and call out aloud, "*Yā līl*" (What a night!)

I'm selling them comfortably, I hold the glass
And I didn't want to sell them for fifteen a head.

And not for eighteen and not for twenty
I said, "If they are not sold in one day, they'll be sold in two days."

Please, auctioneer, go on, work well
My sheep are fat and plump, they do not live off thin air.

I feed them beans and barley and all the needful
And their tail fat, oh Compassionate one, weighs four *qantars*.[18]

But what a pity my wife woke me up from sleep
And said to me, "Oh my father, what are doing sleeping today?"

Get up, that's enough, you sunk in sleep
The sun is shining, get up, go snatch a walk.

I was awakened by the noise from my sleep, I found myself in bed
No market and no money and no sheep.

What is this curse? I closed my eyes
I drew in my head and covered myself with the blanket.

I stuck out my hand and I said to him: "Please, auctioneer, sell
At any price, don't let up, Look, I'm in a hurry."

"Give them for fifteen, give them for ten.
The money, but now—this isn't the time for chatter."

The wife heard and came lamenting:
"What's wrong with my husband, is he off his head?"

I said to her, "That's enough, shut up, you stupid woman.
You're good enough to be a beast going round and round
milling."

"Twenty sheep would have been a great help to us
May God have revenge on you that because of you I lost
them."

The *Malzūma* of *Fṭā'ir al-mākina* (The Matzo Machine)

This *malzūma* centers on the new invention at the end of the nineteenth century of a machine that could make Passover matzot, thus replacing the exhausting work of preparing matzot by hand. This invention sparked a halakhic controversy among the Jewish sages in Europe and North Africa; the fear was that the religious rules for baking matzot were not observed in the machine-baking process, and thus there was doubt that the matzot were kosher. A dispute arose over these matzot among the Jewish communities in Tunisia too, as is evident in this *malzūma*. However, the author expands on the subject beyond this question and refers in detail also to the social and folk aspects of the tumult around preparations for Passover, mainly from the viewpoint of the needy. This author is not known, but it might be Ṣemaḥ Halevi, at whose printing house it was published, as noted at the end. Ṣemaḥ Halevi, a member of a European family that had settled in Tunis, was born in 1869 and was one of the most important intellectuals and journalists in Tunisia around the turn of the twentieth century. He was one of the foremost figures in the development and proliferation of Judeo-Arabic literature.[19]

> Over the machine matzot
> This year we suffered at length.
>
> "Woe is me!" said the impoverished wretch
> "When Passover is approaching me and I am worried
> I don't know what to do
> The hardship is heavy on me."
>
> And I greatly fear the disgrace
> Which in my eyes is more than the slaughtering
> I cannot be haughty
> With reserve, that's how I was brought up.
>
> We heard about the machine and we rejoiced
> And we said we have won relief from the hard work
> With God's will it will not shame us
> This year will be blessed for us.
>
> This year all is dear
> What will be with the poor person
> The prices have increased and the people have drawn back
> And what they have is little.
>
> Came the iron machine
> Produces matzot, a new operation
> Quickly kneads the flour
> Turns on a thick spindle.

Quickly is the dough done, kneaded
Like the macaroni machine
The matzo comes out ready measured
They said: "It has a nice taste."

Thin, cracked pieces
When they are drawn out pierced
Like the act of an overlooking window they are done
Or ladders for painting.

These matzot are small and light
Tasty and eaten without garnish
It has nothing to say to *al-Fonograf*[20]
And it has nothing to say about us.

This is new enjoyable work
Matzot of France and Livorno clean work
Bird food a light biscuit
That is what is pleasant for us.

This is what will be suitable and proper for the poor person
The engineers thought and proffered advice
They said: "This year there will be order in the loaves
Our fathers before us turned it around above us."

When they departed hurriedly
From Egypt with the utmost speed
They baked loaves and made them miraculously
Without piercing it in a machine.

Our machine works easily
And makes matzot by this method
Produces thin loaves
Pierced with apertures without a machine.

Our machine will knead by measure
Pours out in an instant from the sack
An oven and belts, wonderful things
Something our old folks and our forefathers did not know.

Our machine is narrow in design
There is no need for piercing and twisting of fingers
All this is gain and an advantage for the funds[21]
Even the bakers among us.

The poor miserable person too gains
Instead of a *raṭl*[22] he buys two
As two newspapers have written
This thing is enough for us.

Our machine has become an attraction
Everybody is densely packed
In the whitewashed passages there is noise and hubbub
And policemen guard us.

Our machine cost a high price
The pregnant women longed to see it
And all this for the benefit of the poor
Let it be said: "The Lord granted us and we enjoyed it."

This year we shall eat plenty
A long time we shall enjoy the sweetness
By distribution of food more than usual
May God enrich us next year.

But a great doubt arose in people's minds
And everyone began to discuss it
They said, "We have no need for this thing
Our shame will increase and we've had enough of it."

Some said, "We're eating leavened
And we have no need for this scandal
If the ordinary person doesn't buy from it
We will be exposed and the neighbors will talk about us."

We shall be put to shame and disgrace
Among the people and the residents of the house
Seawater will not wash it off
It will also be a mark of shame upon us.

The water of the seas will not expunge it
The poor person and the modest will be embarrassed by it
Tears flow from the eyes
And he will say, "Please, my God, save me."

Save us from the disgrace and the exposure
O merciful one, O possessor of mercy
How shall I hide from the eyes?
This thing is hard for us.

Please, Lord, the earliest in your world
Who is pleased with the eating of the matzot.
No one gives his opinion of me
In your mercy be merciful with us.

Our lives are laid low like dust
With us the bran is like flour
Let us celebrate the festival
Content with what God gives us.

Let us just get our bread
Loaves, and we shall steep them in water
Eight days will pass with what there is
We are worried with the approach of Passover.

Where our masters guide us we shall go
They will not leave us worrying
We have no wings to fly
Please, God, pity us.

See our strain and see our state
And do not forget us from before you
You alone are the securer
We have not trust in the community.

Please, compassionate one, be compassionate with us
Our eyes are ever raised to you
We shall all celebrate with joy
Send us Rabbi Nissim.[23]

Work wonders and miracles with us
As in the days of the Exodus of Israel from exile
We shall all celebrate rejoicing in truth
And shall forget what we suffered.

The *Malzūma* of the Girl Diamanṭa

The tale of this *malzūma* seems to be an event that actually took place. A Jewish girl from a poor family at the end of the nineteenth century went to do housework. She was able to retain her innocence in the face of the seductions of the younger brother of the householder for whom she worked. The author of the *malzūma*, Ḥai Ṣarfati, also known by his nickname Okhū Bāyā, as noted in the words preceding the poem, was one of the foremost intellectuals of the Jews of Tunis in the second half of the nineteenth century. According to Daniel Ḥagège, Ṣarfati was the first of the writers in Judeo-Arabic.[24] The *malzūma* was published on a separate sheet in Tunis (1889?).[25]

Although the story of Diamanṭa was common among the Jews of northern Tunisia in the late nineteenth century, it spread quickly among the women in other Tunisian communities, including in southern Tunisia, in such areas as Gābes, Djerba, Taṭawīn, and Mednīn. This was undoubtedly out of identification with the young girl. The great popularity of this *malzūma* is attested by the facts that in recent years oral versions of it have been recorded from illiterate female storytellers from these southern communities and by the fact that professional singers perform it at wedding parties. The oral versions are only slightly different from the printed version. Needless to say, the version given here is the published one. The structure of the *malzūma* is a regular *zajal*.

The *malzūma* of the girl Diamanṭa, author Ḥai Ṣarfati, May the Lord preserve him and keep him alive, known [by the name of] Okhū Bāyā

> There is a girl, very lovely
> Her beauty has no equal.
>
> Beautiful, perfect in her deeds
> She has a tongue sweeter than honey
> Her father is utterly poor
> Her work is to turn the silk.
>
> Every day she labors at her work
> Struggles for her clothing and sustenance
> Her father and mother depend on her
> She spends a great amount on them.
>
> She works day and night
> Behaves faithfully and with grace
> Her relatives are poor and her father poverty stricken
> She works for them like a slave.

One day a well-to-do man saw her
Took her in to work at his house
He had a wife and three children
And a younger brother, single.

She worked for him the first two days
The bachelor saw her and she caught his fancy
He said crude things to her,
"I'll always be rich for you."

He said to her, "I'll be good to you,
You'll get a whole *durō*[26] from me."
She let his words drift away in the wind
And ran away home to her father, hurt.

Her father said to her, "Why are you back?"
She replied, "I want to stay at home,
Even knowing that bran is my food
And I'll drink from the well."

Her father was silent, didn't speak to her.
Her master asked after her and did not find her
He went at once to her house
He found her working at the silk.

He said to her: "What's up with you? You didn't tell me,
You didn't ask permission from my brother or my wife.
Tell me, who was it who offended you?
You'd better inform me clearly."

"Sir, I'm not offended,
May your fortune magnify, greatest of merchants,
I don't feel like working at houses,
Not yours and not anyone else's."

"Work[27] is according to a person's will,
You were not bought to be a slave
If you have had second thoughts[28]
God will let us hear good things about you."

To get back to the bachelor:[29]
From the moment she left he found no relief
His tears ran like drains
He was sick with love and his tears streamed.

He wept and his tears were on his cheeks
The greatest physicians came to him
No doctor knew of his disease
They said, "What should our advice be?"

He declined greatly, and his condition worsened
Even his bones grew hollow
The doctors wearied of the medications
And didn't know the remedy.

The physicians huddled together—six of them
They said, "His grave is ready."
He opened his eyes and said, "Bring Diamanța
Through her I shall get up well."

His brother heard what he said
He said to Diamanța, "Do a kindness,
Come with me to my brother now,
You will see all good things from me."

She said to him: "Sir, listen to me,
I'll go with you, but promise me,
If your brother recovers he will take me for his wife
And write out a [marriage] bill at the scribe's."

He said, "Go with me and your will shall be done
I'll write out the bill for him
But come with me to the house
And whatever you have in mind shall be done."

She went with great love
Saying, "God, give salvation."
She sat a moment before the sick one
He opened his eyes and found the world valueless.[30]

He saw her, groaned, and died, poor fellow,
And she weeps and her heart grieves
She and his brother cry out both
Their fire intensified and burned within them.

Love is hard and cruel
It kills those who have it and it has no doctor
He will die burned out and the agonies with it
More than slaughtering the ram.

The greatest of the physicians answered:
"There is a miracle in this love."
He saw the pulse, he discerned the beat
And he said, "There is still a solution."

The doctor held his fingers
Took out a knife and incised his forearm
At that moment all his ribs trembled
And he even regained his soul a little.

They brought Diamanța and let her blood
Four doctors supported her
They put her flowing blood on his
It flowed in his blood and he recovered well.

Have you seen his love and his greatness
How her blood entered his body
His brother called out his name
And said, "God, you are the overseer."

He lives after he died
The people said, "Wondrous things
A great miracle with love
Love works and everything happens."

The doctors gave a prognosis concerning him:
He will marry her after two months.
He heard that remedy
He was happy and regained back his powers.

Two months later he took her to wife
He held a big wedding and rejoiced in her
He entertained in his house her relations and her parents
And dressed them in felt and silk.

The doctor had performed a great act
And this was no small excitement
The bachelor, he presented him with a hundred liras
And added to this a large gift.

He added to it a watch and an expensive ring
Made in Paris workmanship
They were worth a hundred English pounds
Words of truth have no derision in them.

The *Malzūma of Qāʾim wa-nāʾim* (Falling Asleep on One's Feet)

The subject of this *malzūma* is the Jewish hospital built in Tunis in 1893.[31] The construction underwent many tribulations and the writer of the *malzūma* tries to arouse the Jewish public in the city to bring about the hospital's full and proper renewed functioning. The *malzūma* was published in a special eight-page booklet, without indication of the publisher but only of the year: 1914. The author's name is not given.

We'll tell a whole story
And I shall relate what happened
In rhyming verses and *malzūma*
About the condition of the hospital
In clear Arabic words
For great and small
How its state became lamentable
After it had been dignified and well-appointed.

The start of its foundation was in the Association
Of good and devoted people
Who thought about the betterment of the community
For a long time, years
They gathered together and made a pact
To cure the miserable people
On the one hand—a good act for the Lord of heaven
And on the other hand—help for the community.

All beginnings are hard
Especially in the matter of wages
As much as a man will toil and be weary
As much as tribulations assail him
He will lift up his eyes to God and request
That he see light after the gloom
The hospital was completed and erected
In word and deed.

In Dār al-Pāshā [32] in the fresh air

The Jewish Hospital is located
The patient arrives there
He'll find everything available
He'll be treated without shame
He'll be cured and will reach the goal
From the administration and the diligence of the workers
And the utmost perfection.

But there are people who don't know
And haven't really grasped it
If they fell ill they didn't go there
In their eyes it was considered the Angel of Death
They say, "You go in there ill
And come out in a coffin
Medicines are not given
Until he becomes feeble and turns into a shadow."

He'd prefer to die at home
And not be neglected in a hospital
With his family and children
And not a shameful death
He has no hope for recovery
Straight to the grave
There is the beginning of his end
There his luck will fail.

We shall not bother our heads about this thought
And what the doubters think
But only a few enter it
It does not satisfy the thirsty
Three thousand is its budget
Every year calculated
For costs and expenditures
And for total purchases.

The hospital functioned in this way
For eight years
The movement was meager
With budget and limited expenditure
In the end it expanded
May God do well for the benefactors
People with resolution and diligence
People of wisdom and wealth.

When they saw its benefit
A support and shoulder for the poor
All rushed to its aid
And their minds were set on maintaining it
Each according to his power and ability
As far as his heart and pity moved him
Until its circle grew large and wide
And made to expand opinion and sense.

In truth it pleases the mind
And widens hearts
Its budget rose up
To a turnover of forty thousand
Anyone clever and thoughtful
Ran to the splendid hospital
He competes with the others and is jealous of them
And persuades the people.

If you want to enjoy a vision before your eyes
Go and gaze at the hospital
Go and visit it any time
You go out of your mind
The patients walk about in it
They have no fear in their hearts
Even the rich man in all his glory

Will go to the hospital when he is ill.

Life there is easy
Accommodation is of the best
There is strong illumination
Good and remedial treatment
Sheets of *kriyya*[33] and blankets
Mattresses and pillows
Soup and fresh eggs
And milk in pitchers.

Food according to the patient's taste
Anything you ask for will be provided
Anything you desire and want
Goat's milk or beef.
Silver dishes
Dazzling the eyes brightly
Glass utensils that they use
Brilliance, clarity, expensive.

People long to stay
Without any illness and without any injury
There is accommodation and rooms to stay over in
You sleep pleasantly and happily
On a wool mattress and a pillow
You stretch out along and across
There is contentment and sweetness
There are pleasures and coddling.

There is eternal Garden of Eden
There is life and cure
There the gold coin
Will not suffice, all of it
Generous deeds on all sides

And vows without number
Without charge to the Association
Every month honestly.

After all this
Money is left over
For expenses in their entirety
And pay for the workers
They are not kept waiting for their wages
Founders and members
Eight hundred who joined
The Hospital Association.

At the fine parties
Their collections are huge
In al-Wād and Ariana[34]
And Tunis the mother of the cities
The government granted them assistance
And tickets and security
Are always in abundance in the cupboard
Which will fill a sack.

They moved out of the old building
And settled in al-Ḥalfāwīn[35]
A great, enormous house
A joy to the watchers
Pleasant fresh air
And seventy beds were made
They were decorated with the finest adornment
They built it and spent the money.

They planned in their minds
For this precious purpose
To go and travel quickly

To France the city of Paris
A committee and an Association were designated
To bring the money and the gold coins
In order to devise
Building a hospital with it.

Some of the money arrived
And was deposited
By the Alliance[36] who gave
Seventy-five thousand
From Tunis they received more
Almost twenty thousand
They began to operate and to act
And they relied on God.

It was managed nicely
Especially advanced
It was spotless like the Garden of Eden
Everything new not old
A pity that this pleasure passed
And it fell into ruin and is gone
Everything that we yearned for has passed away
The wheel has turned.

The first beds were replaced
And the thinking was substituted also
This Association that entered
Was busy with nothing but disputes
Work and order were abandoned
Until everything fell to pieces
It was gripped by quarrel and strife
And the income declined.

Its grandeur came to an end

Cobwebs hung from it
And patients begged people to come and save them
From the fleas and the bedbugs
What had seemed like a joy
Turned into worrying about food
Where are the pleasure and the well-thought-out things
And where is the expenditure of wealth without accounting for it.

The decorations became old
And the sheets became ragged
The blanket was torn
And holes went through it all over
The beds all rusted
And cracks formed in them
And the ceramic utensils
Were replaced by plates and jugs.

No one was left to succor it
All the male nurses left
The wool was replaced by sea wool
Old and full of dust
The pillows which were excellent
Became brittle as flint
The cloth of the mattresses where is it
And the mattresses became holey like a sieve.

The situation is still gloomy
And the grief adds anxiety
Until the wheel stops
Its shame cannot be hidden
After its wonderful history
The hospital has become a stigma
Its story is told for a disgrace

And the gossip surrounding it has increased.

The hospital is in a bad way
Speed a cure for it
Fight for it those who dwell far off
Say: "Bring syringes"
Save it from this catastrophe
Do not say: "We have a dead thing on our hands."
See, its salvation is close
And you will still have a living thing.

Save it with all the remedies
Hurry to it people
We have been given the task of saving it
Get to manage it
As before, we shall restore it to its proper state
Nothing will be of use to us except resolve
And we shall built it anew
They gave us for it a hundred and a *riyāl*.[37]

The rich ones did not take part
And they do not give their heart
They do not save it from depreciation
They are occupied only with what benefits them
For pleasure they will run fast
And they see nothing else
And the good deed they ignore
Trust in them is stupidity.

But how we labored
Orderly and with organization
In the three years since we came in
We have established something marvelous
And although halfway through it was hard for us

And something difficult came upon us
Know all that we succeeded in
From simple pottery we made a pitcher.

The hospital is in great trouble
It arouses the compassion of enemy and friend.
Its condition is very bad and it is spoken about
And it's no good lying about it
They insisted of our assistance organization
That it should go on helping us in part
Even if only a thousand francs a month
With it we would put the situation right.

The committee had pity and commiserated
And they found that the situation could brook no delay
Instead of the sum they had thought about
They gave more
So as to ensure their welfare
Fifteen hundred every month
With this sum they would finance
This whole year entirely.

What is this situation, a catastrophe!
This was a little cake that does not satisfy the hunger
The devoted people were concerned
Their words were serious, they were heard
They wanted to get rid of this shame
They took counsel on the subject
A new fine hospital
In the cities became a legend.

They said, "Make an effort, friends
The situation cannot bear silence
Gather together at this moment

We shall assemble and contemplate in truth
We shall show them dedication and courage
Lest they say that our activity has passed away
Come, this is the last shift
Like the camel driver."

Come let us finish what we started
Before the time of the disintegration
The matter is in our hands
Salvation is within us
We shall drive away the worries and the distress
And our Jewish brothers will rejoice
Make in the hospital
A rose and a jasmine and a fill.[38]

We shall submit our request to the government
We shall clarify our wish in a letter
In the proper and polished form
Without confusion, every word in its place
We have land and money is being received
And donations of the good practical people
May our request be favored
We toil for a good cause.

They formed a committee and applied
And were received well
They spoke with the General Secretary
Their heart was sure about what they wanted to obtain
Each of them was happy and they enjoyed greatly
The enterprise of the hospital was to be completed
All was to be completed in full
It would lack nothing not even a pin.

The gentlemen gathered their forces at the right time

And threw themselves into action
Their labor and the sweat of their brow
God will reward them with goodness
When unity prevails among them
Everything is realized with certainty
They will work and the Lord will help them
Every act for the sake of heaven will be easy.

4

The *Qinot* (Laments)

As noted in Chapter 3, the *qinot* (laments; sing. *qina*) and the *malzūmāt* were the most important genres in Judeo-Arabic literature in Tunisia in the first half of the twentieth century.[1] In this chapter we present five *qinot*. The first three *qinot* are satires written in the 1930s about modernization and change over time. In them the sharpest criticism is leveled against those who scramble for elements of the alien secular culture, which causes neglect of Jewish values, disintegration of the family cell, and destruction of Jewish society generally. The last two *qinot* were composed on the tragic, untimely death of the Jewish actress and singer Ḥabiba Messica; they evince the mythic approach to her image.

Satires on Modernization and Changes of the Day

The *Qina* of Fashion and Attire by Jīhīn

This *qina* was printed in a special eight-page leaflet by the Imprimerie de l'Orient in Tunis in 1926. The author is mentioned on the title page by nom de plume only: Jīhīn. We have not been able to identify him or her. Every strophe is followed by its transcription into the Latin alphabet, which implies that it was directed also to Jews who could not read Hebrew characters.

Refrain
A lament for women and young girls
And fashionable dress and competition
Sluttishness and the tight attire and short-cut hair
Kohl and rouge in the city streets.

What is this bad condition
The women naked, O people
A skimpy tailored suit
They go about in it in the city.

A light and nice suit
And its vision is sweet to the eye
In Bḥēra[2] she'll walk out clattering
And the men there lust
You in your eyes as if full
And only two garments going up and down
She'll think herself a *Parisienne*
And show off her goods to the people.

She shows off her fancy goods
To lusting men
So that she'll be known among them
And they latch their eyes onto her
She no longer protects her honor
And hasn't given a thought to religion any longer
She is drawn to the fashion, dragged along
And all this is due to rivalry.

O, over wicked fashion
The woman's head has become mixed up
She has gone wild about clothes
She doesn't miss even a thing
She doesn't forgo anything

Tailors and trims without reckoning
A suit costing five hundred
Its color removes distress from the heart.

Her husband is at a loss
Whence will come the money
And if he doesn't have silk dresses made for her
She'll be angry and send him into a depression
She is bound to make him bitter
And she'll have an affected man
She'll be bereft of common sense
And the strife between them will increase and grow.

Every month a new outfit
Where will the money come from?
The husband is plagued by serious trouble
And he is like a baby chick
He doesn't earn a *soldi*[3] except with a groan
And worry is planted in his heart
Every outfit one of a kind
With the required perfection.

Her husband can't satisfy her appetite
He lives among people respectably
She goes to her boyfriend so that he may give her
Everything the moonlight lady asks for
Every evening he'll meet her
She spends the evening delighted and happy
She has sold her body and presented it as a gift
So that she might dress well, O people.

She chases after the latest modes
To be the epitome of beauty
To be the one and only in her generation

She makes up and rouges her cheeks
Her gown is décolleté, of fine tulle
The breasts are exposed on her
What a hard thing to bear!
They are bare in the center of the town.

A tight-fitting dress
Bosom naked and showing
Every man who sees her
Becomes giddy and in a whirl
Made crazy by her shapely figure
Everything visible to the eye
And what's more is that she's easily overtaken
Fire rages in the heart.

Willy-nilly he "gets the hots for her"
And shoves her from her path
He sees her as a passing cow
Certainly it gets his blood up
He mouths fancy words
And his heart pounds
She'll fall at once at the man's feet
It is a grave prohibition, gentlemen.

If the woman were modest
No impropriety would come about
She would be constantly bustling about her chores
And the man would go off on his way
He wouldn't approach her, and turn off his course
He would keep a great distance from her
But today, you, woman, are going astray
You have lured him to corruption.

What do they have, they are all adulteresses

All of them painted and rouged
Foundations and basic behavior have diminished in their value
Everything is tossed out without measure
All are built to a plan
Their cut is made like a picture
High bosom is very much its model
It removes concern from the heart.

Even the elderly women don't refrain
From this attire and making up their faces
They have ceased behaving like women of their status
They have descended to the epitome of evil
They paint themselves with lipstick and rouge themselves and tart up their faces
After they have already gotten rusty
And what's more they are dying to fill their bellies
This is the nadir of misfortune.

They adorn themselves and paint themselves with rouge and henna
Wanting to restore their youth
Instead of being refined in silk garments
They stroll in Bḥēra for a short while
With bare arms and thighs
They want to show their wares in public
They even burst into song
And are drawn after the city fashions.

The hairdressing salons have multiplied
The young girls and the women throng them
They crop their hair to half
And use a razor blade to straighten it so as to be attractive

After it was long they make every trace of it disappear
They visit the coiffeur every other day
They turn a man's head and confuse him
All because of the fashion and the rivalry.

In short, they have become utterly modern
They have wholly departed from their tradition
They have brought us to the lowest level
No religious immersion and no bathhouse
It is a serious prohibition, madam
Stop, enough of your complaints
Make yourself modest, you daughter of decent folk[4]
Lest people defile you.

The young girls apply themselves and are concerned
For hairdos and dress
They don't save up for a trousseau
No trousseau and no copper[5]
They think of nothing
Only dressmaking and get-ups of various kinds
On chairs they all cluster
In Bḥēra or al-Wād district.[6]

Shamelessly and immodestly
She will widen the slit to twice its size
Before Jews, Muslims, and Christians
She will powder and make up her cheeks with rouge
She'll want to be the most stunning
And go on being attractive
She'll shorten her dress and show her thighs
She'll cast out concern and sadness.

What an evil situation this is
The girls chasing after their bellies

They have sunk up to the neck
The young men do whatever they want with them
They run after that panting one
Playing the mandolin together
She is lost and she is rotten
And she will be a shameful person.

She will be rotten and lost together
Because of the wicked fashions
Everyone who comes will pour into the pitcher[7]
And she will carry the names of the corrupt ones
Until a man from the outside comes along
Not knowing anything, uneducated
To him she'll appear successful, a fine woman
And she's like evil fortune.

The girl stays out late with the boy
Under the porch in the darkness
And she will say that God will fulfill her desire
And she'll win that youth
Everything he wishes she has to comply with
If she refuses his face will frown at her
He'll amuse himself with her of the eyebrow[8]
And the fire of love will rage ever more fierce.

Deterioration of manners has increased in our city
Because of the girls and women of our times
Woe upon us and our life
They have become ruined and made bad
They have ceased to uphold the words of our masters
Whose words are engraved on our hearts
They have grown distant from what is forbidden, O sons,
Which brings expensiveness and lowness.

The *Qina* of the Lira and the Cost of Living and the Women and the Daughters by Jīhīn

This *qina* was also published as a special eight-page pamphlet at the Imprimerie de l'Orient in Tunis in 1926, and it was also composed by Jīhīn. As in the previous qina, after each strophe its transliteration in the Latin alphabet appears.

Refrain
What a load of troubles
The lira has gone up, reached two hundred[9]
However much we earn, it still is little
For our livelihood we are in agony.

The lira continues to get more expensive
And the cost of living is soaring
O, my God, what a mass of trouble
A nail is hammered into our hearts
The slice of bread has lost its flavor
We are all suffering, great and small
Semolina continues to go up in price
At two francs ninety-five.

What are we to do, my brothers
The meat, a kilo for fourteen
From Sabbath to Sabbath I place it on my tongue
We have fallen into a state that's beyond description
The oil's finished, like an empty vessel it shows me
The liter has leapt to eleven
My heart is confused and my burning is aflame
We are suffering for food of the body.

Our heart is confused, what shall we do?
The cost has become hard to bear
All the commodities have become expensive deals

And have disappeared from the markets
The lira continues to go up
And our heart continues to grieve
The citizens can't take any more
And remain silent longer.

What a hard life
Four eggs for a franc sixteen
We never reached a price like that
In the war they were eighteen
Life is bad and cursed
Death—inevitable, but the sorrow for what?
Shaqshūqa and *maghmūma*[10] have become loathsome to us
And the coins fly from the hands.

The coins fly, oh my misfortune
They have grown wings like a bird
Māẓālī[11] is five francs a kilogram
After it was thrown out worthless
What will the poor man do
Concerned for his breakfast.
Everything has become dear
Twenty-notes fly about.

Night and day my heart palpitates
What will be and what will happen
Like the blackamoor my face has darkened
Because of the cost I have gone out of my mind
My heart grieves and has become envious
Expenses outstrip wages
I have to buy to satisfy my needs
But the purses are empty.

The cost of living gets more and more expensive

This is something that mixes me up
I am not able to eat fruit
They have become madly expensive
O, my God, what terrible trouble
A liter of oil for twenty *riyāl*
The whole world is on the brink of destruction
And we don't know where we are going.

The wealthy man has great joy
When he sees that the lira has gone up
At once he raises the price of his goods
And makes many thousands
Every summer and spring
He goes out for leisure in luxury
While the poor man, oh my dear ones,
Because of the costs his status has been thrown to the ground.

The lira goes up by ten
And the rich man adds twenty
When things get cheaper and are less
He'll reduce by a *soldi* or two
In the old days, alas!
The poor man won compassion
But now, what trouble
He clutches the money with both hands.

The rich man gets richer
And the poor man dies of hunger
What life is this, O our brothers,
The goods continue to get dearer
All this is from our flaw
That was planted in our hearts
Remember the Ten,[12] O our sons,
And retain something of the religion.

We are beset by great anxiety
By the cost of living oppressing our heart
Whatever we have earned is little
Fifteen—a kilo of coal
When we remember carrots and greens
At once worry assails us
We need a full pocket
But the money is little in the hands.

A bunch of onions has gone up to ten
And dried peppers to fifteen
The poor man is stuck in distress
Anxieties have magnified around him greatly
He has been cast down to the ground from his position
By the cost of sustenance and clothes
He awaits the spirit of salvation
From the Lord of the Universe.

My common sense has fled my head
My thoughts have multiplied on me
The whole day I have doubts
Distress has taken me over
What life is this, people?
How much is the laborer's anguish
Will these agonies never end
And in our lives shall we see our world.

The women don't want to consider
This cost of living, gentlemen
In their opinion we are penny pinchers
And we lift them out of the river
They spend money without measure
A thing that breaks the heart
They have no mercy on the husband

Instead of one outfit they ask for two.

Because of the dresses I was shown up as an empty vessel
Every month an outfit in another shade
The lifeline is pulled after the fashion
Eyebrows and eyes are painted
The lady never stops drawing out and bringing
And piling up debts on me
Life has become bitter
Shoes alone for ninety.

There is no more grace and mercy
The woman wants to be extravagant
She brings the husband to torture
And throws him into a snare pit
He waits for her outside the market
Until his soul flies off
He longs for death
Because of the women who go astray.

She wants to have a nice outfit made
And her neckline is exposed naked
She fancies herself a *Parisienne*
"Great!" "How nice!"
In Bḥēra she goes about clattering
As if she were like a clump of stuffed intestines
Her powdered neck is filthy
And she has a kilo of powder on her cheeks.

The girls at the height of their tartiness
Don't think about the cost of the cloth
They don't consider the worry
Adorned in the finest of clothes
They run from place to place

And drapes of material in their hands of different kinds
Whence comes so much money
They have in their hands.

How much our masters commanded us
To keep away from degeneration
Woe to us and our lives
We did not accept their words, gentlemen
For you have seen with your own eyes, O my sons
The cost of living, the hunger, the heartbreak
All this because of the wives of our husbands
Who have become liberated.

O, women, protect your souls
And keep away from the forbidden
We are almost lost because of you
And agony hangs on our hearts
That's enough, go back to your good path
So that the decree may be removed entirely
And God will do good to you
When you become proper women.

The *Qina* of the Cinema and Football

This *qina* was published in a special eight-page pamphlet by the Imprimerie de l'Orient in Tunis in 1926. The author is referred to only by the initials Y. B., which might stand for Yosef Bījāwī.[13] After each strophe there is a transliteration in the Latin alphabet for Jewish readers who could not read the Hebrew anymore.

Refrain
Lowness and deterioration of behavior and idleness
At the cinema and at the football match
Our money has become chaff
The passion of women and men.

Who is he who will not complain
About the idleness and low living
There is no earning
And in addition the sickness of competition
For a living it is not enough
And in addition wastefulness and dreadful behavior
And doesn't he go to the cinema
And keep himself away from the football?

Indeed, in God's name, what agonies
On account of this topsy-turvy time
The man is all troubles
He has forgotten the shape of money
Boredom is evident on his face
He passes and his head droops
He will quickly negotiate about the cinema
And will be early for a ticket for the football.

He'll leave his children naked
Bereft of sustenance and clothing
They'll always go about barefoot
They won't taste what the cup is
The cinema is the worst of sicknesses
Enticements have multiplied before us
He sells the mattress and the bedding
For the Capitol or the Royale.[14]

On Sunday he's bad tempered
From the morning caught up in pondering
His hand on his cheek, thinking
What will be and what's going to happen
About expenses he moans a great deal
Better to go to the football
He doesn't understand and he doesn't know

His money is going up in smoke.

He wants his breakfast and there is none to be had
A piece of bread goes round the house
She[15] will tell him: "We haven't any oil
With what will we cook breakfast?
Go at once, don't delay
Bring bread and oil immediately."
The poor fellow goes and does not return
Because he had nothing.

The pocket's empty—what can he do
He has nothing but ten francs
He pays the cost of the football first
It is before every action
The price of a ticket is high, "burns"
Less than two *duro*[16] it doesn't work out
To see one slipping
And the other running stupidly.

He leaves the wife waiting
For her husband to bring her the oil
Hungry, longing to eat
She has nothing in the house
And he imagines himself sitting in the Garden of Eden
He forgets those who banged their heads against the wall
This is the worst of the tribulations
Come upon those of little wealth.

He returns and his neck is twisted
He gets back all tottering
The well-known performance has ended
He arrives with nightfall
On his entrance he picks a quarrel

Raises his voice and the racket
He makes do even with a tomato
And an onion pickled in vinegar.

She says to him: "There's nothing
Look at me, about to die of hunger
Cut down a bit on this frenzy
My heart is in anguish for the children."
He tells her: "I'll tell you why
I've come home unhappy
Lwisti[17] won by rough play
They scored three times."

She says to him: "What good is that to me
When my stomach is empty of food
What have you gained, tell me, in God's name
We owe a year's rent
You soothe me with hollow words
I ask for food, you answer me with a row
Look at your children and understand my feelings
If you are a man among men."

He tells her: "There's a game"
—As if he doesn't hear at all—
"It's all passion and love
Cheers for him who invented it
Very sweet and marvelous
It is played with cunning and skill."
The woman hides from the husband
To the Empire she moves in the end.[18]

These agonies and vanity
Are a new sickness, O people
The world is already mixed up

Idleness, competition, and low living
The bachelor, the daughter, and the pregnant woman
Want to go to the stadium
They ignore the proper thing
And rush at once to the corruption of propriety.

In God's name, tend your families
And take some advice from me
Look after your wives and your children
And don't waste your money
You become emptied[19] and need your neighbor
Who will regard you with a look of scorn
After the glory your fire will die out
And you will become cantankerous poor.

Two *Qinot* on the Tragic Death of Ḥabiba Messica

Ḥabiba Messica has earned, and continues to earn today, a special place in the tradition of the Jews of Tunisia and of the Tunisian people in general, including Muslims. She has become a mythic figure. Therefore we discuss her life and career first before presenting the *qinot* themselves, which were written shortly after her death.[20]

The uprooting of the Jewish communities in the countries of Islam, from their land of nativity, to the Land of Israel began to acquire significant demographic dimensions as early as the 1880s. However, the mass migrations came about only after the establishment of the state of Israel in 1948. Not surprisingly, few of the traditions and myths were preserved in Israel by the Jewish communities from Islamic countries before the creation of the state. The great communities that formed after that event, by contrast, have kept these traditions and myths alive, and not just among themselves; the traditions are also exhibited outwardly, sometimes even with vigor. Two scholars, Shlomo Deshen and Moshe Shokeid, have analyzed the festivals and mass gatherings of Tunisian immigrants in the state of Israel,[21] a phenomenon that has grown stronger in recent years among other communities of immigrants from other Islamic countries and their descendants.

One of the myths sprang up around the figure of the famous Jewish singer and actress Ḥabiba Messica (1899–1930).[22] We first heard of her from a member of the former Gābes community, Moshe Cohen, who was born in 1900.[23] He told of the singer's performances in the capital, Tunis, which he never missed whenever he was there; he even traveled from his town in southern Tunisia to the capital in the north especially for appearances of the renowned singer. In general, it seems, all Jews from Tunisia who had been born in the first half of the twentieth century were acquainted with the legend of Ḥabiba Messica. Subsequently, we pieced together details of Messica's life from oral and written sources, and from them it was possible to visualize this great singer, not only in realistic and authentic dimensions but also as she appeared in the eyes of the people long after her death.

To understand the creation of the myth of Ḥabiba Messica, it is first worth reviewing briefly the special story of her life. This exceeded every accepted traditional framework of the Jews of Tunisia, even when the community was exposed to modern Arab culture and European culture, particularly the French.[24] The Jewish communities in northern Tunisia—Tunis, Nabeul, Sousse, Bizert, Sfax, and others—were but a single component in the overall population, which was for the most part Muslim. Beginning in the mid-nineteenth century, the Jewish communities experienced profound social and cultural changes.[25] In the course of these changes the Jews identified more with the Muslim Tunisians who looked to Europe than with the Europeans themselves. This is evidenced by their imitation of Turkish garb—as was done by the modern Muslims—particularly the red fez.[26] But the breach of the traditional Jewish boundaries into European modernism and, under its influence, Arab modernism found expression precisely in the Judeo-Arabic, not the Judeo-French, press and literature, which began to appear in Hebrew print in Tunis in the 1860s and 1870s.[27]

Ḥabiba was born in Tunis to a lower-class Jewish family.[28] The name her parents gave her was European: Marguerite. It was the custom of many members of the Jewish community there to call their offspring by European names. In this manner, like others, they expressed their attraction to European culture.[29] Marguerite was orphaned in her childhood, and she was taken into the house of her aunt, Laila Sfez,[30] who was a singer in her own right. Under her aunt's influence presumably, Marguerite longed for a career as an actress. And an actress she became, but still more a singer, breathtaking in her special beauty. It was then that people began to call her *ḥabībat al-kull* (beloved of all); the name stuck in the popular and literary consciousness, and Marguerite became Ḥabiba Messica. Ḥabiba (beloved) was loved by the entire Arab public, thereby breaching the bounds of the Jewish society in which a considerable number of women singers were renowned, such as Fritna Darmon and the Chemama Sisters, from whom Ḥabiba learned a great deal. Ḥabiba went still further to break into Tunisian society as a whole, Jewish and Muslim, by joining the theater managed by Muḥammad Bourguiba,[31] brother of Ḥabib Bourguiba, who headed the Tunisian national movement and later served as president of Tunisia for many years.[32] Bourguiba's theater presented distinctly European plays, such as *Lucrezia Borgia*, *Mary Tudor*, *Hamlet*, and *Othello*; as part of the theater company, Ḥabiba toured the major cultural cities of Europe: Beatriz, Monte Carlo, Berlin, and more.[33] However, her incredible success was suddenly cut short soon after she passed her thirtieth birthday. Ḥabiba had resisted the attentions of one of her untiring fans, a 77-year-old Jew of the Testūr community named Eliyahu Mīmūnī; she preferred the company of her young admirers. Indeed, she had pledged her fidelity to her French fiancé, Raoul Marel. Mīmūnī broke into her house in Tunis on the night of February 20, 1930, poured flammable liquid over her, and set her on fire. Ḥabiba fought for her life in the hospital for several hours until she succumbed; she drew her last breath as dawn broke. Her attacker did not survive long, and less than a month after the terrible deed he gave up the ghost following a pain-racked illness.

This condensed account of Ḥabiba Messica's life is based on several articles in French published in Tunisian, French, and Jewish journals since the 1960s,[34] and many details have been omitted. The journal articles themselves are an expression of the mythicization of Ḥabiba Messica's image. But the clearest expression of this process is the film about her made by the Tunisian Muslim director Salma Baccar, titled *La danse du feu*.[35] We also note that, contrary to the affection showered on the singer in her lifetime and the positive mythicization of her image in the following years, in recent years, at the time the film was made (1995), negative sentiments about Ḥabiba had started to surface, in part by the Tunisian Jewish émigrés in France and by Muslims in Tunisia. Neither of these groups approved of Baccar's portrayal of the singer. The Jews were not happy with the way Baccar presented a somewhat negative image of Jewish moral comportment; and the Muslims derived no comfort from the presentation of a Jewish personality as a Tunisian national heroine. However, as the movie director attests, the singer's name has not been forgotten among various circles of the population in Tunisia and of Tunisian émigrés in France. She also testifies that in making the film, she scoured the contemporary Tunisian press and found that the life and death of Ḥabiba Messica had been accorded detailed and continuous accounts.[36] In addition, in the winter of 1996–1997 an exhibition was held in Paris of Jewish music in Tunisia, at which the songs of Ḥabiba Messica, among others, were played.[37]

The performer's mythicization actually began during her lifetime, with her success in drawing Jewish, Muslim, and Christian admirers and lovers. Many of them would follow her everywhere she went, and they filled to overflowing the halls where she appeared. Because of this, they were nicknamed *'askar al-līl* (the night army) or *ṭuyūr al-līl* (night birds). Ḥabiba's reputation was sweeping and incredible: a diva of Arabic song throughout North Africa, in the full sense of the term in Western society since the 1960s. Not by chance, apart from *ḥabībat al-kull*, she was known by another Arabic epithet, *malikat al-ṭarab* (queen of the musical emotion), and by the French nickname *l'oiseau du feu* (the firebird).

Ḥabiba was gifted with the basic components of rare artistic talent in the sphere of singing and acting; she had an amazingly beautiful face with its European features, graceful manners, and a kind heart. But the mythicization of her image in the eyes of her admirers—Muslims and Jews alike—apparently went beyond these elements and was augmented by the willingness and courage of a Jewish girl, born to a lower-class family and orphaned in childhood, to strive for unlimited greatness. And of course there was also her success itself in her appearances in the cultural halls of Europe, in those days the model for imitation in all areas of life. Without doubt, her admirers identified with the basis of her weak image: a woman and Jewish. Yet Ḥabiba succeeded in casting off the social and religious fetters of tradition and proved that it was in her power to tackle with unquestioned success European culture also—a story that also appealed to her fans. It is said that, contrary to the Muslim religious tradition (and also classical Greek theater) in which youths played women's roles, Ḥabiba Messica was determined "in the face of all the storms in the world" (*contre vents et marées*) to play the part of a man in a certain play. She was fortified by the figure of the adulated French Jewish actress "Sarah Bernhardt, then aged 75 and using a prosthetic leg, who played the parts of timorous virgins."[38] In this manner Ḥabiba expressed the secret wishes of members of Jewish and Muslim society in Tunisia, and perhaps also in other countries of North Africa, at a time when their attitude toward European culture was ambivalent: on the one hand, admiration and the desire to imitate, and on the other hand, suspicion and hostility.[39]

Naturally, Ḥabiba Messica's tragic demise only served to complete the canvas of her amazing life and to strengthen to the point of collective pain the absolute identification with her image. Something had been done to her that the mind could not tolerate in any manner or form, not only in the moral aspect of the affair—a senseless murder—but also in the intellectual and cognitive aspect: the destruction of this perfect and lovely creature, a deed devoid of reason or purpose. Indeed, all the journal articles depict the collective hysteria that enveloped Tunis entirely, without distinction of religion and faith, as word spread of Ḥabiba's shocking death; the outpouring of grief was also immortalized, of course, in the two Judeo-Arabic *qinot* written on her death. The Muslims broke the fast of Ramadan, and Bīshī Salāma, one of the well-known Muslim singers of the day, wrote a dirge especially for her funeral ("Souzat Ḥabība")[40] (Ḥabiba's funeral was attended by thousands of people in a procession that stretched several kilometers).

Our concern, however, is mainly with the mythicization of her image within the Jewish community, and this is the concern of most of the sources at our disposal, written and oral. The most remarkable thing about the identification with her image in the historical consciousness of the Jews of Tunisia is that there was no explicit Jewish element in this identification, for Ḥabiba Messica broke the commandments of the Jewish religion without a second thought. Certainly, the singer never was accepted as honorable in traditional Jewish society; moreover, Ḥabiba appeared before enthusiastic audiences who were not of the Jewish faith, and she lived an independent life and was thronged by lovers—Jews, Muslims, and Christians. Furthermore, in her ensemble there were several Jewish musicians from Tunisia and nearby Tripoli; at least one of them, who was from the pious Djerba community, converted to Islam to get away from his Jewish fiancée, who was jealous of Ḥabiba. Despite all of this, no member of the Jewish community or its rabbis dared to denounce Ḥabiba in public regarding her private life, which was far indeed from the conservative norms of the community. As one writer put it (translated from the French), "Who will go and cast a stone at the undisputed queen of Tunis?"[41] It was said, for example, that on the thirtieth day after her death, the rabbi of the Tunis community resolved to conduct a memorial service for her. Some members of the community protested to the rabbi over the holding of a religious ceremony for one who showed no concern for the values of the religion and tradition. The rabbi replied with a religious argument that convinced everyone and overcame the opposition: In Jewish tradition it was acceptable to purify an unclean object by passing it through fire, and because Ḥabiba had been burned, she had achieved perfect purification. The memorial service was indeed held, attended by a large crowd.[42]

Mythic female personalities are known from the later history of Jewry in Tunisia and North Africa in general. We need only recall the saintly Sūlīka Ḥatchuel, who was martyred in Morocco; the poet Frēḥa, in whose name a synagogue was established in Tunis; the girl Diamanṭa from Tunis, who preserved her purity as an unmarried girl; and the righteous young woman from the Būshāyef family in whose name a synagogue was established in Tripoli, to which people made a pilgrimage to beg for relief from illness and to hasten their going to the Land of Israel.[43] These women, however, bore in their personalities a clearly national and religious Jewish element, identification with which is not surprising. This is not the case with respect to Ḥabiba. Even if we want to go back to the ancient history of the people of Israel and compare her image to another Jewish female success, namely, Hadassah, who became Esther in the court of King Ahasuerus; despite the well-being and prosperity she brought to the people of Israel through her closeness to the monarch, the sages judged her negatively for sinking into the royal Persian court.[44]

Nor is this all. The mythicization of Ḥabiba Messica did not end with her tragic death or soon after it. On the contrary, it became only more intense, especially through the *qinot* written for her. One of them, penned by Shim'on Ben Ya'aqov Ha-Cohen,[45] was published by the Imprimerie de l'Orient by Abraham, son of Ḥai Ṭawīl.[46] This *qina* is also preserved in the oral tradition and was committed to paper by David Cohen in his book on the vernacular Arabic of the Jews of Tunisia, without his knowing of the published version.[47] The *qina* is also common in various versions told by Tunisian women immigrants living in Israel to this day.[48] The other *qina*, which does not have an author's name associated with it, only the pen name Datan, was published by Makhlūf Najjār, owner of a famous printing house in Sousse.[49] Ḥabiba Messica is also well-known among the Jews of Morocco, and the *qina* for her serves as the melody for popular songs in this community.[50] We note that Tunisian Jewry, more so than the other Jewish communities in the Islamic countries, including Morocco and Yemen, commonly responded to events in its history with popular poetry; this is especially true with regard to folk writings.[51] Makhlūf Najjār's printing firm was extremely active in the 1930s and 1940s. It produced hundreds of booklets of tales and poems in Judeo-Arabic, mostly works translated from various languages, including literary Arabic. Most of these booklets were distinctly secular literature and were widely distributed; hardly a single household among the Jews of Tunisia did not read with captivation the stories and poems from this printer. Only in the late 1940s and 1950s did rabbinic circles, mainly in Djerba and Gābes, begin to express opinions about the danger, as they saw it, stemming from these carnal works for the preservation of the moral level according to the values of Judaism.[52]

The two *qinot* were published in Judeo-Arabic, and all their strophes were also set in a Latin alphabet transcription of the original text. This gives some idea of the pronunciation of the original. In any event, this practice was highly uncommon in the hundreds of booklets published in Judeo-Arabic by the printers of Tunis and Sousse, and it was done solely because the late singers' fans were from the three religious communities in Tunisia. Furthermore, Makhlūf Najjār, the printer of the second *qina*, was careful—unusual for him—to print on the title page the title of the booklet in three languages: Judeo-Arabic (in Hebrew script), French, and Arabic (in Arabic script). The Judeo-Arabic version says, "A *qina* of the artiste Ḥabiba, being verses of a poem and bitter cries / for the excellent actress adored by the admirers / who was murdered and lost in her youthful years / and caused tears to flow from the eyes."

As we stated, one *qina* was preserved in the oral tradition. The reason seems to be that it is spoken in the first person, that is, in the name of the singer Ḥabiba herself, bewailing her bitter fate. It is also written more colloquially, whereas the other *qina* is more literary. On this account the first-person *qina* does not include words in praise of Ḥabiba herself as a renowned artiste, beloved by her audience, as the other *qina* does. Instead, it tells the story of the catastrophe, the funeral, and the burial with great precision. It adds many details unknown from other sources, in starker colors and with vivid descriptions so real that at times they turn the stomach. The plot of the *qina* draws on two sources: one is clearly Jewish, the other Arabic. The Jewish element is the famous lament of Hannah and her seven sons, which was widespread among the Arabic-speaking communities, including that of Tunisia, whose women customarily recited it on 9 of Av. Hannah too keens for herself and describes the disaster that has befallen her: "Hear me, Ḥanna, what befell me / and look at what has passed over me."[53] The Arabic source is a genre known as the poet's lament for himself, and it is known as early as the most ancient Arabic poetry before Islam. Even the Arab poet and anthologist Ibn ʿAbd Rabbihi (Spain, ninth century) wrote about it at length in his book *al-ʿIqd al-farīd*. So too did Israel Levin in his book *ʿAl mot* in reference to a poem of Shemuel Ha-Nagid.[54] In this *qina*, as in the other, the singer is perceived as a righteous woman; therefore the anonymous (male or female) writer has her speak these words in the last strophe of the *qina*: "The travail of my agonies is done / With the best of the Garden of Eden is my rest."

Naturally, the major contents of the *qina* are an account of the act of murder, gushing words in praise of her gifts as an artiste, and fierce expressions of grief over her untimely death. But apart from these, the writer of the second *qina* to Ḥabiba Messica evidently approaches her as a saintly figure, a stance that may well reflect and explain the Jewish community's attitude toward her. At the end of the enumeration of Ḥabiba's talents as an artiste, the writer states, "Even in charitable acts she excelled / helping all who were in distress." The lines of the penultimate strophe open with a common anaphora in laments: "Who will comfort," "Who will give forbearance," which is intended to demonstrate the enormity of the catastrophe. But the expression of the lamenting poet in the last line is surprising: "And who will console me, even me / other than You, Lord of all flesh!" Moreover, in the closing strophe, the author refers to Ḥabiba as though she is a perfect saint, and in distinctly religious contexts: "The supplication before God that He have mercy on her / and let her reside in Paradise / and that He feed her from the best of the Garden of Eden / for the fortune she gave as charity / and with good recompense may her reward be abundant / for her support of bride and groom / and to seal this lament / I say: Fortitude, please, Lord, fortitude!"

The personage of Ḥabiba Messica as a fully progressive individual, even a remarkable person and one worthy of our admiration, is still alive and well even to this day among Tunisian Jews. All of them know about her extraordinary voice and her wonderful performances before Arabs and Jews alike—those who did all that was within their power to hear her sing. They still have not forgotten her special musical performances, such as the long trill when pronouncing the words *yā līl*, which especially enthralled her Muslim listeners until they broke with their teeth the mouth of the beverage bottle from which they were drinking.[55] A stinging proverb often heard from the mouths of Jewish women of Tunisia and directed at men in their "latter years," *'Amrōs yeṣīr / al-shāyib yirja' zġīr* (the old man will never return to being a young man), is taken from one of Ḥabiba's songs, and the words were intended for the murderer Eliyahu Mīmūnī.[56] In like manner the bearers of tradition have mentioned Ḥabiba's kind heart, her acts of charity, and her practice of doing special performances for which all the proceeds were dedicated to a bar mitzvah celebration for the needy or to a bride's annuities. Whenever Ḥabiba's name is mentioned in social gatherings, it becomes a synonym for any terrible personal tragedy. Legend tells that Mīmūnī, whose great, unrequited love for Ḥabiba led to his burning her and to his being treated as a pariah, built at Ḥabiba's request a palace in the middle of the sea and that, despite this, she still spurned him. The account of Ḥabiba's funeral procession has also been embellished, such as the story about the people of Tunis emptying bottles of perfume in abundance upon her bier, until at length, rivers of fragrant ointment flowed over the ground. Trading houses were closed for three days, and foreigners who were not from her immediate family mourned for her, refusing to shave themselves and shutting themselves in their houses for seven days.[57]

However, what appears to be most astonishing of all is that, for the sake of perpetuating her name and memory, as is customary among the Jews of Tunisia for someone who has died childless, a Torah scroll was dedicated near the place of her death, and eventually this scroll was taken to Israel and is kept for her memorial and the public's use in a Beersheba synagogue named after the Tunisian holy man Rabbi Ḥai Ṭayyeb Lo Met (the name means "Rabbi Ḥai Ṭayyeb did not die"). This Torah scroll was discovered a few years ago by Yemima Lavan, an art historian of Tunisian Jewry, who had seen a Torah scroll in the Beersheba synagogue whose cover was embroidered with the initials H. M. When Lavan inquired about the initials, the old caretaker said that the community of Tunis had dedicated the scroll as a memorial to the beloved singer, and he even told her the details of Ḥabiba's life story. Casings containing Torah scrolls throughout Tunisia are made of wood, but the casing for Ḥabiba's Torah scroll is overlaid entirely in pure silver and is topped with an ornate crown.[58]

Aside from the *qina* for Ḥabiba Messica that David Cohen selected to represent the genre of folk dirges compiled in Judeo-Arabic in Tunisia, beautiful pictures adorn the booklike albums representing Tunisian Jewry, such as *De Carthage à Jérusalem: La communauté Juive de Tunis* (published by Bet Ha-Tefuṣot, Tel Aviv, 1986) and in Allali's *Les*

Juifs de Tunisie. We have already noted the special film about Ḥabiba directed by Salma Baccar and the numerous articles about her published in several French literary magazines, usually with a pronounced emphasis on her extraordinary uniqueness, success, and fame, and, of course, her tragic end. Ḥabiba's voice has not been silenced, and from time to time her name, life story, and voice are still broadcast on the air, on different programs in Arab countries.[59]

The *Qina* for the Tragic Death of Ḥabiba Messica: "Fī tūnis ṣārat ghrība / isma'ū yā nās bi-al-thbāt"

Refrain
In Tunis, something terrible has happened!
Hear O people, a true account
Concerning Mīmūnī who killed Ḥabiba.
He burnt her with alcohol!

On Thursday, during the morning hour,
I had returned to my house without incident.
My body was tired and lithe.
I said: "I'll take a quick nap."
I called my handmaid, and gave orders to her.
I said to her: "Whosoever there might be of the people,
If they shall ask concerning me,
Tell them: My mistress is asleep."

I went inside the room; nothing was on my mind.
I took off my clothes.
I felt as if the world was gloomy.
My heart was worried and oppressed.
Sleep was not pleasant to mine eyes.
I could not bear the acute cold that came over me.
I put more covers over me and became warm,

Until I fell asleep.

Sleep had taken hold of me, in spite of my wish.
No man was with me in the house.
After about an hour,
I could not tell what had smitten me!
Mīmūnī had done his despicable act!
He poured out alcohol and oil.
He lit his burning flame.
His intent was to kill me!

I was awakened from my sleep, and I became terrified!
I felt the great heat!
I found the fire taking hold of me!
Smoke was billowing in the midst of the house!
Then, behold! The enemy overcame me!
That which I dreaded came upon me!
I was shouting, but my soul choked!
O, how great is my calamity!

My soul fluttered in the smoke.
O, how hard it is to take this cup!
The burning on me never ceased!
I shout: "Save me! O ye people!"
Woe to me because of Ḥabiba who is perished!
How she struggled to no avail!
Mīmūnī's treacherous act had been done.
He wished for my burning.

I struggled to save my soul.
I jumped from my bed in dismay.
He pushed me; he wouldn't let me go!
My eye accidentally hit the dresser!
I immediately fainted and felt terrible

He stepped then on my neck
From the shouting, my voice became hoarse.
He did not pity me in my suffering.

Forthwith they opened the door unto me,
The moment they heard the sound of screaming.
They found me thrown down in an awful state,
Burnt and my eyes put out.
In a trice, the firemen came in,
And the policemen presented themselves.
I told them what had happened to me
And they made a written account of what happened to me.
They brought a horse-drawn carriage and took me up.
The policeman gave orders
They took me to Ghānim's Clinic.
The features of my face were no more, and had blackened!
When the physicians came and looked upon me,
They said: "She's in a critical condition!"
Thereat my eyes darkened!
The time of my death has arrived.

Their remedies were of no avail.
They cried over me incessantly.
The fire had already taken hold of me.
Ḥabiba Messica is going to her death.
This was God's will for me.
It's engraved against me upon my forehead and it has
been inscribed.
I'll die spotless and pure,
So that I'll attain my rightful place.

Early Friday morning,
My spirit departed and was put out.
When people had heard what happened to me,

Small and great wept over me;
Over my tragic death
And over the pain that I felt.
A severe burning came over me.
It was not put out, except with my spirit's departure.

In a coffin they placed me.
They took me out in an instant.
To the old cemetery I was brought.
They laid over me flowers.
My name they had written in the *Dépêche* newspaper.
My picture appeared in its midst
Mīmūnī told what he had done to me.
Everybody could read about my terrible ordeal.

Papa cries beside my head,
While my aunt laments and shouts!
My lover has fainted over my coffin,
Bewailing with a heart-rending cry:
"I cannot bear the separation from you!
I shan't forget your good deeds!
What a pity over your likeness, which goes to the dust!
Profound is my loneliness!"

O poor me, when they took me out!
Both small and great wept over me!
The horse-drawn carriage doth carry me,
Covered over in my silken scarf.
Children recite over me,
And the tears of their eyes trickle down!
Even the world wept over me,
And was shaken at my funeral!

In linen sheets they brought me,

While bouquets of flowers were in their hands.
All of the people accompanied me;
Jews, Christians, and Muslims alike!
The heads of the community honored me,
Dressed in their suits!
My friends, also, did not estrange themselves from me.
Everyone came to my burial!

They passed with me beside my house.
I left it and was parted from it.
It had emptied itself of Ḥabiba.
In the best of my years I had been picked!
I shan't see it again, neither turn that way again!
Lo! I am passing away from the world!
Bring in the people! Let them recite and pray!
Let them give charity at my funeral!

They brought me to the graveyard,
And carried me upon their shoulders.
In sooth, 'tis all full!
They encircled my grave row upon row.
They sought forgiveness from our God.
They then buried me and poured out dust.
I rested from the treacherous world.
I had gone to my mother.

They buried me and I attained my rightful place.
My afflictions had come to their full measure.
In the best of paradise was I drawn,
Where no account is given, neither punishment!
They have restrained themselves on account of my parting,
Both loved ones and friends.
This was the end of my life and my time on earth.
Come visit me in my place!

A Lamentation for Ḥabiba Messica: "Yā al-aḥbāb qeṣṣa ghrība / tkasser qlūb al-ḥjār" (O beloved ones, a wondrous story which will break hearts of stone)

Refrain
O friends! A terrible event
Breaks the hearts of stone!
That which happened to the artist Ḥabiba!
She was burnt alive before her time!

He that hears this lamentation
Will shed tears profusely!
Ḥabiba Messica, poor thing!
She was a creation made for happy occasions,
O ye inhabitants of sheltered Tunis!
She saw the greatest of sights!
With her loss, grief has come over us,
While tears have been poured out like rain!

Hear ye this tragedy!
Incline thy ears attentively!
Ḥabiba was for us a light!
The mere mention of her caused a man's household to stir!
She returned late one night, like the moon.
She returned home and said: "I am tired."
How evil is this calamity!
She came to a treacherous end at the break of dawn!

She went into her bedchamber tired.
She prepared her bed for sleeping.
She fell asleep while she was at ease,
Just like at other times.
The treacherous act came brutally upon her,
A cruel man on a dark day!

He set her on fire and excruciating heat,
And cast her down into grievous sorrow!

He entered her room and drew nigh unto her,
While she was in deep slumber.
He poured gasoline all around her,
While no man kept watch over her.
He performed his treacherous act, and overcame her
With a heart harder than brass!
What a requital he came to requite her!
How cruel he had been to God's creation!

Ḥabiba shook in terror.
She saw a burning fire rising up in flames!
She found herself going up entirely in flames.
Trapped by a human being.
What means this treachery, the bringing on of this
evil disaster,
O Lord, who sits upon the throne? O Judge!
Her companions have all become mourners!
Grief has grown in their heart!

The news has spread since the morning hour,
While Tunis is entirely in shock!
They heard about the sad act.
In the eyes of the physicians there is an evil foreboding,
Considering that the burning came with ferocity.
Hope is lost and vanquished.
They made known the fateful hour.
They said: "Ḥabiba's life is in jeopardy."

They took her to hospital
In a condition that would alarm the most stout-hearted!
Upon a stretcher they brought her,

While a crowd of thousands pressed to see her!
They sent for her family and informed them.
They were far away from Tunis.
They hurried off, thinking to save her!
They found the situation grim; hopeless.

Ḥabiba persevered for a day and a night,
With suffering that could bring even the cruel unto tears!
They could not find the advice to heal her.
The physicians showed openly their despair.
What a pity over such a beautiful body!
How had she gone on a sudden!
The light of the illustrious stage
Was lost on a moonless night!

Ḥabiba is dead, O Lord of mercy!
Artistic talent has perished! For us it is lost!
Everyone shouted: "O, Lord of vengeance!"
Profound treachery without a cause!
She was great at acting!
Her fame had spread to other lands!
Her acting was always impressive!
No one ever gave her a word of criticism.

Unto the city of Tunis and her sister towns
Has come the bad news.
They wept over Ḥabiba and her youth.
They heard about the burning, even the act of Satan!
Their heart grieved over her likeness and her life,
And over the low-down treacherous act made against her.
They lamented but could not restrain themselves
Over the Fate who betrayed her.

Let us lament over this illustrious artist,

The greatest ever produced in the field of acting!
She had ever been known by her acting.
Night was never too long.
In the theaters she was victorious!
She was outstanding, and none compared to her!
She was lauded by her acts of benevolence,
Helping all those in distress.

The death of Ḥabiba came by surprise!
No one imagined such a thing!
She was the crown of every banquet!
Her name stands out among friends.
Artistic talent took a fall to the lowest grade!
The telling of her story would require a book!
They neglected the care of all vessels!
They said: "Artistic talent has greatly been damaged!"

The separation from Ḥabiba shocked us.
It stunned the heart of all of us!
All of us were saddened at her death;
Jews, Christians, and Muslims.
Who can heal us?
Patience, O Lord of the universe!
In the theaters, she electrified us!
Like a whirlwind in the midst of the sea!

Ḥabiba has passed away from this world.
Her funeral procession was long-lived.
The poor with the rich were present.
Neither the small, nor the greatest of princes, was missing!
They said: This world is transient.
Time is treacherous; it picks its harvest!
After she had been an uplifting to many!
What a pity she dwells in the grave!

Her bier was conducted at eventide
By thousands upon many thousands of people!
In every street were stationed policemen
Who would position the people by rows.
When they arrived in the middle of their course,
Her coffin was carried by hand.
They escorted it as they would a bride bedecked in
ornaments,
While tears flowed down upon their cheeks!

When they reached the gravesite,
With obsequies not seen for a king,
Women and men were scratching their cheeks,
Shouting: "O Lord! Compassionate God!"
They said: "Would that money had redeemed her!"
They had paid it now and taken it on loan!
They poured over her grave and over her,
Precious ointments, musk, and the essence of citrus blossoms!

Who is it in Tunis that did not weep
Over Ḥabiba, the perfection of all good attributes!
Theater, after her passing, will no longer be pleasant.
Let us say the truth and not be afraid.
Her betrayal perplexed me, enraged me!
My heart was sore and became faint.
If the performance were now made free of charge,
Only in vain would it please me to come back late at night.

Only in vain would it please me to come back late at night
During those festivities at night,
After the death of Ḥabiba, whose blood was precious!
As for him that betrayed her—God is his judge!
She had a noble role in the theaters.
Her acting would captivate the heart.

Her death I could never have imagined!
One of the rustics had betrayed her!

After this awful incident,
The accused immediately fell ill.
The government's arm had been broken,
And his investigation was called off.
Heaven had decreed a perfect decree.
Before all hearts could blacken,
He died a death of torment,
And hadn't remained even a month after her.

With his death, all retribution had been completed.
Words had come to an end; reproofs had ceased.
As for my God, thus His vengeance was accomplished,
Stopping the work of all judges.
Beloved Ḥabiba is dead,
She that possessed tranquility and generosity.
A phonographic record of her songs is now sought after.
They had been left mourning and in sorrow.

Her songs on record are being sought after,
In Tunis and in all countries.
Hearts are robbed by her memory.
Every phonographic record of hers is praised!
In France and in Germany they are deeply loved!
In every place her name is known.
Who will comfort her moaning relatives,
Those dressed in black color?

Who will comfort her mourning relatives
Over her untimely death?
Who will comfort the lute and the playing band
Over the actress who'd intoxicate a man's senses?

Who will comfort the men of the pub
Over the singer who'd drive them mad?
And who will comfort even me,
Save you, O Lord of all flesh!

The one request of the Lord is that He'll have mercy upon her,
And that He'll cause her to dwell in the Garden of the orchard!
And that He'll cause her to eat from the goodness of the Garden of Eden,
Because of the money that she gave away as charity!
And with a good reward may He abundantly requite her
For having supported the bride and bridegroom!
Now to conclude this lamentation
I will say: "Long-suffering! I beseech Thee O Lord, long-suffering!"

5

The *Ghnāyāt* (Songs)

The *ghnāyāt* (songs) differ from the three genres discussed in the previous chapters, the *piyyutim* (liturgical poems), the *malzūmāt*, and the *qinot* (laments). Their origin is not Jewish, nor were they performed particularly at Jewish events. The *ghnāya*, the most suitable equivalent of which is a song, is actually an Arab-Muslim song that was performed in coffeehouses and at amusement places in Tunis and other cities in northern Tunisia. For example, it was usual for *ghnāyāt* to be sung after a theater performance, and as we will see in Chapter 7, the role of female Jewish singers in Tunisian singing was considerable. Many of the songs were imported and rendered by singers from Egypt, as noted expressly on the numerous separate sheets, leaflets, and booklets in which the *ghnāyāt* were published. But some of them were presumably local folk songs transmitted orally among the Muslim population, from whom the Jews got them. We have evidence of this only from the communities of Tripoli, Tunisia's neighbor to the east,[1] but in many respects the Jewish communities in Tunisia and Libya were quite similar and they experienced much migration between them, especially from southern Tunisia to Tripoli. In any event, entertainment flourished in Tunisia at the end of the nineteenth century. The great participation of Jews in entertainment, either as performers or as members of the audience, was one of the major features of life in the Jewish communities in northern Tunisia at that time.[2] It was a rupture of the boundaries of the Jewish quarter and participation in life all around, not necessarily in the economic domain but in the world of culture and the spirit. Of course, this was a time of great hopes for equal rights, economic progress, and education, all under the influence of the events taking place in Europe and in the lands of the Ottoman Empire. Apparently this phenomenon underlay the gap that opened between the Jewish communities in northern Tunisia, which were open to foreign influences and allowed the Alliance Israélite Universelle to operate among them, and the Jewish communities in southern Tunisia, mainly Gābes and Djerba, which jealously adhered to their conservatism and rejected the Alliance.

To serve the northern communities, the Jewish printers in Tunis, such as Ṣiyyon and Mordekhai Uzan, began to publish short booklets, usually of eight pages, in which *ghnāyāt* were copied in Hebrew script. Neither these compositions nor the language in which they were printed falls under the definition of Judeo-Arabic literature or language.

The themes of the songs are the usual ones in their genre, almost entirely about love, such as the well-known medieval Arabic poems to which the sages of Jewry objected. They called them *ash'ār al-ghazal* or *shire 'agavim* (carnal poems) in a tone of sharp censure intended to prevent as much as possible their penetration into the Jewish domain.[3] But the sages of Jewry were ineffectual and certainly could not prevent the practice by which sacred Hebrew songs sung in the synagogue or on other paraliturgical occasions were written to the melodies of these carnal poems. This custom had become a veritable onslaught, starting with the work of Rabbi Israel ben Moses Najara (Israel Najjāra) in Safed in the second half of the sixteenth century. Furthermore, the halakhic doctors and the religious sages in the communities of the Middle East and the Spanish exiles who were asked about this matter usually expressed a positive opinion of it. Many of the editors of anthologies of liturgical poems published in the nineteenth and twentieth centuries in North Africa and the countries of the Middle East state clearly in their introductions that one should take a highly positive view of the setting of liturgical poems to the foreign melodies of the Arabic "carnal poems"; thus members of the Jewish communities were kept away from the original content of those songs, but their tunes were not prohibited. The Tunisian poets were no different in this respect from poets of other communities, as can be gathered by references to the melodies of Arabic love songs in the headings of several of the liturgical poems given in Chapter 2.

But the subject discussed here is quite different. Two factors appear to have merged to generate the flood of publications of Arabic love songs in Hebrew transliteration. The first factor was the great demand for the songs by many in the Jewish communities of northern Tunisia. As noted, these communities played a part in the life of entertainment and understood the Arabic of these songs, even though Arabic was not identical to the dialect they spoke. But they did not know Arabic script and were unable to read texts written in it. On this matter we note that the Muslim dialect was easily distinguished from the Jewish dialect, even by someone not familiar with the Judeo-Arabic dialect in Tunisia, because its highly characteristic Hebrew element was completely absent; also, the transcription of the Arabic emphatic *qāf* is not the Hebrew emphatic *qof* but the letter *gimel*, in accordance with the Muslim pronunciation, such as *tirizgnī* and not *tirziqnī*. The second factor was the development of the press and economic considerations of the owners of the printing houses, who certainly made a handsome profit from the booklets of *ghnāyāt* that they printed and distributed. Be that as it may, this has to be seen as a more significant shift than is usual in the Jewish tradition, one whose closest parallel in Tunisia at that time was the printing of Muslim and European "carnal" stories translated into Judeo-Arabic; this practice was also fiercely opposed by the sages of the Jewish communities of southern Tunisia.[4]

The printers seem quickly to have grasped the great economic potential in publishing the Arabic *ghnāyāt*, because to the Hebrew transcriptions they added ones in the Latin alphabet, verse after verse, undoubtedly for the use of anyone unacquainted with Hebrew script, namely, Muslims and perhaps also Europeans domiciled in the cities of northern Tunisia and even Jews who could not no longer read Hebrew texts. Moreover, the Jewish printers generally published series of *ghnāyāt*, in sets of booklets, of which we know at least five: (1) *Mujmiʿ al-aḥbāb* (Gathering of Friends), by the printing house of Ṣemaḥ Halevi, founder of the modern Judeo-Arabic school in Tunisia;[5] (2) *Nuzhat al-khāṭir* (The Pleasure of Man), also published by Ṣemaḥ Halevi; (3) *Ṣawt al-mughanni* (The Voice of the Singer), by the printer Ṣiyyon Uzan; (4) *Ẓahw al-aṣḥāb* (The Joy of Friends), also by Ṣiyyon Uzan; and (5) *Bustān al-ʿushshāq* (The Lovers' Orchard), by the Castro printers. All were printed in Tunis. Large collections of *ghnāyāt* were also published. It is estimated that the number of individual publications was more than a hundred, containing several hundred songs.

The different printers engaged in fierce competition, or at least two of them did: Ṣemaḥ Halevi and Ṣiyyon Uzan. In the booklet *Ghnāyāt b-zīnak yaʿṭū al-amthāl* (Tunis, n.d.) Ṣemaḥ Halevi accuses other printers of encroaching on his domain (on the back of the title page) but does not name them.

> Beware of forgery!
>
> Some short-sighted people, black-hearted, took it into their heads to deprive us of our livelihood, and to take away our bread, and conspired to ruin their fate by doing harm to another, so they got into this business of copying and forging, and they produced something ugly and despicable that it is beneath them to become notorious for except on the Carnival, a festival in which people daub their faces and blacken their visages and go crazy in the streets unashamedly.
>
> But our friends who hold dear our pen know that this work and all our printings are well written and proofread and are printed in modern type at our printing house especially for this purpose. And without doubt they will ask for the proper version and spurn the faulty one.

Sure enough, Ṣiyyon Uzan's response was not slow to follow. He vaunts his product as against that of Ṣemaḥ Halevi, also without naming names. This is what he wrote in Part 5 of the series *Zahw al-aṣḥāb* (Tunis, n.d., back of the title page):

> Where are you, profligates!
>
> We inform you, our brothers, lovers of art, that all our *ghnāyāt* are perfect in essence, unlike the *ghnāyāt* of others which (are printed on [light] silk paper of perfume wrappers). They do not have complete verses of any *ghnāya* because the paper is small. But our friends know the value of our series (such as the series of the book of *ghnāyāt zahw al-aṣḥāb*), which are large and printed on good heavy white paper and all the verses of the *ghnāyāt* are complete (they are not of the forged ones in which you will often find verses of early *ghnāyāt* imposed on new *ghnāyāt*, as others do), and it is worthwhile not buying what they have, but they will be better off purchasing only the series printed in this format (i.e., on this paper) and not to acquire or buy those series in the small format. Moreover, our *ghnāyāt*, which we have published, are all new, printed in modern script and in French. Those are the *ghnāyāt* that are found at our premises, and are not to be found at the premises of another:
>
> "Allah Allah, O My Mother, Daughters of the Bedouin Wanted to Journey"; "Please . . . , Your Anklet Has Been Placed on the Heel Bone" (to the melody of "You Arouse Hope in the Mouth"); "O My Headscarf, Leave the Kerchief of My Head"; "Tattoo, O Tattooer"; "I Love You Very Very Much O Girl"; "The Nightingale Sang on the Branch of the *Fill*."

Without doubt, most of the published *ghnāyāt* were original writings of that time, not by Jewish writers but by Arab authors. Their content was usual, namely, on the subject of love. These *ghnāyāt* were written to the melodies of other famous songs, which were also published separately.

In fact, the Jewish printers acted here as publishers for non-Jews, a matter naturally of great significance for Jewish-Muslim relations at that time. This illumines still more why the *ghnāyāt* were printed in the Latin alphabet.[6] But the importance of the Jewish printings in this regard certainly increases the preservation of Arab Muslim compositions from Tunisia around the turn of the nineteenth century.[7]

Nevertheless, Jews also wrote *ghnāyāt*, although to the best of our knowledge these were not love songs but songs of morality, a kind of *tokheḥa* (reproof), like the *malzūmāt* and the *qinot*. Common to these *ghnāyāt* is thus not their content but their structure; typically, the poems are not particularly long, certainly far shorter than the *malzūmāt* and the *qinot*, and have four-line verses with the rhyme scheme ab cccb dddb. Two characteristics are typical of the *ghnāya* with respect to form: (1) The first line in every verse is usually shorter than the others; and (2) one or two words in the last line of each strophe are repeated in one form or another in the first line of the following strophe. The meter of the short line is six feet, and in the others it is less stable: seven or eight feet. Every *ghnāya* was written to the melody of another known *ghnāya*.

Ghnāyat al-mā wa-al-ni'ma (Songs of the Water and the Bread)

The *ghnāya* "Yā mūlānā," by Victor Halevi,[8] was published in a special eight-page booklet at the Internationale printers (not Jewish?) in Tunis, with no date. The text on the title page reads:

> The *ghnāya* of the water and the bread, in eighteen strophes in an accomplished rhyme and with lucid words, tells of what has happened in our lives regarding the cost of living and its being situated in drudgery, to the melody of "Ya merjāna." The *ghnāya* is apt for these times, by its author Victor Halevi, may God the Creator of man preserve him, amen.

The Muslim *ghnāya* "Ya merjāna" was published by Mordekhai Uzan in Tunis (n.d.) at the end of a booklet that contained "Ghnāyat al-faḥm" (The Song on the Coal). To display the formal similarity, as against the difference in content between the two *ghnāyāt*, we cite the Muslim *ghnāya* first and then the Jewish one.

The Muslim *Ghnāya* "Ya merjāna"

O coral, O coral, O coral
Only I shall stay at home.

I love beauty
The face powder and rouge both
I said to him: "I have naught, light of my eyes."
He said to me: "My pockets are full."

I want to kiss
I love the henna and the make-up
I said to him: "I have no money, O betrothed."
He said to me: "My sacks are full."

In my room
Trousers and a green belt
He found me soothing my little girl
He said to me: "I have come to you, the lovely one."

In my bed
Trousers and a silken girdle
He found me calming my little boy
And I am singing to him with my voice.

In the courtyard
A suit and a modern comb
He said to me: "I desire love."
I said to him: "My father is with us."

The Jewish *Ghnāya* "Yā mūlānā"

Please our God, please our God, please our God
Quench your servants' thirst.

Behold I have become hard-pressed
Because of life, see, I am confused
How much have I stood in a queue
I have come worn out and weary.

For semolina two queues
A tail holds by both ends
Right and left
And a policeman stands beside us.

A policeman behind us
Guards honesty and justice
But people are pushing and shoving
Until I am covered in sweat.

My sweat pours down
From standing and rising early
Woe is me, I have lost my life
And I was not more active at home.

No activity remains to me
Pressed by the utmost stress
There is no blessing in money
And the cost of living is beyond us.

Sustenance has become more expensive
It really is unbelievable
The prices have skyrocketed
We have hoped, and our hopes have lasted long.

I shouted out: "I'm in pain
From the scarcity of coal and oil
Now water is rationed
And most of the taps are empty."

The taps of those living higher up are emptied
My heart is seared by the shouting
O my God what shall I do
Every woman asks from her neighbor.

When the water comes
Those living lower down are saved by the God of
Heaven
And those higher up have nothing
They long for a full jug.

They fill jugs
From higher up women and men come down
Each has a box, a jug, a pitcher
To quench their thirsty body.

This is not enough
Whatever they fill will not suffice
You'll fill pots and pans and will not leave any over
So that they will cool down from the heat.

A great heat
The water comes in a trickle and slowly
To Ḥalq al-Wād[9] it flows every evening
Until the next day, so it may be said that it was supplied to us.

I didn't know
Which way to go or where to turn
How weary I am and have suffered
And still I am tired and anxious.

Let thought end
By God's will and let it be like a dream
The price will go down and the worker will rejoice
And we'll say: "God has saved us from suffering."

Bread will be cheaper
Oil will be cheaper and coal and meat
And cloth and everything
And the poorest will live with us.

The hardships will end
And we shall live a peaceful and contented life
We shall enjoy well-being with bread and water
And our body will be sated to satisfaction.

God of Heaven
Will give us from his bounty, liberally and not sparingly
Long live the government of France
And may He save her from all her foes.

Two *Ghnāyāt* by Rabbi Hwātī Srūsī to Mark the Liberation from the Germans and the Establishment of the State of Israel

The author Ḥwātī ben Ḥai Srūsī was a native of Gafṣa in Tunisia. He emigrated to Israel after the establishment of the state and lived in the town of Lod, where he died in 1976. His book *Ben aḥisamakh*, which is a collection of his diverse writings on the Bible and the Talmud, was published in Jerusalem in 1976. At the end of the book (155–60) the author appended two Judeo-Arabic poems from the booklet *Pode u-maṣṣil* (Redeemer and Savior): (1) a poem written to mark the liberation of Tunisia from the German occupation with a sketch of the Gafṣa community under Nazi rule in 1943;[10] and (2) a poem written on the occasion of the establishment of the state of Israel. The two poems were not meant to be recited as part of any liturgical or paraliturgical framework, and we believe that their place is in the *ghnāya* genre. We think this because a composition by Shim'on ben Ya'aqov Ha-Cohen, called "Ghnāyat Khammūs Jānā" (The Song of Khammūs Jānā), is identical to these poems in structure and content (the tribulations ensuing from World War II owing to the Nazi occupation of Tunis).[11] This is yet another manifestation of the secular *ghnāya*, namely, its use for a national religious purpose in a poem with many artistic features of thanks to God for redemption from adversity. The structure of the poems is the most simple.

"Naḥkīlkum mā jrā fīnā bi-tfāṣīla"

I saw fit to print here a new poem that I composed at the time of the war of the Germans, may their name and memory be blotted out, who came to the city of Tunis and came to the town of our dwelling Gafṣa, may it be established on high, amen, and we suffered many tortures and blessed be the Redeemer and Savior for out of travail we came to well-being thanks be to God for He is good and His loving-kindness is eternal.

We shall tell you what befell us in detail
What the Germans brought down upon us in a month
and a night.

The Sabbath
The community gathered in the synagogues
To pray to the Dweller of the Heavens
That He received our prayer without delay.

We led the groom
To the synagogue with a *piyyut* confidently
Everyone rejoiced and his heart was glad
And we did not think of this plot.

We thought nothing
As we said and completed the Morning prayer
And for the commandments we declared as usual
And we took out the Scroll as was our custom.

The Scroll was taken out
And laid on the Ark for a moment
Until we heard disturbing and frightening news
They said: Gafṣa is under siege.

The Germans entered
And we all lost our minds in panic
We returned the Scroll without completing the reading
And we fled to our homes in a short time.

We fled to our homes
And the Germans entered by way of the railway station
And countless Gentiles after them
And shouting "Long live Germany" with terrifying noise.

"Long live Germany"
There entered men twenty in number
And the Gentiles lifted them onto the horses
Clasping them and kissing their helmets.

Clasping them
They began to loot the Mobile [gas] station at once
And the plunder of the Jews they did the next day
The Lord knows what happened to us that night.

The Lord knows
Praise God, He took preventive measures to my distress
On Sunday morning He saved me from my agony
And the Americans entered in force.

The Americans
Entered Gafṣa with complete confidence
And took the gang of Germans prisoner
And condemned the looters to death.

They came on the highway
And all the Jews received them with applause
And with joy we thanked the true God
Who always keeps safe the nation brought low.

May he keep us safe always
The Americans are in Gafṣa
Chewing gum and sweets they scatter in every street
Chocolate and sugar and tea in large quantities.

Great abundance
Innumerable packets of cigarettes
Even the little girls and boys
Everyone united without trickery and pretense.

Their hearts united
Girls and boys collect the sweets every day
Cigarettes tumble off the lorries
May God shower them with bounty and blessing.

May He reward them
The soldiers left after three months
And the Germans, what they had done to Gafṣa and plotted
The Americans made it a trap for them.

They made for them
The Americans thinking to themselves
They would reduce the force in Gābes
And the Eighth Army would enter easily.

Monday night
All the Americans leave
We went to the commander with a heavy heart
And asked him to take us away that night.

We asked of him:
"We are afraid that the Germans will torture us"
Give us lorries and take us away.
He did not pay attention to us, not a word and not any talking.

He did not accept what we said
And our heart filled with fear and anxiety
There were Jews that fled in the darkness
And we were left to troubles and lack of rest.

The troubles and the agony
All night sleep evaded our eyes
Early in the morning the mine exploded
And the distress became destructive and sickening.

Toward morning
Fear fell upon all the Jews
A small vehicle entered in the evening
To carry out this transfer.

On Tuesday night
All the vehicles and tanks entered
And the Gentiles were in great joy
They said: "Blessed be this night."

That night was a festival
And they made terrible threats against the Jews
And with them the stupid Germans
We fled and left the houses abandoned.

We left the houses
Full of good things without number
They went in looting, large and small
And with them the Germans with carbines.

With them the Germans
And all the Jews fled to the houses of Ḥāj ʿUthmān
Thinking we were entering with a quiet heart
We thought he did the good thing entirely.

We thought he did
But in the morning he changed
And drove all the Jews out of his house
We were in trouble and in a panic.

Trouble and fears
The Muslim said: "Now rumors are spreading
Whoever takes in Jews will be put to death
He caused it to himself and brought it upon him."

He can and did
They are plotting to kill us really
Of small and great not one will survive
And we left his house hurriedly.

We left his house
And our faces paled in fear
And everyone worried about his wife and his children
And our tears stream down our cheeks.

Copious tears
All had benefited from our great goodness
We saw no favor from the sheikh and from the *qāʾid*[12]
They who sent the ants among us.

They destroyed us
The *qā'id* sent a platoon and they took us out
And there in Maḥmūd Rājib's hotel they placed us
On the dear and honored Sabbath night.

On the Sabbath night
They brought Germans to us in hundreds
Wanting us to perform vile acts
We felt our hearts sink in trembling.

Heart sank
And every German had a fraternizing Muslim with him.
"Give us what's left of the rings and the *maḥbūb*s"[13]
That's how they left us and went down into the town.

They left us
And our tears rolling down our cheeks
We found no merciful and compassionate one to comfort us
And we found no one to protest to.

We found no one
Even the lice poured onto us
We found no wheat and no flour
A quarter of a loaf per person day and night.

A quarter of a loaf
And all of that filled only with sand
And its dressing a crushed piece of carrot
For the entire week and the Sabbath.

Week and Sabbath
We saw no Scroll and no synagogues
By day and by night we are in distress
They plunder us and conspire to kill us.

By treachery
They plundered the beds and finished in the cupboards
The rooms full of good things
And they finished off with all the furniture.

They looted the clothing
They looted the jewels and finished off with money
And they continued and went down even into the cellar
And they swept it clear of everything in it.

They looted the jewelry
They looted the ceramics and made off with the pottery
They stole all the ceramic vessels and all the glass vessels
Stoves and chamber pots and utensils for washing.

Every one of them plundered
They left not a cat and not a dog
Even the coal and the wood
They carried them off in sack and saddlebags.

What a disgrace is this
Not enough what they plundered from the houses
They even went down into the wells
And searched them with an oil lamp.

What a weird thing it is
They even went into the yeshiva
They tore up the books and looted the *Hechal* and the *Teva*[14]
They took up the mats and broke the lamps.

They looted openly
They finished off with shutters and doors
We lift up our eyes to You, the Compassionate One
Take out our righteousness soon.

In a short time
The Germans entered Gafṣa with confidence
And quickly passed through Feriāna
To reach them without delay.

The main thing is to arrive
They reached Mount Darnāya and stopped
They found the forces guarding the mountain
They attacked it with planes and heavy bombs.

They made an assault on it
They didn't know whence this trouble had come upon them
They didn't know where to go and where to hide
On the third day they regretted the action.

On the ninth day
We saw the Germans coming back down the road
They made for the railway station in confusion
And were caught on the mountain summits as if in spiders webs.

The mountain summits
And they left eight men in Gafṣa
They scurried off in lorries like animals
And wrenched the doors in the darkness of the night.

In the darkness and in the press
The Germans fled on the Thursday night
The planes pursued them in their search for them
Dropping flares and then bombs.

They dropped flares
And we saw that all the world was lit up
We all thought that the town was destroyed
From the racket of the grenades and the noise.

With terrifying noise
For an hour and a half the planes bombed
And we are in trouble, for all of us are confused
They repeated it on Thursday in the same way.

On Thursday evening
The planes came in proudly
They caused a great uproar in the bread queue
And brought them swiftly to the grave.

They brought them to the grave
And praise to God of the Jews, not one was hurt
Only Aaron and Khmiyyes and Lakhḍar
Were lightly wounded, not seriously.

They suffered wounds
The Protector of us is always merciful
But the Italians and the Germans
Were hit and were wiped out with burning fire.

The fire consumed them
They left fleeing fast
And on Goat's Hill they stationed their forces
And here they left a few dead Italians.

They left Italians
How the enemies mistreated us
It was not enough that they began with plunder
But every day they concocted a pretext.

Every day
They held a lively market and public announcements
They sold the anxieties and bought the disgrace
Our property was flung about in all directions.

Our property was sold
The eyes see it and the heart ached
They planned in their heads and found a wide space [for it]
In Gābes and Sfax and Tunis the capital.

Even to Gābes
A month and a day and we are under pressure[15]
And every one of us is imprisoned in his place
Until the pleasant Wednesday night.

Wednesday night
The artillery opened up at seven
And we were afraid with the utmost terror
Until morning the town was in uproar.

In the morning at ten
The Germans and the Italians fled in distress
The Americans became aware of this victory
And entered at one o'clock with pride.

They entered at once
And assembled us, all the Jews
In the square in front of the well of the consul
He climbed onto the well and photographed the scene.

He climbed up and photographed
And left at once for the railway station
He caught up with the enemy exhausted on Goat's Hill
They drove him out of there fast.

They pushed him out humiliated
They at once turned towards Sfax
The two forces soon overtook him
They pushed him to Tunis a long stretch of road.

To Tunis they pushed him
And opened fire on him from three sides
And like a bird in a trap they catch him
Trapped and defeated and fallen and lost enfeebled.

Fallen and lost
He deserved it the treacherous dog
How many plots he wrought against the Jews
God requited him as he deserved and will requite him
still more.

He requited him quickly
For leaving us naked and starving
Sleeping thrown down on the ground
The lucky of us stretched a rag.

He paid him back properly
And the troubles and hardship were lifted from us
And in the land of Tunisia good things multiplied
Oil, wheat, sugar, coffee, soap, and indigo.

He compensated me
A recompense by expelling him from the land
May our exile totally end
And we shall be a pure and exalted state.

The Lord requited him
For all his evil deeds
How he mistreated the humiliated nation
Expulsion and robbery and wicked deeds.

Supreme [God] requited him
The Germans daily are retreating
And sleep and eating have begun to be sweet
They have taken Tunisia from him and ended in Sicily.

They ended it
And even Italy they have invaded
They concluded a cease-fire and left it
And the Germans were left alone in trouble.

Left angry
Day and night the whole time and they hesitate
They didn't know whether to continue with the war or to submit
Their blood is scorched and they are enmeshed in a problem.

Their blood is scorched
Three free countries united against them
Russia added to their troubles
Their end will not come in a short time.

In a short time
Trouble and oppression will be lifted from us
The Messiah will come to us and we shall make a celebration
And we shall return to our honored land.

The city of Zion
The herald will come to us and our eyes shall see
The Temple and the Canopy will be built
And the Messiah with crown and diadem.

With a gold crown
And all the nations will fear him
The flag will flutter on the wall
And then we shall rejoice and be glad.

"Dawla mā ḥlāhā"

State, how pleasant it is!
May God exalt it!

On the Sabbath night
Our state was declared
Irrefutable and exalted
And our God is with it.

At midnight
The candle lit up
The State of Israel
Our God named it.

The fifth of Iyar
How dear is that day!
Our state is a bouquet of flowers
And a coin we have minted it.

Mr. Truman
Quickly and rapidly
With full trust
Sent and congratulated it.[16]

Mr. Stalin
After a couple of minutes
Recognized at once
The state and its government.

All the countries
Recognized all of them
The Jewish state
O, my God, set your eyes on it!

France the famous
Acted well
Forged the way
May God reward her.

Our state was declared
Let our flag be hoisted
O, God our Creator
Brought us to it.

Our state is marvelous
Wise and intelligent
In a short time
God exalted it.

Our new state
Sweet and pleasant
On the blessed night
God strengthened it.

O exalted God!
Give a sign
Help and an indication
That I might go and see it.

Land of freedom
It is dear to me
I shall come to it soon
And I shall breath in its air.

How lovely is the sojourn in it!
May God sustain it
We shall eat its produce
And drink its waters.

The gates of our land are open
God has liberated it
Its prayer is acceptable
It will go up to its heavens.

Land of the fathers
Perfect in attributes
And all the good things
There you will find them.

Our Jewish land
And the language is Hebrew
On every path
You will hear its clamor.

How pleasant is the state!
Perfect and desirable
Please, Lord God
Perfect its peace.

The President
Ḥaim Weizmann
The Compassionate stood at his side
And power—he took.

David Ben-Gurion
And the Irgun group[17]
Overcame the Leviathan[18]
It fled and left it.

Lord our God
Break our enemies
For the sake of the Hagana[19]
Which put its enemies to flight.

On you I call
Please my God, save
Moshe Sharett
And all its ministers.

In the land of my fathers
I shall work with all my might
I shall bare my arms
I shall plow its turf.

I shall sell all I have
And I shall journey there
I shall work hard
And I shall build its ruins.

Please honest people!
Help with men[20]
And contribute wealth
Nothing is equal to it.

Please, my God, do more
And send the son of David
That he may reign and be grand
In its palace and its edifices.

I, Srūsī Ḥwātī,
Have set forth my array of words
My speeches are done
And peace upon the reader of them.

6

Essays on Ideology and Propaganda

As far back as the Middle Ages, Jewish communities in the Middle East and in North Africa maintained the tradition of engagement in literary and spiritual pursuits not arising directly from study of the Bible and rabbinic literature. Not surprisingly, therefore, the rabbis of these communities were actually at the forefront of those in the second half of the nineteenth century who preached expansion of knowledge and education; no deep split occurred between Orthodoxy and Enlightenment. In general, ideological secularization did not take root in these communities, although observance of the religious commandments was certainly diminishing. The rabbis even gave their blessing to the opening of modern schools, and the Alliance Israélite Universelle society could act almost unhindered in these communities. The two heads of the religious court in the Tunis community, Rabbi Abraham Abūqāra and Rabbi Abraham Ḥajjāj, did not object to the introduction of foreign languages into the curricula of traditional Jewish schools. They actually concurred in the opening of an Alliance school once the society undertook to preserve the proper spirit of Judaism.

In those days far-reaching reforms were improving the legal status of the Jews of Tunisia. Even after Tunisian independence in 1857, the bey Muḥammad ibn Ḥusayn (1855–1859) instituted the *'Ahd al-amān* (Pledge of Security), which, in his government, was called *Qānūn asāsī* (the Basic Constitution), whereby equal rights were granted to the

Jews. Although it was influenced by the *tanẓīmāt* (reforms) in the Ottoman Empire, the *Qānūn asāsī* was a far more traditional document than either of the two major Turkish *tanẓīmāt* documents (the *Khaṭṭ-i sherīf of gülhāné* and the *Khaṭṭ-i humayun*).[1] Muḥammad Bey's successor, his brother Muḥammad al-Ṣādiq (1859–1882), actually started to implement the provisions contained in this constitution. Under Muslim pressure he was obliged to abrogate the basic constitution, but this in no way lowered the expectations of the Jews of Tunisia in political, social, economic, and cultural terms. These hopes were in fact realized almost in full after the country was occupied by France.

All at once the Jews of northern Tunisia were swept up into new ways of life. These were free and variegated, and all the mental and spiritual forces, pent up for almost a millennium under the oppressive rule of Islam, burst out in a torrent. Often this release was unchecked by the traditional leadership, which naturally lost a considerable part of its supervisory authority. The model for imitation in the eyes of many of the Jews of northern Tunisia was thereafter the culture of Europe, mainly France, especially because France had brought the ideas of liberty, equality, and fraternity to the world about a century earlier during the French Revolution. This process of reform also caused grave manifestations that were highly negative with respect to Jewish tradition and preservation of its ethical and national values. These were in fact symptoms of assimilation, the consequence of naive, absolute faith in French humanism.

Against this tendency, which apparently spread throughout much of the public, two groups took a stance in the Jewish community and began to work for the curtailment and elimination of assimilation. The first group was the traditional religious leadership, the rabbis, who regretted having licensed the Alliance to open schools when they realized that the education in them was one of the chief causes of the drift away from traditional Judaism. The second group was in fact the heads of the Jewish Enlightenment themselves. Although they admired the spirit of progress and education, they understood that this did not have to be bound up with the loss of the Jewish outward appearance in either religion or nationality. Both groups set about preventing assimilation through the publication of theoretical and propaganda compositions, in which they called for the preservation of Jewish tradition. It is worth noting that, despite it seeming self-evident, in none of these compositions is there any treatment of Eretz Yisrael or migration to the settlements there. This is because the time was the 1880s, before the rise of the Zionist movement founded by Theodor Herzl. Nationalist themes in the activity of the Jewish Enlightenment in Tunisia—regarding Eretz Yisrael and, even more, the study of the Hebrew language—began to find expression only early in the twentieth century, under the evident influence of Zionism.

As a response to these events, a new literary genre arose, one of theoretical study, which joined other new genres of Judeo-Arabic literature in Tunisia between 1850 and 1950. These writings, principally those of the intellectuals, provide on the one hand an account of the sociospiritual life of the Jews of Tunisia in the period under review. On the other hand, they reveal the ideas and innermost thoughts, the spiritual, social, national, and religious perceptions, of the intellectuals, who in no way wished to blur the Jewish image of the members of their community. In any event, not surprisingly but as an innovation of the Jewish literature that had previously characterized Tunisian Jewry, the language of these essays was Judeo-Arabic.

In this chapter we present passages from three compositions, a fraction of the large number of essays published, that offer insights into the character of this important genre; to date these writings have not enjoyed adequate illumination, perhaps none at all, in the study of modern Tunisian Jewry.

Shuva yisrael (Return, Israel)

Shuva yisrael is a 36-page booklet published in 1886 in Livorno. Its title page reads:

> The Book "Return, Israel." This book, as its name states, is meant to show the ways of repentance to our brothers, our people, God preserve and sustain them, the ordinary people who are ignorant of the matter of the prohibitions of the Torah or of our Sages. All have been assembled within this booklet and are written in the Arabic language, so that it will be in reach of all equally, with Heaven's help.

The booklet consists of two chapters in Judeo-Arabic. Pages 1–5 give fourteen conditions of repentance referring to the following misdeeds: misdeeds against a wife; Sabbath desecration; foul language; prayer; dress unseemly for a woman; cursing the religion of Moses; sitting idly in coffeehouses; male homosexuality; disparagement of the Sabbath and festivals; negative treatment of one Jew by another; disregard for the three traits of the Jew, namely, rewarding good deeds, reticence, and generosity; intercourse during the woman's menstrual period; shaving the beard; and belittling of the Torah and the learned. The second chapter was a warning publicized by the rabbis of Tunis concerning the duty of observing the commandments.

In the manner of rebukes, the description of the state of affairs is highly derogatory, although not entirely detached from actuality. All the negative manifestations were certainly not rife among many in the community; on the other hand, these matters seem to have been written out of heartache over the worst excesses in terms of Jewish ethics. The translation of the second chapter follows.

> A statement of reproof and a reminder and warning and a correction to our brothers, the Jews of Tunis, may the Almighty maintain it, amen, may God preserve them and sustain them, written by the *dayyanim* of Tunis, may God help them, amen, in the year 1883.
>
> Now, gentlemen, we the undersigned will inform you, and we shall warn you, and we shall warn and caution you, first and foremost, with the help of God and His mercy, the right

way in this world and the world to come. Now, what is required of you, may God bless you and lengthen your days, we require of you that each one of you who recognizes himself as a Jew, a son of Israel, a son of Abraham, Isaac, and Jacob, peace be upon them, that he rebuke himself and rebuke his friend, and remind him that he is a Jew. Enough, enough for you of this wicked way and of the wicked deeds that are evident nowadays. That is the way of desecration of the religion, our precious religion, good and pure, viz., the religion of Moses our master, peace be upon him.

At this time there are Jews who desecrate their religion, smoke cigarettes on the Sabbath, write on the Sabbath, sell and buy on the Sabbath; and sometimes there are those who cook on the Sabbath, and worst of all is desecration of the Sabbath in public, in the alleys and streets of the city, such as one who rides in a carriage on the Sabbath, pays the hire of the carriage, and the train fare on the Sabbath, in full view of all. And one who owns a carriage or a motor car, or animals for the carriage, uses them on the Sabbath. Also one who makes Jewish employees work as servants on the Sabbath is a sinner and one who causes others to sin, just like Jeroboam, son of Nebat, making people desecrate their religion on the Sabbath. All of them transgress that commandment of the Ten Commandments that God, blessed be He, gave us, to rest on the Sabbath, we and all that we have; even our animals must we withhold from toil on the Sabbath. For we, the seed of Israel, we have two marks whereby we are Jews: one is the circumcision; one is the Sabbath. And now they have utterly erased one mark, the mark of the Sabbath. The people of Tunis who deviate from their path are left with the mark of the circumcision alone.

Furthermore, the condition of the Tunisians is grave in that some of them have begun to eat prohibited foods, foods from taverns, smoked foods, meat from the hunt, meat of Muslims and of Christians, animal corpses and impure animals, meat cooked in milk; and after eating the meat, at the end of the meal, they eat Dutch cheeses, drink libation wine, and so on.

Even worse is the situation of the Tunisians with respect to prostitution and fornication. This is beyond belief, in that the matter of prostitution has increased greatly. It is so bad that ten- and twelve-year-old schoolboys, who formerly followed the path of their predecessors—boys of that age did not know about whoring—now their situation has deteriorated to the point that these boys have become procurers. They act as procurers in this matter of prostitution, apart from the matter of the licentiousness of unmarried women.

Then there are wicked people, doers of evil, who spend money extravagantly in order to commit sins with married women, the sin of adultery, a heinous transgression for which the penalty is death in every religion. Moreover, if the married woman becomes pregnant illegitimately, she will bear a bastard child, born in sin in Jewry. But Jewry has a fine reputation and honor among the nations, as being people of pedigree. This evil-doer procreates many bastards in Jewry, Heaven forbid. Now, gentlemen, we have set forth before you ten percent of the evils of the Tunisians in this matter of prostitution. The condition of the Tunisians has gotten even worse, down to the level of bargaining over girls and virgin daughters of poor people. They are bought for cash; one who will sully the girl begins to commit a sin with her from the start, and she still a virgin.

The state of the Tunisians has gotten worse in the worship of God, blessed be He. They do not pray, they do not don the phylacteries and wrap themselves in the prayer shawl around their heads for many years. They do not enter the synagogue until someone dies on him, and then he goes to the memorial day. He does not want to make up a minyan with the congregation, so that it will not become known that he is a Jew. He does not say Grace after meals; he does not wash his hands before eating, nor make the blessing on the bread. He just eats like an animal and gets up from the table. Even the Muslim community is preferable: when they eat, they mention the name of the revered God.

The essence of what we have to say about the exacerbation of the poor state of some of the Tunisian Jews cannot be estimated, in that we greatly fear that this activity will wax very much among our Tunisians. Finally the young sons of Jews in Tunis will follow what they see, go in that way, and all will replace their religion for glitter and all will become Muslims. They will be proselytes for glitter, and it will be all one to them if they bear the name of the community of the Muslims so that the name of the Jews will be removed from them. May God not bring this upon us and not bring the people of Tunis to these wicked deeds.

Our ears have heard the history of the predecessors. Our late ruler the *Mushīr* Muḥammad al-Ṣādiq Pāshā Bey,[2] God's mercy upon him, appointed the late rabbi, the head of the court before us, his honor our teacher Rabbi Abraham Ḥajjāj,[3] may his soul be bound up in the cluster of life, and placed in his hand the seal of the Ḥakham Bāshī [chief rabbi]). Our above-mentioned ruler said to him, "Rabbi, what is this way of the Jews of Tunis? They have become greatly corrupt and have departed from the integument[4] of Jews, and they have not remained Jews?! Now, Rabbi, give your view on how to act and to constrain the Jews so that they repent from their wicked deeds, and if God will it, my hand on your head."[5] That is what our lord, the late governor, said to the aforementioned rabbi. And our present lord, may his days be prolonged, 'Alī Pāshā Bey,[6] in Tunis, may God sustain it, amen, always has been considerate of the Jews and the customs of their religion. For example, when he was in his palace built at the village known in Tunis as al-'Abd Aliyyā, which is in the town of al-Mārsa, he wanted all the Jews to reside with him in that village, and chose only proper Jews pious in their faith. Anyone who was not a proper Jew, or any Jewess who was not proper but lewd, he would not allow to dwell near him in Mārsa in the aforementioned village. Our above-mentioned lord, long may he live, wished our Jewish people to act according to their religion, so that if there was litigation between a Jew and a non-Jew, at once our master would send an agent of the felicitous government to force the Jew to accept the rule of his religion and his Torah, the Torah of our master Moses, peace be upon him. Our aforementioned lord, long may he live, never agreed to harm religions; he wanted everyone to be in his own faith—the Muslim in his faith, the Christian in his faith, and the Jew in his faith.

Now see, gentlemen, even other communities comprehend the gravity of the wickedness of the Tunisian Jews. This is a great desecration which has no remedy except only if the gate of repentance be open, if the way to return to Him who created them, may His name be blessed forever, be evident to the Tunisians. But apparently the Tunisians want to imitate the Jews of the Christian countries in Europe and do as they do. We, the undersigned, know the obvious truth, and we can swear great oaths that Tunis has become more grave and worse than all the countries. Every single country, from Africa to Italy and to France, all talk greatly about the evil of the Tunisians, women and men, and denounce it. Tunisia has become a disgrace throughout the world; it has become the unchastity of the earth, like Egypt of old.

Some Tunisian Jews think that the felicitous renowned government, the government of France, may its glory be elevated, which is the protector of the government of Tunisia, benefits from the deeds of the Tunisians and from the distortion that the Jews of Tunisia, may the Supreme One preserve it, amen, work upon their religion. We the undersigned inform you that by no means, Heaven forbid, does the government of France speak so. In days gone by, the Kol Yisrael Ḥaverim society, the Alliance, may it stand in justice, God preserve them and sustain them, sent strong letters and wrote to the religious judges of Tunisia to impose control over the Jews of Tunisia who were engaging in heinous acts, all that we have written in this declaration. Moreover, there was a man who took a journey to France, a good and fair man. There he saw with his own eyes, and we heard from him a clarification of matters. This was that the government of France, may God, blessed be He, preserve it, amen, does not wish for a distortion of the religions; it wishes only that the Jew be in his religion, the Muslim in his religion, and the Christian in his religion; this confirms what we said. Namely, that the authorities of France, may its glory be elevated, in Paris and in Marseilles, when the Jewish communities there needed to build a synagogue for Jewish worship, the first in Paris, the Jews built a very fine synagogue which cost them close to 5 million francs. This was reported in the newspaper *Ha-Maggid*, a Jewish journal. The felicitous government of France helped the Jews in their religion with this building of the aforementioned synagogue with a sum of 1 million francs. Likewise Marseilles, when they needed to build a synagogue that cost the Jews 450,000 francs, the above-mentioned felicitous government helped at its own expense with a sum of 80,000 francs. This matter was published and verified throughout the world, about this help to the Jews in building their synagogues so that they may pray in them and serve God, blessed be He, in them.

All this shows and proves with very true testimony that they want the Jews to remain in their religion and do not desire the distortion of the religions. Even in the countries of Africa the government of France, may its glory be elevated, helped the Muslim community to build a mosque in Algiers, a splendid mosque. All this is verification and confirmation of our statement that the government of France does not desire that any one of its communities distort its religion, not Jews, not Muslims, and not Christians.

The essence of our words to you, our brothers the Tunisians, may God preserve you and sustain you, is that we warn you, may He [God] bless you: Enough! Turn from the evil course and return in repentance, with God's help and mercy. Know that we have it in our power to impose very great penalties on anyone who does not cease to transgress all as we have written and recorded above, subject by subject. But as the Jews of Tunisia are dear to us, we do not wish to speak to you, Heaven forbid, harsh declarations from the outset, but only good declarations, in gentle language, according to the saying written in our holy Torah, "When you draw near to a city to fight against it, offer terms of peace to it" [Deuteronomy 20:10]. Take up our word for good life and peace. These are the words of the writers and the undersigned in the week of [*Ki tissa*: Exodus 34:10][7], "And all the people among whom you are shall see the work of the Lord; for it is an awful thing that I will do with you." Also the week of [Exodus 31: 16], "Therefore the people of Israel shall keep the Sabbath, observing the Sabbath throughout their generations, as a perpetual covenant, between me and the people of Israel." This day 20th of Adar I, 1883, in Tunis, may the Supreme One sustain it, amen, signed by us, the younger of the flock, with great strength and peace:

> The first signatory, head of the present court, his honor, our teacher, Rabbi David Ben ʿAṭṭār, may his memory be for the life of the world to come[8]
>
> Servant of God Eliyahu Ḥai Būrjil, may his end be good, Amen
>
> Servant of God Ḥayyim Būrjil, may God preserve him and prolong his life
>
> Servant of God Abraham Wakīl, may his end be good
>
> Servant of God Seʿadya Nattāf, may his end be good, Amen
>
> Servant of God Shalom Lishaʿ, may his end be good
>
> Servant of God Yehuda Jarmon, may his end be good
>
> Servant of God Mordekhai Smāja, may his end be good
>
> The young servant of God Ben Zion Gez, may his end be good

Neṣaḥ yisrael (The Eternal of Israel)

Neṣaḥ yisrael is a 64-page booklet containing two equal parts with consecutive page numbering.[9] It is written entirely in Judeo-Arabic. The title page of Part I reads, "A book of the Eternal of Israel. Published by the Neṣaḥ Yisrael Society, founded in Tunis on the New Moon of Adar in 5648. The first booklet. Printed in Tunis at Uzan and Castro Printers 1888."[10] The Society's regulations appear at the end of the Part I (pp. 30–32). At the end of Part II, from page 58 on, many dozens of names of the founders and members of the Society are listed. Page 64 contains details of the Society's income and expenditure. The overleaf of the title page for Part I is a notice in Judeo-Arabic:

> We inform you that the booklets to be published by the Neṣaḥ Yisrael Society will be distributed gratis, and if anyone wishes

to pay any sum to the above Society, it will be received from him as support for its aims and not for the booklets. Therefore, anyone who has not obtained the published booklets can go to the printers Messrs. Uzan and Castro, located below the ascent of Qā'id Michael Uzan, may God preserve him and prolong his days, and he will find them there. The address of the Society is Neṣaḥ Israel, Tunis.

The Society founders took actions to promote the spirit of Judaism in correct measure, mainly because there were Jews who wished to break away from the Jewish tradition. The booklet reprints passages on subjects such as unity, Talmud and civilization, and Hebrew language, all with an obvious didactic leaning. We present here translations of the first three chapters of Part I.

1. An Appeal to Readers

How despondent is our heart and how it aches when we see countless books and daily papers that besmirch our name and invent groundless things about us. They regard us as men of corruption and swindling, and by their lies and vile language they have turned the meaning of the name "Jew" into "twister" and "exploiter," one who devises plots against the property of people in order to take it over and works to do harm so that no good will come of it. When a crisis occurs in commerce or any damage arises in a given state, they at once are certain that the cause of it is the Jews, and the citizens believe them and hate us still more, and want to do us harm. And if we reply to them, and prove their lies and wickedness to them, they go on striving to harm us because they know the truth, and they do it with malice. Our answers will not avert them from their dishonest ways because their hearts are harder than iron and truth and decency toward people will not grow in them. And if we are silent, their words will be confirmed, and consequently great injury will be caused to us.

But this manifestation is an ancient ill to which our fathers and our fathers' fathers grew accustomed since our land was destroyed and we were dispersed among the nations. If in any era people appear who recognize our worth and believe in our justice and our way with God and man, and cast aside the cloak of ignorance, hatred, and evil from people, and draw us closer to themselves replete with warmth and respect, we cannot trust that that era of freedom will last forever. In an instant the breath from the mouths of those lowlife ignoramuses who hate us will gather to cloud our sky, and we will no longer be able to enjoy the light of freedom—except when our God brings us the spirit of victory and removes from us the clouds of evil. Then the sun of justice and law will shine on the world, and a man will no longer hate his fellow, who was created like him, because of his religion and origins. But what causes anguish in our heart and unaccustomed tears to flow from our eyes is that our own brothers are fleeing their origins and are ashamed of the word "Jew." They make every effort to hide their name and to clothe themselves in garb that is not theirs; they believe that indeed they have become "European" in reality, so that the shameful and base word "Jew" will not be referred to them. But time has moved them and proved to them that they are going in the path of darkness, that the owner of the costume will strip them of it and will not believe any fabrication, because he will look to the origin, not at the name or the deed.

After search and investigation, we realized that the origin of the disease that has taken root in our nation, which is steadily spreading like a scurvy, is ignorance of proper Judaism among those people. They run from its banner and do not feel that its principles, founded on true tenets, will not collapse; that they are based on justice and faith, truth and uprightness, mercy and kindness, freedom and love of fellow men. If they have not drunk from its waters or enjoyed its fruits, how will they hold it in esteem? If those who have grown up in its bosom hate it and turn their back on it, how may we expect those who are not of its faithful to consider it worthy? Or to love its adherents when its light has grown dim? In particular, when they see that some of its sons have departed from the right path, they infer that our Torah, or even our very creation, results in negative things; they do not grasp that in every people there are good and bad. This is so because hatred inheres in their body and they cannot see us as human beings but consider us brutish and despise us. They find no one who throws off his disguise and reveals the light of "Judaism" in full, until its sons return to it and cease straying from it. Then its opponents will appreciate it and cast the sword from their hand and turn to peace.

Seeing this, we the undersigned, bemoan the situation in which we are immersed. We fear the consequences, namely, that if this situation continues, the good for which we Jews [are known] will be lost, and no shred of it will remain to us. Only the name Jew, denuded of its roots; and we will incur upon ourselves humiliation and an insult to justice.

Therefore, we have assembled and founded a society called Neṣaḥ Yisrael whose goals are:

1. To reveal the hidden light in the Torah of Israel and to inform people of its elevated quality, so that they may respect it, and no longer belittle it, as has been their wont.
2. To indicate to anyone who is a Jew that according to the commandments of our Torah we are bound to love and cherish every being, even one who harms us, and we may not requite him according to his deeds.
3. To inform every Jew of his value and the value of his forefathers, so that he cease keeping his distance from them out of ignorance.

4. To set out before our brothers all the good that the people of Israel have done, and the benefit that has grown out of it for individuals and for all.
5. To expand education and culture in our people.
6. To bring our people closer to each other.
7. To restore to the true path anyone who has sinned against his fellow, because in the eyes of the nations we are seen as one man, and when one of us strays, this causes harm to us all.
8. To invest effort in the education of our children so that they are given everything that is required for any Jew.

To achieve this purpose of ours, we feel it is fitting to publish a booklet every month that will contain items as mentioned above and we shall distribute it free. If we obtain more support, we shall do more to bring us closer to our beneficent goal. We hope that our brothers will be of assistance to us, and that our God will succor and prosper us. Amen.

2. Unity

No man can achieve what he deserves except with the help of his fellow, and one who says that he can arrange his affairs without the aid of others is a liar. All creatures are like a machine assembled of several parts, and we see that it does what we require of it. But this is only as a result of the complex of its parts, while each part alone accomplishes nothing of what we expect from it. Similarly, every man in himself, without the participation of all cannot get what he deserves in the course of his days on earth. Only through sharing by all and mutual support will he achieve his desires. We may add and clarify our words that every creature must perforce eat, drink, sleep, and work, etc. But the soil does not bring forth baked bread for him, so all he need do is eat it. He has to sow seed, and then execute many tasks in order to have bread to eat. This process cannot be accomplished by one man, but with the help of another, be it by financing or physical labor. Anyone who isolates himself from society isolates himself from life. Similarly, when anyone who comes up against some difficulty, if he does not seek advice or a suggestion from his fellow, he cannot resolve the difficulty. Therefore, we see that any body formed for the purpose of a certain benefit will achieve its goals if all its members act single-mindedly. What one person lacks another will provide, and what the second lacks a third will provide, without contention among themselves. The dissolution and downfall of a body occurs when its members stop being of a common mind about the same goal, and each one of them strives and works to suppress the view of his comrade without addressing the truth. This circumstance is certainly a great detriment to the generality of that body; we have seen that inner dissent caused all of us great damage and would have brought catastrophe to our people had we not reunited as a single body and joined together as one soul.

This was in the time of Ahasuerus, when these were the precise words of the wicked Haman to the king: "There is a certain people scattered abroad and dispersed among the peoples in all the provinces; their laws are different from those of every other people, and they do not keep the king's laws, so that it is not for the king's profit to tolerate them" [Esther 3:8]. Sire, there is one people among the nations whose branches are disparate, and whose opinions are divided, to the degree that they have no special religion and law of their own. But they learn from every religion and law, and they share part of all, and they do not keep the Torah of their God. Therefore, this people has come close to its end, and God does not wish them to remain on the face of the earth. "If it please the king, let it be decreed that they be destroyed" [Esther 3:9].

Accordingly, Sire, let it be decreed that they be destroyed, because there are destroyed by God, and my master the king will gain respect and worth when his decree to destroy a whole people all over the world becomes known. Without doubt, divisiveness would have resulted in our destruction on earth, but for Queen Esther. She knew the cause of the injury, and hastened to repair it by ordering Mordekhai: "Go, gather all the Jews to be found in Shushan, and hold a fast on my behalf" [Esther 4:16]. Go and collect together all the scattered branches in such a manner that even if you require of them to fast three days night and day they will obey you and will not defy you. "Then I will go to the king, though it is against the law," etc. And when all the scattered branches are gathered, and the separation and divisiveness ceases, we will have no transgression in the eyes of the Lord, just that we do not go in his laws, and if he wishes to destroy us on that account, we will be destroyed. This is what Esther was able to set right for the scattered nation, and it was she who stood fast for us in order to save us from the slaughter, and we overcame the foe. Therefore, she appointed for us these days for all of us to fast, and to prove that we are a single body, in sorrow when it comes upon us. And then we send gifts to each other and gifts to the poor, which proves that even in the time of our joy and well-being we are a single body and will not split asunder. How grave is the matter of dissolution! And how pleasant and precious is cooperation and proximity within us, and love of every person for his fellow. All this, Sublime Providence knew and commanded in the Torah, "Love thy neighbor as thyself."

3. Ḥoni the Circle-Maker and Judaism

At this time, when some of our people are moving away from us, and becoming intermixed among other nations, and are ashamed to bear the name Jew, and our dear language is entirely unknown to them, and all this because of lack of recognition of our honor, it seems to us right to present the readers with the works of the wise writer Rabbi Reuven Asher Brodes,[11] may God preserve him and prolong his life. He addressed the Miqra Qodesh [Holy Scripture] Society, which was founded to propagate Judaism in Lvov. This is an excerpt from his speech, as published in *Ha-Maggid* of last year, issue 37.

> All have learned about the tale related in the Talmud about Ḥoni the Circle-maker, who pondered on the verse "When the Lord restored the fortunes of Zion, we were like those who dream" [Psalms 126:1], namely, that it could not be that a man would slumber for seventy years. One day, going out to the field, he found a man planting a carob tree. He approached him, and asked, "When will this tree yield fruit?" The man replied, saying, "In seventy years it will yield fruit." Ḥoni the Circle-maker reflected, and said to him, "Why then do you labor so to plant a tree of whose fruit you will not eat? Do you think that you will live seventy years more?" The man answered him, saying, "Just as my forefathers prepared for their children and grandchildren, so do I labor and prepare for my progeny and the next generation to eat of the fruit of the tree I have planted." Then sleep overcame Ḥoni the Circle-maker, and he slept under the tree, and a strong fence was around it, so that wild beasts would not damage him, for a spell of seventy years. Then he awoke from his sleep, and found a man eating of the fruit of the tree. He asked him. "Did you plant the carob?" He replied, "No, but my grandfather is he who planted it seventy years ago." Ḥoni said to himself, "In that case, I have slept for seventy years." He got up, and went into the city, and no

> one recognized him. He entered the yeshiva and found them revising Halakha in his name. He said to them, "I am Ḥoni the Circle-maker." But they did not believe him and said, "We have indeed heard of you, but we do not know you." Then Ḥoni sighed and said, "God, death is better than life. Why have I such a life? I must find society or I shall die!"

Gentlemen! Who will not see in these words a likeness to the people of Israel, and what has befallen them in the age of their imprisonment? Our early masters, who would hide and disguise their words and their ethics in the garb of riddle, also concealed in these words the living figure of the Jewish nation. We too were asleep for very many years, we too slept in the clefts in rock, and were not given leave to enjoy and to rejoice in the sweetness and pleasantness of the sunlight; we were not given leave to intermingle among people and to rejoice in the days of our life on earth. The gates of learning were also closed before us, and we were left asleep in the darkness for many years. But our Creator, who neither slumbers nor sleeps, preserved us from our enemies and they did not annihilate us. Still, we slept until the time came when the sun of freedom rose and awoke us from our sleep, and we saw strangers eating the fruit of knowledge planted by our forefathers in days of yore. Our hands were those that planted this tree thousands of years ago; we were the first to plant the tree of liberty and fraternity and amity among all human beings. It was our Torah that commanded, "Love thy neighbor as thyself" [Leviticus 19:18], "Love the sojourner" [Deuteronomy 10:19], "You shall have one ordinance and one law both for you and for the sojourner who sojourns among you" [Numbers 9:14], "Proclaim liberty throughout the land, to all its inhabitants" [Leviticus 25:10]. It was our Torah that planted these precious plants, the Tree of Knowledge and the

Tree of Life, of whose fruits all dwellers of Europe are eating. And now that we have advanced so as to live among people, how distressing it is to see that even our sons deny us! Those sons, whom we have brought up at our knee, do not know us. If we enter the schools and universities and remind them that they are our children and are related to us, they will reply, "We have heard the name Jew, sure enough, but the fact that you founded liberty, taught love and fraternity among human beings, and so on—we do not know that. We are Europeans; what have we to do with that old people that came from Asia? We do not know you, and we shall take nothing from you!"

Our brothers who are versed in Judaism and know what it behooves us to do are deep in sleep beneath the fence and do not know that in Europe they are making use of the light of Judaism, and many are walking in this light. They do not know that everything stems from our hands and that they have acquired it from us. They continue to sleep in darkness and do not awake to put this matter right. And Judaism, in seeing its children receding from it, says, "I have come to the end of my life—either society or death!" And what shall we say? Ah! Just a little more and we shall see ourselves as two peoples. On the one hand, we shall see our children receding from us and joining our enemies outside; on the other hand, we shall see people asleep, without the spirit of life in them. On the one hand, they seek to add one protective fence to another; on the other, they have torn down the fence safeguarding the garden of Judaism. Our children do not recognize us, while our adults do not acknowledge the light emerging from our Torah. The natural scientists say that for any thing to exist on earth, light and heat are needed together. So too our people, may they last forever. We see the light and the heat, but we see them separate. Our children enjoy the light, but their heart is cold, while within our leaders their heart is warm but the light is far from them.

Therefore, dear brothers, those among you who are able to bring filaments of light from one side to light up the other, and to take a few degrees of heat from this side to warm away the cold on that, make every effort and do not refrain from bringing in those who are distant from each other. Then we shall be one society and we shall be able to say to them, Society, not death!

This is the essence of Mr. Brodes's lecture. We are sure that these words, which came from the heart of a lover of his people and a yearner for its strength, will find paths in the heart of listeners and will bring forth from them good fruit, the fruit of knowledge and life.

Ba zeman ha-yeshu'a (The Time of Redemption Has Come)

Ba zeman ha-yeshu'a is a tiny booklet (7 × 11 cm) of 56 pages. Its title page states: "'I first have declared it to Zion, and I give to Jerusalem a herald of good tidings' [Isaiah 41:27]. A book containing learning and every Jew is obliged to read it once daily. It is published by the activists Shalom bar Ḥanna, Shalom bar Esther. Revenues from it are intended for the purpose of charity. Al-Sharqiyya Printers, 40 Maltese Street, in Tunis [n.d.]." The author of the booklet is Shalom bar Ḥanna, who name is printed on the last page, but we are unable to identify him. Shalom bar Ḥanna may be a pen name, concealing the author for some unknown reason. In its aim this booklet belongs with the two previous ones, but it has two interesting innovations.

First, the preaching and rebuke about the need to protect the religious tradition and the national legacy are set out in a distinctly literary manner: a sermon from Elijah the Prophet appearing in a quasi-prophetic vision to the author in a dream in a resplendent synagogue whose like he had never seen in Tunis. In keeping with the homiletic genre, the booklet is replete with biblical texts and rabbinic Midrashim. Note in this context that the author's words are directed at the issue of observing the commandments, and they do not refer to the importance of progress and enlightenment, although they do not, of course, come out against them; nor is such a tendency evident by inference. But it is clear that religious ideas actually reinforce the national leaning, as evidenced first of all from the title of the composition, "The Time of Redemption Has Come," and naturally also from the image of Elijah heralding salvation.

The second innovation is that for the first time in Judeo-Arabic literature in Tunisia, and most unusually, the author does not refer to the Jewish community in that country alone but to the four communities in the North African countries: Tunisia, Algeria, Morocco, and Libya. This seems to be a development in national thinking and the correct perception of the common cultural denominator of these, as distinct from other Jewish communities. We present the translation of the Foreword here.

> My dear brothers and members of my people!
>
> I have neither intelligence nor understanding, I have no skill with the pen or knowledge, I am "a common man!" But I am spiritually bound to undertake a mission several times stronger than my powers. It is this: to spread among my brothers, dwellers of North Africa, what my eyes have seen and what my ears have heard. But unfortunately this did not occur waking but in a dream; and as this dream came to me three nights consecutively, these being the nights of Rosh Hashanah and Shabbat Shuva, I trusted in God, be He praised, and I began with this work which I hope will be crowned with success and victory.
>
> I said that I was in a dream, and for three nights I saw one single vision. It is this: I saw, and behold I was in a synagogue whose like I have never seen in Tunis or in its vicinity, and an aged man, his face showing marks of grandeur and honor and

a white beard flowing down to his waist, stood at the Ark and preached.

"Who is this preacher?" I asked.

"Rabbi Elijah!" those present answered me.

At once I turned my ear to hear the words of the preacher.

> Since the time of the destruction of the Temple to the present day the Divine Presence is garbed in black, and will not radiate and will not take pleasure until He sees the Children of Israel observing the festivals as is proper and observing the Sabbath as is right; and on the Day of Atonement He appears and seeks forgiveness for the people of Israel. But the time is long and still we, children of the Holy One blessed be He, nevertheless have sinned, have transgressed, have been corrupt in our way; we have forgotten the festivals and have done away with the Sabbath. We have neglected prayer and the service, and have put aside the phylacteries, and we have even forgotten our name! We swore an oath and we have refuted our oath to our ancestor Jacob our father, peace be upon him. He assembled his sons and grandchildren, and said to them, "I fear, my sons, that you will intermingle with the Egyptians, you will learn their black deeds, and then this will hinder your redemption." Whereupon they replied in a single voice, "Hear, O Israel (our father), the Lord is our God, the Lord is one." And he responded in his heart: "Blessed be the name of His glorious kingdom for ever and ever."
>
> And even though Rabbi Meir Ba'al Ha-Ness, peace be upon him, tried to speak for us, saying that we are "children, even though corrupt," why should we be corrupt, and by our wickedness prolong our exile?

Truly, we are children to the Lord, but a recalcitrant son deserves punishment not kindness, and why should we not alter our dark way and repent, so perhaps God will have mercy on us, and redeem us from exile?

Remember, in Egypt, although Israel sank through fifty gates of defilement, still they did not change their name and retained their names always: Abraham, Isaac, Jacob, Reuben, Simon, and the others. But today, for the many transgressions, these names have been discarded and instead preference is given to Paul, Pierre, Jean, and other foreign names.

Likewise their wives were always good and always kept away from the sin of impurity. But today? Something sends a shiver through the body, and one cannot describe what takes place! Formerly, they hastened to marry their children young, but today, because of the *dota* (bride price), the youth forgets himself and wastes his time in idleness and profligacy. He does not think of marrying until such time as it may not be possible for him to beget children; and he also forces the young women to dare to place themselves in the hands of Gentiles. That is considered a very great desecration! Yet the world stands on three tenets: fertility and multiplying, worshipping in good faith, and study of Torah. Out of these three, for the first there is no pretext, as everyone can marry and does not have to wait until he accumulates furniture, which in the end he has nowhere to put. The rich man can help the poor in this, so as to propagate the seed of Israel, and thus corruption of behavior will be prevented and the downfall of the daughters of Israel among the Gentiles will be reduced. And if the rich man makes the effort to choose from among the poor girls, this is a highly praiseworthy act; similarly the rich woman from among poor boys—she too has great reward and her children will emerge prosperous and good.

The second commandment is also without a pretext, and every person is required to act in justice and faith. But as for the third, one may argue: I have not the time to study Torah, as I am overburdened with my work! But indeed, this too has a way out: he need only employ another who is God-fearing and poor, and pay his wage, and then it is considered as if he himself has studied.

These are evidently easy things to accomplish. As every Jew is obliged to pay the tithe, why should it not be easier to take the step of marrying? Why should we not hasten to fulfill the commandment of the Holy One, blessed be He?

The Jew is recognized by three things: circumcision, name, and the phylacteries. As for circumcision, we certainly will not suspect any Jew of not being circumcised. But the name, that is a matter subject to debate. As I have told you, there are many who have forgotten the ancient Jewish name and have replaced it with a "new" foreign name. This fact continues to prolong the bitter exile for us.

The commandment of the phylacteries? My body trembles when I see what is happening, and I shall state it out loud and clear: I have sinned, I have transgressed, I have erred before the God of Israel! I see a family rushing and hurrying and delighted to prepare phylacteries for their son when the time comes for him to enter into the religious covenant [bar mitzvah]. But to our great misfortune, today the son has donned the phylacteries and tomorrow we see him folding away the prayer shawl and the phylacteries. He will only remember the prayer shawl [alone] but once a year [the Day of Atonement]. Why did you hold this celebration, my sons? If your intention was to succeed in performing a commandment, I may tell you that you have committed a great sin, because when your son enters the religious covenant, he is deemed an adult man, who is required before God to uphold all the commandments of the religion. And if you shut your eyes and do not insist that he recite prayers every day and don the phylacteries on account of which you held the celebration, you are loading sin onto the neck of your son and onto your own neck!

On the day of the bar mitzvah your son is considered to have received an award, but this is not an award given by one man to another or by a government to a person, but a heavenly award, a spiritual award, a divine award. If we see a man who has received an award from the government, and he wears it day and night, why do we see that one who has won the spiritual award puts it away in the closet and treats it like a memento and nothing more? For the heavenly award is more honorable and privileged than the earthly award! Therefore, urge your sons to wear the spiritual award every day, to uphold the commandment "And they shall be for frontlets between your eyes"; for this commandment will hasten the "end of exile."

Similarly, expunge the sin of slander, because it kills three souls: of the slanderer, of the listener, and of him about whom it is uttered! Is there anything graver than killing a soul? Graver than idol worship? Slander is graver than these.

> As for keeping the Sabbath, this is something that every Jew is obliged to do without fail, and in keeping the Sabbath he will be preserved from all evil. If the people of Israel keep two successive Sabbath days properly, salvation will come at once.

And now the preacher turned his face to me, looked at me, and said: "Perhaps you should be ashamed of yourself?"

"What have I done, sir?" I asked in fear and trembling.

"Every night you read *Tikkun ḥatzot* and weep without the presence of any person and without any kind of instruction, even though you are not a scholar or a learned person! Your deed has brought you here!"

"Am I to stop what I do?" I asked, my eyes filled with tears.

"No, but repent in your way, repent, and engage in the task that we wish to impose on you. You are a son of Africa, and your name is Shalom [peace]. Spread what I shall tell you through these four lands of Africa: Tunisia, Algeria, Morocco, and Tripoli. Say to the Children of Israel dwelling in these countries, in my name, Elijah, study every day—either before the morning prayer or after it, or after the afternoon prayer—once every day, the following study": (the reader will find it after the Foreword).[12]

"I am ready, sir, to do what you have told me," I replied, and thereupon I heard behind me a voice crying,

"The time of redemption has come! The time of redemption has come! The time of redemption has come!"

Two days later I set out on this mission, and I trust in God that it will bring forth the desired result.

And peace from your brother, the humble servant of God Shalom bar Ḥanna, may his end be good.

Brothers, Children of Israel, I have fulfilled my mission, and God helped me, for he sent on my path two people renowned for fearing heaven, namely Messrs. Yosef bar Esther and

Shemarya bar Ṣvila. These two assisted me with all their might and did not let me collapse under the burden. This fact proves that God, praised be His Name, made it easier for me in performing this hallowed task. And now, having insisted yet again that I am the least of men, I ask my brothers not to be amazed that this matter has come through me. I am devoid of all wisdom and all culture, and I will greatly rejoice if through me the errant return in repentance, and by them I receive any requital; they are the causes of it.

At the end of my book I make mention of the rules I was ordered to state. The first rule: Every Jew is required to respect every scholar, because only in wise men will we be respected and respect for them is our respect, and certainly no scholar is to be left without anything for his sustenance. Likewise we must help the charitable societies, in the first place the religious societies such as the Ḥevrat Talmud Torah, Or Torah, Keter Torah, Shema Israel, Bar-Mitzva, just as we shall not forget the Bridegrooms' Society, etc., etc. We must urge our sons to pray daily, and God will answer us at all times, as we have been taught, that He "will act for the schoolchildren." It seems that my brothers will listen to me, even though I am a "common man." Namely, I have no worth and no honor, no knowledge and no understanding.

Finally, I say to you: do not forget that we are the Children of Israel, and we have not held fast except through our grasp of the religion and upholding its requirements. Therefore, remember this virtue, and you will certainly not forget the duty imposed on you. Thus God will help you in all your affairs, and will assist with every benefit that brings advantage to all, regardless of faith and religion.

And peace. Servant of God, Shalom bar Ḥanna, may his end be good.

7

The Drama and the Theater

It can hardly be said that drama was a genre of Judeo-Arabic literature in Tunisia. Nevertheless, Jews played an important role in the development of theater in general in Tunisia, and Jewish theater troupes had repertoires in all the languages in use at the time in Tunisia: classical Arabic, Judeo-Arabic, Hebrew, and French.[1] Most of the Jewish theater productions, however, were dramatized versions of various tales performed mostly in Judeo-Arabic. But it is uncertain whether those texts were sent to a printing house to be published or remained in manuscript form for future use by the audience and actors. We do have some slight evidence of printed dramatized versions, but this is not enough to justify stating that a drama genre existed in Judeo-Arabic literature. It seems that no original Judeo-Arabic works were written from the outset as plays. Nevertheless, the intensive activity of Jews in theater should not be overlooked; here too we refer principally to people from the northern communities rather than people from the southern ones as being active in the various facets of stage productions and also as the audience. We learned from much oral testimony that the participation of Jews in theater productions in general (where some of the Jews were outstanding) and in Jewish theater was great. From an overall cultural viewpoint this activity should therefore be seen as part of the new activity of the spirit whose language of communication was Judeo-Arabic and which characterized the Jewish communities of northern Tunisia beginning at the turn of the nineteenth century. For this reason we expand the framework of our discussion somewhat and devote this chapter to a comprehensive consideration of the activity of the Jews of Tunisia in the sphere of theater and drama.

Beginning of the Theater in Tunisia and the Role of the Jews

It is well-known that the play as a literary genre and theater as a medium for social entertainment were absent from the Arab world in the Middle Ages, although certain frameworks for public performance existed as religious texts (e.g., the tale of the death of Ḥasan and Ḥusayn, the sons of ʿAlī) or for amusement (*qaraqoz*, i.e., shadow play).[2] Only in the nineteenth century, under the evident influence of European theater, did activity in this area begin in the Arab countries (Lebanon and Egypt), and the writing and the acting were conducted in Arabic.[3] In Tunisia the birth of Arabic theater was fairly late, 1907, according to Hamadi Ben Halima.[4]

However, during the nineteenth century, theater performance was quite widespread, although not of original works in Arabic but of works imported from Europe, chiefly France, and troupes from Italy performed before the rulers of Tunisia as early as the second half of the eighteenth century.[5] Tunisian Jews, more precisely, Jews from the Livornese community (the Grāna), who lived mainly in the capital, Tunis, seem to have played a considerable part here.[6] The Jews of the Grāna community had originally migrated from Livorno, on the coast of western Italy, for the purpose of trade, and the community remained separate from the old, established Tunis Jewish community, with the marks of social superiority. Only in 1906 did the two Jewish communities in Tunis become united, although the social distinctions did not disappear.[7] Members of the Grāna community were the first to join the Jewish Enlightenment movement in Tunisia in the second half of the nineteenth century, and they worked above all to disseminate culture and education among the Tunisian Jews through extensive publication of diverse literature in the local Judeo-Arabic dialect.

The medieval Jewish world also did not recognize the play as a literary genre or the theater as a cultural, spiritual, or recreational activity. The first Hebrew play is in fact a translation of the Spanish piece *La Celestina* by the Marrano Fernando de Rojas; it was translated by the Jew Yosef ben Shemu'el Sarfati, who died near Rome in 1527.[8] Hebrew theater was born in Italy in the seventeenth century, with the impressive work of Yehuda Somo of Manuta, who wrote the first original Hebrew play, *Ṣaḥut bediḥuta de-qiddushin*, and indeed staged it. He also wrote an instruction book for dramatic art in Italian (which has not survived).[9] Such activity did not wane among the Jews of Italy in the following centuries.[10] During the seventeenth and eighteenth centuries several original plays were written in Italy and the Netherlands (in the latter by descendants of Spanish exiles), such as *Yesod ʿolam* and *Tofte ʿarukh* by Moshe Zacut, *Gemul ʿatalia* by David Franco Mendes, and *Maʿase shimshon* and *Migdal ʿoz* by Moshe Ḥayyim Luzzatto; these plays were clearly influenced by foreign literature, although we have no evidence that they were performed.[11] By contrast, the allegorical Hebrew drama *Naḥat ru'aḥ*, by Yiṣḥaq Palache of Algiers, was performed in Algiers at the end of the eighteenth century.[12] Another dramatic piece should be mentioned here, *Nazāhat al-mushtāq wa-ghuṣṣat al-ʿushshāq fī madīnat tiryāq fī al-ʿirāq* (The Pleasure Trip of the Enamored and the Agony of Lovers in the City of Tiryāq in Iraq) by Abraham Daninos of Algiers. This piece was printed in Algiers in 1847 in Arabic characters.[13]

A direct line seems to run from the theatrical activity of the Italian Jews until the nineteenth century to the import of theater into Tunisia at that time.[14] The earliest piece of information on this is a deed signed in Livorno in 1826 between an impresario and his company of Venetian actors, who had not been paid after a season in Tunis. The source we possess says nothing of the impresario's religion, but it is fairly reasonable to assume that he was a Jew.[15] This source does state explicitly the Tunisian Jewish origin (*un israélite tunisien*) of the proprietor of the theater, Théâtre Tapia. This is in connection with the words of a Swiss officer in the service of the king of Les Deux-Siciles that he had applauded the members of this theater, which "was set up at that time in Zarqūn Street in the city of Tunis with a stage and a curtain. The theater was a vaulted warehouse, quite roomy, a good part of which was made vacant. A corner for a balcony: several rows of chairs, benches, and at the end, in a semi-circle, 'boxes' separated by sackcloth. Lighting was by oil lamps, which dazzled the eyes."[16] In 1860 the Théâtre Tapia took on a more general and more national name, Théâtre Carthaginois. The Jewish Tapia family was well-known in Tunis, belonging to the Livornese community.[17] The penchant for Italian culture emerges clearly from the repertoire of the company, whose actors were known as the Italians: *La Traviata* in 1856 and *Bal Masque* in 1859. The company also performed outside Tunisia, and in a Cairo appearance the singer Adelina Patti acted in Filippo Marchetti's *Ruy Blas*.

The founder of another theater, which operated in Tunis for thirty years, was also a Jew of Livornese origin, David Cohen-Tanuji (1835–1928).[18] His many travels in Europe, presumably on business and particularly to international trade fairs in 1855 and 1867, brought him into contact with European dramatic art, and he resolved to create a European theater in Tunis. Cohen-Tanuji built a special edifice, in keeping with the finest European architecture, on Bone Street at the corner of Constantine Street. It had seating for 400 and special boxes and balconies. The theater opened in December 1875 with Benjamin Goddard's *Ruy Blas*, attended by a representative of al-Ṣādiq Bey and several consuls, including the Frenchman Théodore Roustan. Gounod's *Faust* was apparently first performed in this theater in Italian, as was Donizetti's *La Favorite*.

However, soon the Italian leaning, which generally typified the economic, political, and cultural ties of Tunisia (including its Jews) to Europe at the time, was replaced by a tendency toward French culture. In 1879 Cohen-Tanuji's theater staged the premiere of Lecocq's French operetta *Giroflé-Girofla*; this was followed by Lecocq's *La Petite Mariée*, Hervé's *Le Petit Faust*, Offenbach's *La Jolie Parfumeuse*, and Audran's *La Mascotte.* In 1890 the theater became known as La Scala, and in 1892 it took on the highly charged name Folies-Bergères: Concert du Chat Noir. Through this change from serious drama to light entertainment the theater altered its character to a music hall, and its management was taken over by someone else (Jo Galano). At the recommendation of the Commission des Théâtres of the French administration in Tunisia (taken by France in 1881), the new managers introduced important improvements in emergency safety arrangements and added dressing rooms for the actors. In 1895 the oil lamps were replaced by gas lighting, and in 1898 all safety regulations of the Commission des Théâtres were satisfied. In 1905, after thirty years of splendid activity, the theater's doors were sealed and the building was demolished.

The link between the Tunisian theater and the French theater naturally grew firmer after 1881; a Jewish connection existed here too. In 1886 the famous French Jewish actress Sarah Bernhardt and Madam Agar of the Comédie Française played in *L'Aventurière*, presented at a new theater established in 1883 in a wooden structure located near the Tunis municipality building. This theater did not survive long; it burned down in 1889. Still, the legendary figure of Sarah Bernhardt exerted enormous influence on the actresses of Tunisia, who wanted to be like her. Later in this chapter we shall see that Ḥabiba Messica shared this desire, but so did Arab actresses. In fact, Rashīda Luṭf was acclaimed as "the Sarah Bernhardt of Tunis" in 1925.[19]

Three more theaters were built and functioned in Tunis before the establishment of the first Arab theater: (1) L'Arèna, an Italian theater later renamed Politema Tunisino, with an Italian manager, Napoleone Zanetti (the theater was destroyed by fire in 1897); (2) the first municipal theater, founded in 1885 by a Greek named Gringa and later renamed *Te'atro* Paradiso; after it burned to the ground, it was rebuilt and at first was called Théâtre Française and then Théâtre Municipale, and it was managed by a Frenchman, G. D. Douchet; and (3) the Rossini, an Italian opera house, which opened in 1903.[20]

We have presented this list to highlight the considerable role of Jews in theater life in Tunis in the nineteenth and early twentieth centuries and, no less important, to show that the theatrical entrepreneurs were not members of the Arab majority but members of the Jewish minority or European foreigners, first Italian and later French. However, Hamadi Ben Halima opines that all these plays could not possibly have been performed only before members of the Italian or French colony in Tunis. Arab intellectuals who had ties with Europe and its culture and who knew Italian or French were presumably among the theater audiences and enjoyed productions of operetta, comedy, and farce. As proof of the Tunis intelligentsia's receptivity to European theater at that time, Ben Halima cites the works of three leading figures in the political, social, and cultural sphere: the minister Khayr al-Dīn Pāshā, Bayram al-Khamīs, and Aḥmad ibn Ḍiāf.

If this is Ben Halima's assessment of the position of the intellectual minority within the Arab majority in Tunis, how much more does it hold for the Jewish minority, or more precisely the minority within the minority? This was the Grāna community, who kept up their ties with Livorno, their city of origin, together with some Jews from the long-standing Tunis Jewish community who were fervent activists in the local Jewish Enlightenment movement and stood for openness to the surrounding culture, Arab and European. We know for sure that they, in contrast to their Arab counterparts, participated in the establishment of theaters in Tunis and managed them.[21] All of this is according to what we have described earlier regarding the playwriting and theatrical activity of the Jews of Italy (and to a lesser extent of members of other Jewish communities in Europe), whose continuation was evident in Algiers at the end of the eighteenth century and in Tunis in the nineteenth and early twentieth.

Arab Theater in Tunisia and the Role of the Jews

Arab theater in Tunis began in 1907, at the initiative of the French government of the country, when an Egyptian company performed at the Théâtre Municipale. From all the foregoing we should not be surprised that one of the first two original plays presented in Arabic was *Muḥādatha bayn yahūdayān* (A Conversation Between Two Jews), whose subject—the problem of nationalism among the Jews of Tunisia—was most timely then.[22] This question greatly troubled the Tunis Jewish community, which was torn among three alternative national commitments: (1) the tie with the Jewish people and its tradition, especially in light of the Zionist awakening that was putting down notable roots in Tunisia; (2) the link with the French state and its European culture, to which many in the Tunis Jewish community were drawn and which they saw as a model of Enlightenment and proper social life; and (3) the connection to Arab nationalism in Tunisia, which began to develop at that time; some Jewish intellectuals in Tunis believed it was necessary to integrate into the Arab community and its culture. All these commitments found clear expression in the Judeo-Arabic literature in Tunisia in those years. The issue came up for inevitable public debate because of the plan by Tunisia's French rulers to vest in the French courts exclusive authority to try cases involving the country's Jews, a move that generated hostility between the Jewish minority protected by the foreign regime and the Arab Muslim majority population. Another theater production having to do with Jews was *al-Yahūdī al-tā'ih* (The Wandering Jew), based on the famous novel *Le Juif errant* by the French writer Eugène Sue; this play was staged in 1920 by the al-Shahāma troupe, of which Ḥabiba Messica was an important member.[23]

It is doubtful that these plays were published or that they survive anywhere, but we are convinced that many of the Arabic plays performed at that time in the theaters in the genres of the *qiṣṣa* (story) and the *ḥikāya* (tale) were translated into Tunisian Judeo-Arabic and printed at the Jewish printing houses in Tunis and Sousse, especially Makhlūf Najjār's printing house. We possess two attestations, albeit from the early twentieth century. One is a dialogue in the booklet *Monolog ʿalā qad al-līl mā yṭawwil* (Tunis, n.d.) between *al-ʿāshiq* and *al-ʿāshiqa* (the male desirer and the female desirer) in a version suitable for dramatic performance, in both Judeo-Arabic and French translation. The dialogue is called a monologue because it was delivered as a one-man show by Ḥayyim Bshīrī. This is stated expressly on the booklet's title page: "*min famm* [from the mouth of] Ḥayyim Bshīrī." We thus learned in passing that, apart from regular theater productions, there were one-person shows. The other attestation, which is more detailed, is in the booklet *Khlāʿat purim* (Tunis, n.d.).[24] This booklet contains various pieces of parody in Judeo-Arabic, including a sonnet of the kind well-known from other Jewish communities from as early as the Middle Ages.[25] One of the pieces is a "malʿab te'atro" (theater game) called *Sakrat purim* (The Tipsiness of Purim). At the start of this one-act play the actors' names are given (*asami al-mlāʿaba*): Dānā, Hamāma, and *jamāʿat al-baraka* (the blessing company).

The subject of theater and drama among the Jews of Tunisia and their Judeo-Arabic literature is still far from exhausted. A deeper and wider examination will obviously yield highly valuable information. Interesting findings are likely to arise from a comparison of these genres in Judeo-Arabic literature with the Arabic plays presented in the theaters in Tunisia.[26] We present one example of the subject. In the *tajrīda* (book list) of the printer Mordekhai Uzan and his brother of January 1925 (Tunis) two booklets are listed with this blurb:

> *Nuzhat maṣr* [The Entertainment of Egypt], Book I, has within it modern Egyptian poems and monologues and dialogues that are sung in theaters at the present time. At its end the *ḥasīn* mode. Hebrew and French scripts.

> *Nuzhat maṣr*, Book II, contains other modern Egyptian poems and monologues and dialogues, and with them the addition of the *māya* mode. (4)[27]

Another incident that may elucidate the Jewish connection to the world of Arab theater in Tunisia is the prevention of the production of the play *Yūsef ha-ṣaddīq* (Joseph the Just). This tale was a folkloric traditional favorite among the Jews of Tunisia, as attested by the abundance of local Judeo-Arabic versions in many manuscripts and printed publications. In February 1909 the board of the Jewish hospital in Tunis asked Sulaymān Qardāḥī to produce a play as a fundraising effort for the hospital. Qardāḥī is considered the father of Arab theater in Tunisia. An energetic and broadly talented Egyptian, he had arrived in Tunisia at the end of 1908 and established an Arab theater there that presented a large number of plays.[28] He generously acceded to the request and suggested putting on *Joseph the Just*, no doubt reckoning that its popularity would make it a draw for many Tunis Jews. They were the target audience, considering the charitable purpose of the production for the hospital.[29] Incidentally, we discovered that this important Jewish institution in Tunis was familiar with the Arab theater and could see no difficulty in mounting a play for a large number of the city's Jews to attend. But Tunis Muslims (*cercle tunisien*) displayed extreme religious fanaticism, and through the Arabic journals threatened to stage public protests and even to ban Qardāḥī if the play was produced, thereby desecrating the sanctity of the name of "the worthy prophet Joseph." Qardāḥī could not withstand the immense pressure, and he suggested a different play to the hospital board.[30] But sixteen years later a Tunisian theater director, 'Alī ben Kamla, dared to produce at his theater *The Selling of Joseph by His Brothers*, which all other companies eschewed, despite the vicious criticism hurled at him in the Muslim papers, especially because the role of Joseph the Just was played by the Jewish actress Ḥabiba Messica.[31]

Another Jewish theme presented in 1937 at the Joint Tunisian Theater (which existed from 1936 to 1949) was the story of Khālid ibn Yazīd al-Qaysī or al-Kāhina, which relates the capture of North Africa by Muslim forces in the second half of the seventh century from the Berbers, led by the Jewish queen known as al-Kāhina (the Sorceress).[32] The script was by the Tunisian writer Aḥmad Khayr al-Dīn, who was paid the enormous sum of 1,000 francs owing to theater policy of intense competition with other theaters. In the journals of the time a fierce debate raged about whether the play was indeed the work of Khayr al-Dīn. Ben Halima holds that it was an adaptation of *La Kahena* by Emile Roudie.[33]

Apart from Ḥabiba Messica, whose theatrical work we discuss in the final section of this chapter, a number of other Jews were active in Arab theater, so in terms of nationality the Jewish actress was unexceptional; her uniqueness lay in her personality alone. In 1905–1907 the Jewish singer Kiki Guetta was a member of the al-Hilāl musical ensemble in theater performances at the La Rotande hall in Tunis.[34] In 1908 the Libyan-born Jewish singer ʻĀliya Simon settled in Tunis, converted to Islam, and married a major figure of Tunisian theater, Ḥasan Bannān (more about him later), and both joined the al-'Ādāb theater. The first theater company in 1908, al-Najma, included two brothers of the Sāsī family, hairdressers by trade, and their being Jews is in no doubt. In Voltaire's *La mort de Cesar*, produced by the al-Hilāl theater, in which Ḥabiba Messica was an important figure (see later in this chapter), the lead was played by a new actor, the Jewish singer Maurice ʻAṭṭūn. Another Jewish singer-actor, Maurice ben ʻĪs, played in *Majnūn laylā* with the al-Tamthīl al-ʻArabī theater in 1928.[35]

The Jewish quarter in Tunis, most of whose residents were of course Jews, always served as a place for artistic entertainment. Ben Halima mentions this in connection with the decision by a leading person in the Tunis theater world to erect in the Jewish quarter a new building for his theater after the existing one had burned down. That had been a cinema in the Muslim Bāb Swīqa district. In December 1923 the new building, called Le Passage, was opened.[36] Two reasons for the choice of the Jewish quarter for its location presumably existed: the great interest shown by the Tunis Jews in theater and the distance from the prying eyes of extremist Muslims who objected to this form of entertainment.

The relatively large proportion of Jewish men and women in the musical professions (singers, instrumentalists, dancers) and the centrality of the Tunis Jewish quarter for performance entertainment were no doubt due to the fact that in the Tunisian tradition (Muslim and Jewish) the members of these professions did not enjoy high esteem. For example, in his article on the Jews of Tunis between the two worlds, the late Jacques Taïeb, a scholar of contemporary Tunisian Jewry, entirely ignores their occupation with theater and entertainment in general. He is content to mention in a footnote that that this was an old calling, followed principally by Jews of lowly origin. He states that only in the interwar period did many Arab artistes enter the field, although numerous Jewish entertainers of great renown had long occupied its first ranks, such as Shaykh al-ʻIfrīt and Masʻūd Ḥabīb, and young talents such as the singer Raoul Journo and the flutist Wald Shnīshen.[37]

The Arab-Jewish Jawq al-Taraqqī al-Isrā'īlī Theater

Apart from the presentation of Jewish themes in the Arab theater in Tunisia and the participation of Jewish actors and singers in the various companies, for a decade in the early period of this theater activity (1913–1923) a Jewish theater existed called Jawq al-Taraqqī al-Isrā'īlī (Jewish Progress Troupe; in French, Progrès Israélite). The first report of it appeared in the newspaper *al-Zahra* on November 4, 1913 (translated from Arabic): "Young Tunisian Jews have formed a troupe called *al-Taraqqī* headed by the famous singer Mr. David Hajjāj. On 5 November at the *Rossini Theatre* it will present *Ṣidq al-widād* [Love of Truth], a literary and historical drama in four acts."[38] During and after World War I nothing is heard of this company, but it reappeared in 1922, now with Jewish and Muslim members. The leading lights of the company were (1) the artistic and musical director, the Jewish singer Maurice 'Aṭṭūn, who had left the al-Shahāma theater ('Aṭṭūn was also the father of the famous Tunisian singer Ḥanna Rāshid and husband of the singer Fritna Darmon); (2) the manager, the Muslim al-Sharīf ben Yakhlaf, who had been an actor with al-Shahāma (in 1922 he left al-Jawq al-Fukāhī al-Tūnisī [Tunis Comedy Troupe], which he had formed in 1920, to join the Jewish theater); and (3) the company's Jewish secretary and treasurer, Momo Chemama.

The company's first production was at the Rossini Theater on March 11, 1922. It was a four-act play titled *Judith*, with an obviously Jewish theme, written in classical Arabic by ben Yakhlaf. Press reports stated that the cast consisted of sixty Jewish and Muslim actors and that the title role was being played by a new acquisition of Italian origin, the actress Dalila. Other members of the cast were ben Yakhlaf, 'Aṭṭūn, and Gaston Bshīrī, a Jew who subsequently met his death in a German concentration camp during World War II.[39] As was the custom, an Eastern concert was played after the performance. On October 28, 1922, the operetta *Nūr al-ṣabāḥ* (Morning Light) was presented, written by Maurice 'Aṭṭūn, and 'Āliya Bannān (Simon) acted in the leading role.

The 1923 season was busy, particularly with revivals and operettas. On April 3, *La mort de Cesar* was staged. Other productions included *Majnūn layā*, *Ṣalāḥ al-dīn*, *Esther*, *Romeo and Juliet*, *Le médecin malgré lui*, and *The Selling of Joseph*. All the plays were performed in classical Arabic, not French or the local Arabic vernacular,[40] a fact highlighted by the Tunis press as evidence of the profound awareness in the heart of Tunisian Jews of classical Arabic. That year the company was joined by Ḥasan Zmerlī, an important Jewish figure in Tunisian theater.[41]

At the end of 1923 Jawq al-Taraqqī al-Isrā'īlī apparently ceased to function, as it is no longer mentioned in the press; ben Yakhlaf moved to Algeria and Maurice 'Aṭṭūn set up his music hall. In any event the special nature of this Jewish theater lay in its exclusive use of classical Arabic and also, like al-Hilāl theater, in its being a mixed company of Jews and Muslims.[42]

The Theater Ensemble of Makhlūf Najjār

Makhlūf Najjār was a most important figure in Judeo-Arabic literature in Tunisia, chiefly by virtue of his printing house in the town of Sousse in northern Tunisia, where hundreds of publications in Arabic and Judeo-Arabic of various kinds were printed. His abundant enterprise merits a deep and wide-ranging study. One of his other accomplishments was theater.[43] In May 1913 Najjār assembled a group of young Jewish actors, none of them older than 14. The first production was *The Selling of Joseph by His Brothers*, a favorite theme among the Jews of Tunisia, as noted earlier. The play was performed in classical Arabic and was a great success, touring the towns of Sfax and Nabeul and finally playing at the Théâtre Municipale in Tunis. The company reaped further success on its tour of Algeria in 1914. Apart from plays inspired by the Bible, others were produced, for example, adaptations of Molière such as *Le médecin malgré lui* and *Les femmes savantes*. The language of the plays varied among all possible alternatives available to the Tunisian Jewish community: the local Arabic vernacular, classical Arabic, Hebrew, and French.[44]

A brief but most important account of the theater company that Najjār managed was given by Najjār himself in the *Kitāb snāwī* (yearbook) for 1918–1919, which Najjār printed.[45] In its second part Najjār devotes just over two pages to the company he headed:

> **The Najjār Company**
>
> The Najjār Company has won fame all over the state of Tunisia and the state of Algeria. The members of this company are young boys and girls who have presented the loveliest plays on the stages of the great theaters, and they do so in the original Hebrew language. Often present in these theaters were notables of high position and prestige, and they were delighted and greatly amazed at the presentation of the characters with complete faithfulness.

The first play of the Najjār Company was the play *Joseph the Just* at the Sousse theater on 15 February 1913. Now the company is considered to be of great worth to the inhabitants of Tunisia because it stages many plays. Among them are *Joseph the Just*, *Esther the Queen*, *David and Goliath* (in the holy tongue), *Moshe Rabbenu*, *al-Tabīb al-maghḍūb [Le médecin malgré lui]*, *Nāṣir al-jamīl* [The Handsome], *Maḥāsin al-ṣadf* [The Praises of keeping away?], *Charlotte*, *'Āqibat al-baghy* [The End of the Criminal], *al-Ḥakīm al-ṭayyār* [The Flying Judge], *Hārūn al-Rashīd ma'a khalīfa al-ṣayyād* [and Khalīfa the Fisherman], *al-Sāḥir al-'ajīb* [The Wondrous Wizard], *Ghīrat* [The Envy of] *Barboy*, *al-Žūž ṭrash* [The Deaf Couple], *Jamā'at al-surrāq* [The Gang of Thieves], *al-Jahala al-mud'iyyīn bi-al-'ilm* [The Ignorants Who Seem to Be Scholars], *Kāmil Effendi*, *La Georgienne* (in French), and more.

These are the cities in which the company has performed: Sousse, Sfax, Tunis, Nabeul, Ḥalq al-Wād, Marseilles, Mahdiyya, Moknīn, Kairouan, Bizerte, and Monastir. In the state of Algeria: Constantine, 'Unāba, Qālima [Guelma], 'Īn al-Bayḍa, Settif, Blīda, Bajāya, Sūq Harās, and Khinshla.

Each and every time, the company donates the takings of many evenings to purposes of charity, and many are the societies that have enjoyed great and generous assistance.

The manager and founder of the company is Mr. Makhlūf Najjār, may the Lord preserve him and keep him alive, author of the Yearbook.

The first person who lent a shoulder to the Najjār Company and greatly enjoyed the purity and beauty of the language, pronounced in the voices of the these boys and girls is a noble and dear man, the honorable and generous, the late gentleman al-Bashīr Ṣafar, who was governor of Sousse, and on 2 March 1917 he died for the life of the World to Come

> in his fifty-fourth year. May God in his great mercy make it pleasant for him.

Here too we doubt that all the plays listed by Najjār and others not mentioned were in fact published. Most of these titles are know to us as *ḥikāyāt*, that is, stories published by Najjār at his printing house.[46] But we can assume that at least some of the works were published also as plays. This, at least, transpires from Najjār's *tajrīda* of January 1936, which includes a blurb for a booklet titled *Charlotte* (*Charlotte* was mentioned among the plays performed by the Najjār Company in the 1918–1919 yearbook): "This is a vision that leaves the most powerful impression on the heart. It contains secret things between the beloved and the lover. A scene that beggars the mind. It is presented at theaters in five acts. It has thirty pages and its price is 2.00 [francs]."[47]

We also found in several places in Najjār's publications, in *tajrīda*s and at the end of the *ḥikāyāt* he published, the indication "*Joseph the Just* (*Te'atro*)." From this it perhaps can be inferred that the dramatized version of this tale was indeed published. But we should clearly note that we have not come across any publications of this kind in Judeo-Arabic.

Ḥabiba Messica: A Central Figure in Arab Theater in Tunisia

Ḥabiba Messica was born to a family of musicians in 1899. In Chapter 4 we translated two *qinot* about her legendary image. Here we concentrate on her as an actress, something that has been almost totally forgotten. In what follows is our translation of Ben Halima's summary of this performer, followed by details of her career in the theater.[48]

> Of all the vocalist-actresses [*ṣāni'a*] Ḥabiba Messica alone lives on in the memory of Tunisians. She aroused the enthusiasm of the entire prewar generation. At a time when the

artistic life was a disgrace for a woman, she won admiration and respect from the city's cultural elite.

She was born in about 1899 to a family of musicians: her father was a simple instrumentalist, and her maternal aunt, Layla Sfez, was a fairly well-known singer in 1915. With her she studied the art of singing, and learned how to play the piano. At the age of twenty Ḥabiba embarked on her artistic career as a vocalist at weddings. Later she was attracted to the theater. Her teacher in this area was Muḥammad Bourguiba. Thanks to him she attained the level of the greatest comedies and played leading roles in world-famous dramas. She wrote out her lines in Latin script.[49]

Some people hold that she was more talented in acting than singing. Although she played the piano and violin flawlessly, her voice lacked beauty and her range was not as wide as that of Layla Sfez. She did not excel in any special way of her own: like other singers of the time, she was content to sing popular Tunisian melodies, and also the fashionable Egyptian *adwār* and *ṭaqāṭiq*[50] taught to her by Ḥasan Bannān.[51] She performed Tunisian songs in a voice that was a mixture of timbres, and did so with considerable success.

If all the last generation saw Ḥabiba Messica as its ideal woman, this was not for her talents or even her beauty; it was simply for her kind nature. Only her captivating heart, her wisdom, her appearance, her fine bearing, and her private life can explain the fascination she held for the men who clustered around her all her life. Contrary to other artistes, she remained within the circle of the city's elite. She lived in fabulous luxury, but her generosity was legendary.[52] She was burned to death at the hands of her admirer Eliyahu Mīmūnī on 20 February 1930, and was laid to rest at the Būrjil cemetery.

News of her passing caused general shock. The funeral she was accorded is still spoken of: the whole city followed

> her weeping to her final resting place. The most expensive perfumes were poured onto her body by her sorrowing adorers. Her body was borne on their arms, a high honor, rarely granted to any except a chief rabbi or a person of great piety.[53]
>
> The Chief Rabbi Būqāra delivered the eulogy on the subject of "fire purifies everything,"[54] and the poets bewailed her with moving verses on frequent occasions.[55] A lament (chanted by the mourners at the deceased's home before the funeral) was composed.[56]

The interwar years were the golden age of Arab theater in Tunisia, when European theater was pushed aside and the status of Egyptian theater companies and actors steadily diminished. Their place was taken by the growing stature of domestic theater, which reflected local habits and cultural tastes. This was expressed among other things by the increasing use of the local Arabic vernacular[57] and portrayal of themes drawn from local life. During the first half of this golden age, namely the 1920s, Ḥabiba Messica was a foremost celebrity of Tunisian theater—according to Ben Halima, "La plus grande actrice que le théâtre arabe tunisien ait connu: la chanteuse israelite Ḥabība Messika" (the greatest actress that has been known by the Tunisian Arab theater was the Jewish singer Ḥabība Messika).[58]

Ḥabiba Messica began her career with al-Shahāma, one of the two leading theaters in the early twentieth century (1912–1922). The troupe was headed by two of the most important figures in this sphere, Muḥammad Bourguiba (1881–1930)[59] and the Egyptian Ḥasan Bannān (1883–1969).[60] After a slump in its fortunes the theater began staging productions again in 1921 with the original play *al-Samaw'al*, which presented the life of the renowned Jewish poet who lived in Arabia in the sixth century, the time of the pre-Islamic *jāhiliyya*. Bourguiba acted the lead and Bannān was a singer. That year Ḥabiba, just 21 years old, joined the theater, playing Julie in the drama *Ṣalāḥ al-dīn* with Bourguiba (Richard the Lion-Hearted) and Bannān (William).

This play was notable for its obvious nationalistic tendencies, showing the superiority of the Arab Muslim world to the European Christian one. The play was one of the first performed by an Arab theater in Tunis, thus fulfilling the theater's nationalist educational purposes. Al-Shahāma company also presented classic dramas by European playwrights, such as Shakespeare's *Othello*, in which Ḥabiba played Desdemona.

But Ḥabiba did not concur with these nationalist leanings. In January 1907 a quarrel erupted between the actors and the theater management over the repertoire. In fact, the actors, especially Muḥammad Bourguiba, wished to enlist the theater in the cause of nationalism in Tunisia, like the al-'Ādāb theater managed by Shaykh al-Tha'ālibī, whereas the management preferred to please the rulers of the French protectorate. In the end, members of the management were replaced, and Bourguiba was appointed artistic director of the theater. In January 1922, when al-Shahāma and al-'Ādāb united under the management of George Abyaḍ, most members of al-Shahāma left, among them Bourguiba and Ḥabiba, apparently because they believed that enlistment to the nationalist cause was not beneficial for the theater. They founded a new company called al-Hilāl. This company, which functioned from 1921 to 1923, was the first entirely independent theater in Tunisia; it was not accountable to a managerial board. Many important actors belonged to the troupe, but its life force was Ḥabiba Messica. Among the important parts played by Ḥabiba in this theater was Layla in *Majnūn laylā*, a play about the two famous lovers at the time of early Islam; Bannān played the role of Qays. Ḥabiba also took on the role of Ophelia in Shakespeare's *Hamlet*, with Bourguiba in the title role.

Al-Hilāl company could not survive longer than two seasons (1921–1923) in the face of the powerful competition of the joint theater under Abyaḍ's management. Although al-Hilāl did not create Arab theater in Tunisia, it was special in that Muslim and Jewish actors worked in it together and, as stated, its key personality was

Ḥabiba, who was not willing to submit to any supervision, including Egyptian. Al-Hilāl disbanded, and most of its actors, especially Ḥabiba, joined the al-Tamthīl al-ʿArabī company under the artistic direction of Ibrāhīm al-Akūdī.[61]

This company, with which Ḥabiba acted until 1928, encountered many obstacles, including the refusal of the Tunis municipality to allow Arab companies to use city theaters. Under public pressure the municipality agreed to allocate the auditorium to Ḥabiba's company once a week, on Thursdays, when French companies generally performed. Other problems for the company arose from the temperament of Ḥabiba, its foremost figure. At that time she was popularly known as *l'étoile des théâtres*, and the payment she demanded was the then astronomical sum of 500 francs per performance. The management had to pay her this figure willy-nilly, even though top-ranked actors in the Tunisian theater at the time earned a monthly salary of 150 francs and lesser performers got 100 or 50 francs.[62] Ḥabiba's position was so secure that she could get any role she wanted, even if it might cause a scandal or provoke anger in Muslim circles; this was especially likely when Ḥabiba played male roles, such as Romeo in *Romeo and Juliet*, Radames in *Aida*, and even Joseph in *The Selling of Joseph by His Brothers*.[63] Note that at that time Ḥabiba was still only 23 years old and that women acting in theater productions aroused the fierce objection of conservative groups, to the point of cancellation of performances in which women were to act.[64] Several Arabic plays in which Ḥabiba was cast were adaptations of French dramas, such as *Ḥayāt al-maqāmir* (based on *Trente ans ou la vie d'un jouer* by Ducange and Dinaux) and *al-Mujrim al-barīʾ* (based on *Roger la Honte* by Gaston Leroux). Because of the competition with other theater companies, al-Tamthīl al-ʿArabī began in the 1925–1926 season to diversify its repertoire with the addition of European plays in French, such as Victor Hugo's *Le roi s'amuse*; the reviews stated that the European actors in the cast were better than the Tunisians.

While working with al-Tamthīl al-ʿArabī, Ḥabiba also acted with ʿAlī ben Kamla's popular theater, which functioned from 1924 to

1928. One of her roles in 1925 was Joseph in a production of *The Selling of Joseph by His Brothers*, and she sang in concerts arranged by ben Kamla, together with Ḥasan Bannān and Sayyid Shaṭṭa. In June 1926 she took part in *Tasbā*, presented by al-Nahda al-Tamthīliyya al-'Arabiyya company, which moved to Tunis from Bizerte; she acted in the same play produced by al-Tahdhīb al-Sfaqṣī theater in 1928.[65]

Ḥabiba's European education and her great success as an actress prepared her for appearances in well-known theaters in Europe. In January 1927 a new theater company was formed, al-Mustaqbal al-Tamthīlī (The Theatrical Future), by several actors who had left al-Tamthīl al-'Arabī because of an internal dispute. The theater produced a number of plays in 1927, but it did not become really active until 1928, after Ḥabiba decided to join it. The great success of the young company was due to her acting in a new play, *al-Nasr al-ṣaghīr* (The Little Eagle), an adaptation of Edmond Rostand's *L'Aiglon*, in which she played the Eagle. Ḥabiba won accolades for her performance, and the play was rerun several times by public and press demand.[66] Ḥabiba acted with this company until she was murdered in February 1930. The crime shocked all circles of the population in Tunisia—Jews, Arabs, and French—as recounted in the two Judeo-Arabic *qinot* that lamented her tragic death (see Chapter 4). The event was also described by Louis Bertrand in his book *Revue des deux mondes*.[67] Her place was assumed for a while by the Arab actress and singer Faḍīla Khītmī, until she devoted herself entirely to the music hall opened by the Jew Maurice 'Aṭṭūn and the Arab Ṣāfia Rushdī.[68] Incidentally, Khītmī, a popular actress for many years and a star of Tunisian theater, was the daughter of a Muslim father and a Jewish mother, and she directed a large dance troupe.[69]

Ḥabiba was not forgotten. In an article surveying Tunisian theater in 1932–1933, the author names the important actors and actresses of al-Tamthīl al-'Arabī company, managed by Ibrāhīm al-Akūdī, and concludes, "The memory of the great actress Ḥabiba Messica remains linked to al-Tamthīl al-'Arabī." He also notes her and Faḍīla Khītmī as the two greatest actresses of the Tunisian theater.[70]

In recent years interest in Ḥabiba has revived. At least two compact discs with recordings of her songs are sold in record shops in Tunisia and France. But most notable is a film about her by the Tunisian Muslim director Salma Baccar. This director shaped Ḥabiba's character according to the fashion of the 1990s, as a nationalist and feminist; it cannot be denied that Ḥabiba Messica carried her feminine personality proudly and with her head held high before her contemporary society, which set the man above the woman.[71]

8

The *Ḥikāyāt* and Deeds of Righteous Men

Anyone familiar with Tunisian Judeo-Arabic prose literature, quite a large part of which is translated from other languages, has no doubt pondered the enormous expansion of the genre of *ḥikāyāt* (stories) since the 1870s, along with other genres of literature in translation such as biblical books and rabbinic literature. The *ḥikāyāt* were published in two distinct main forms: (1) books and booklets containing only stories in Judeo-Arabic and (2) chiefly books of rabbinic literature in Hebrew, with stories translated into Judeo-Arabic added, sometimes at the end but more usually at the bottom of the printed page. The choice of printing format was not random; it was simply for the printer's convenience and the like. The two forms of *ḥikāyāt* were pivotal to the spiritual history of Tunisian Jewry in the first half of the twentieth century. They reflect the different natures of the Jewish communities in northern and southern Tunisia and the change in their relationship beginning in the 1930s. The difference between the layouts at root expresses a difference in attitude toward secular literature, particularly love stories or poems. But let us preface the actual matter under discussion with a review of the position of the Jewish sages on the theme of love in Jewish literature down through the ages.

The Theme of Love in Jewish Literature

The infiltration of the theme of love between man and woman into Hebrew literature, whether poetry or prose, incurred at least from talmudic times negative reactions from the religious-spiritual leadership. Suffice it to say that the sages did not include the Song of Songs in the sacred canon until it was exonerated of profanity and granted sanction. This came about in the famous adage of Rabbi Akiva, namely, that "all the hagiography is holy and the Song of Songs is the Holy of Holies" (*Mishnah*, *Yadayim* 3:5). Allegorical interpretations by the sages in various midrashic works, such as the Aramaic translation of Song of Songs and the Midrash on it (*Midrash Rabba*) served only to reinforce Rabbi Akiva's statement. When the Jews came under the influence of Arabic literature beginning in the seventh century, they began to write love poems in the style of Arab poets and even to sing erotic Arabic songs at their celebrations. Echoes of the harsh criticism leveled at this practice with respect to love poems are heard in the apology offered by Shemuel Ha-Nagid (993–1056) in his poem "Ṣvi na'im" in his own *Dīwān*.[1]

> My friends, hear my poems, for my soul,
> As you know, is close to the fear of God
> And it has the meaning as the meaning of
> the Song of Solomon
> In "My beloved is pure" and "Eye like a pigeon."

So the theme of love present in his poems does not refer to the earthly love between a man and a woman but to allegorical love, as in the Song of Songs. The meaning of the allegory is given in the preface to the *Dīwān* by Shemuel's son Yehosef Ha-Nagid; Yehosef dismisses the criticism aimed at his father's love poems (translated from the Arabic): "And although some [of the poems in the *Dīwān*] contained words of lust, his intention in it was a metaphor for the congregation of Israel and its other, which were similarly expressed in metaphor in some of the books of Prophecy. . . . And whoever found within his words something different from what he intended—the fault lies with him."[2]

The Spanish Hebrew poet Moshe Ibn Ezra (1055–1138), who cleaved almost blindly to the ways of Arabic poetry, including the *muwashshaḥ* poems, also expressed regret toward the end of his life over the poetry of this type that he had written in "the carelessness of youth." He hoped that "God will perform a boon to anyone into whose hands they have come but he has kept away from mentioning them and has taken pains to put them aside."[3] Moreover, the *Ge'onim* of Babylonia and Maimonides ruled unequivocally that the erotic Arabic poems and the Hebrew ones written after them were not to be recited at Jewish celebrations. Rabbi Hāye Gaon (939–1038) was asked the following question by the Qābes community in southern Tunisia: "Now it has become customary in our place here in the houses of groom and of bride that the women play on drums and at dancing, and bring Gentiles and rejoice with harp and violin and organ—is it permissible or forbidden, and is there a difference between these instruments or not?"[4] In his famous *responsum* Hāye Gaon said that it was not forbidden to speak praises to the Lord at occasions such as these but that one could not speak

> words that are not of this order but are melodies of the love of a man and his fellow and to exalt a handsome man and extol a hero for his heroism and so on, like the way of those of the Ishmaelites which are called *'ash'ār al-ghazal'* [songs of lust]; either with an instrument that it is forbidden, or even only by mouth that it forbidden. . . . And if women are alone with no man present, even then this practice is ugly. And likewise if women are with them ready to make music it is better that they avoid doing so for it is wanton and an opening to several of the worst sins with harps and violins and instruments such as organs and flutes.[5]

Maimonides and Rabbi Shmuel ben 'Eli, the head of the yeshiva in Baghdad in the second half of the twelfth century, wrote similarly.[6] In general, in medieval poetry we know of the "compunctious poet" who at the end of his days repents of having written poems of passion and so on.[7] The aversion of critics to secular love poems and secular poems in general intensified still more in the thirteenth century, clearly under the influence of Maimonides; an example is the book *Ha-mevaqqesh* by Shem Tov ben Falaqera.[8] Note that the Muslim religious sages also harshly criticized the Arabic poems of passion (*ghazaliyyāt*) and wine (*khamriyyāt*) and the accompanying music to these poems; one such critic is Ibn Qayyim al-Jawziya (1291/92–1351/52).[9]

The sages' criticism—in keeping with certain political and social developments of the time—did in fact result in the elimination of love poems from Jewish literature in Spain with the almost complete disappearance of courtly poetry. But in its stead a new genre sprang up in Hebrew literature, the *maqāma*.[10] In it the theme of love reached a far higher level of development than that in poetry, with vulgar, tart expressions not found even in the Hebrew *muwashshaḥ* poems. The demand for this rhyming prose was immense, in complete contrast to the love poems, whose growth and consumption were for the upper classes and their circle, which naturally were fairly restricted. The spiritual leadership apparently did not look on this genre with favor either. Not without reason did Don Vidal Benbenesht (fourteenth–fifteenth century) consider it his duty to append an allegorical interpretation to his love story *Parables of 'Efer and Dina*; the allegory was intended, according to Ḥ. Schirmann, "to clear the wrongdoer," "since the tale of *'Efer* was liable to vex some of the readers."[11]

The exile from Spain and the convulsion it caused among the exiles in no way reduced the consumption of love literature, stories of desire and eroticism, in those communities. This was not just in Jewish Italy, which continued the tradition of sensual writing on these subjects; stories of love and passion were not always remote from the style of the *Decameron*, as attested in the works of the Hebrew poets of Italy such as Immanuel of Rome (thirteenth–fourteenth century) in his *maḥbarot*[12] and the brothers Jacob and Immanuel Frances (seventeenth century) in their poems.[13] Striking evidence of the enormous demand for love literature emerges from the Hebrew printing of that time. To supply the needs of the communities of exiles, the minority of them in Italy and the majority in the Balkans and Turkey, almost all the Hebrew *maqāma* literature was sent to print at the dawn of Hebrew printing in the fifteenth and sixteenth centuries. For example, the slim volume of the *Parables of 'Efer and Dina*, whose author is not among the foremost figures in medieval Hebrew literature, was printed no less than six times between 1517 and 1590 in Constantinople, Rimini, Rome, Ferrara, and Salonica.

This consumption of love literature is what caused Rabbi Yosef Caro, the great *poseq* (decider) and author of the *Shulḥan Arukh* (Safed, second half of the sixteenth century), to come out forcefully against the corrupt habit (in his view) of reading the *maqāmāt* of Immanuel and similar licentious material.

> Rhetoric texts and parables of profane discourse and the words of lust as in the book by Immanuel, and also books of wars are forbidden to be read on the Sabbath and on weekdays likewise forbidden, on account of *moshav leṣim* (frivolous company), and he who does it transgresses the commandment of "do not turn to idols" [Leviticus 19:4], namely, Do not displace God from your minds. Words of lust are all the more so, since they stir the evil inclination, both he who composed them and he who copied them; and needless to say the printers who cause the multitude to sin. (*Oraḥ Ḥayyim, Hilkhot Shabbat* 307:16)

Without doubt, Rabbi Caro's condemnation caused a considerable reduction in the demand for love literature in the communities of the East, and consequently the *maqāma* literature was no longer sent to print in Italy, Greece, and Turkey in the seventeenth and eighteenth centuries.

An expression of this is also found in the essay *Pereq be-shir* on Hebrew poetics. Its author is Rabbi Yehoshua Benbenesht (Constantinople, second half of the seventeenth century). The rabbi absolutely forbids secular poetry in its entirety and certainly erotic poems.[14] The attitude became even stricter when the Jewish communities throughout the Diaspora turned inward following the mighty messianic collapse of Shabbetai Zvi and his forlorn conversion to Islam together with many hundreds of his adherents. Yet although the sages had the power to censor this literature by moral supervision of the printing houses, they could not prevent the recital of erotic poems at wedding parties and other joyful celebrations. Here too one example will suffice. These are the words of the great preacher Abraham 'Antebi, the rabbi of the Aleppo community:

> Come see, my brothers, my friends, how much punishment is due to one listening to the poems of lust, which are all words of passion and lewdness. It entices to thievery and inserts into the man who hears them, and all the more so who recites them, the evil inclination like venom in a snake. Furthermore they are accompanied by drunkenness; still more, if women stand crowded to hear the singing with men, I have no doubt that they will not leave that company pure of iniquity . . . especially in those generations when the masses of the people assemble with such gladness if verses like these are recited to them. It is like it flogs them and chastises them and when they start, wickedly, the licentious words, joy enters their hearts and they get up to play and goats caper. How great is the power of the evil inclination.[15]

Judeo-Arabic Prose and the Jewish-Muslim Divide

The political changes that occurred in the countries of North Africa in the nineteenth and the first half of the twentieth century were in essence the penetration of the European powers and the social and economic changes experienced by the Jewish communities in those lands in the nineteenth century. At root these changes constituted the lowering of the spiritual walls separating Jews and Gentiles as part of the process of the granting of equal rights. These developments made it easier for those communities to absorb foreign literature translated into Hebrew or the languages spoken by the Jews, chiefly Ladino and Judeo-Arabic. The book *'Ose pele* (The Miracle Worker) (Livorno, 1869–1870), by Rabbi Yosef Shabbetai Farḥi, presents moral tales and stories from Jewish history, such as "Solomon's Tale," "The Miracle of Purim," "The Scroll of Judith," "The Scroll of Antiochus," "A Jerusalemite Tale," and "The Story of Bustenay." By contrast, the famous Livorno printer Israel Costa was bold enough to publish a small book titled *'Aravim be-tokha* (Arabs Within It) (Livorno, 1875), which contains stories from a non-Jewish source and whose content was by no means self-righteous religious morality but pure pleasure. This is stated on the book's title page: "The book *'Aravim be-tokha* contains stories and tales from the land of the East. Some have been translated from the languages of peoples around us and some the author's spirit produced to gladden the human heart and to give to the foolish ones cunning, to the youth knowledge and intellect, and some will delight the sage after his toil and labor with Torah and wisdom." Needless to say, the heroes of the stories are not Jews; in fact, the main source for the collection is the *Arabian Nights*, although the publisher exercised extreme vigilance in not translating the spicy erotic tales so typical of this Abbasid work.

These developments did not bypass the Jewish communities in North Africa, including those of Tunisia. This is not the place for an account of the relations between Tunisian Jewry and the government since the acceptance of the constitution in 1857, which assured equal rights (as in known, the constitution was rescinded in 1864 under pressure of the Muslim population). A considerable number of scholars taking a historical approach have dealt with this subject (see Chapter 1). But no less important is the literary, cultural, and spiritual study. It yields fruits of great value for an understanding of the world of Tunisian Jewry in the first half of the twentieth century in light of the major changes that occurred.

In the history of the humanities all over the world, the role of printing is well-known for its propagation of spiritual and cultural norms and for its part in the democratization of learning. The economic ties between the Jews of Tunisia and the Jews of Livorno in the eighteenth and nineteenth centuries, especially the formation of the communities of Livornese Jews (Grāna) in the cities on the northern coast of Tunisia (Tunis, Sousse, Nabeul, and Sfax), resulted in the religious sages of Tunisia sending their books to press at the high-class Jewish printers of Livorno. At first, the published books were intended for eminent scholars in Judaism: *Responsa* and the like. Later, however, the publishers also began to issue books meant for the wider public: prayer books and collections of prayers and various *piyyutim* for the yearly cycle. The trend toward democratization grew stronger when the printing houses began to receive not only Hebrew books but also those containing Judeo-Arabic translations meant for the broader strata of the communities more comfortable with Judeo-Arabic than with Hebrew. The high point with respect to democratization of printed literature was the publication of books of stories translated from Arabic into Judeo-Arabic. Examples are *Sīrat al-malik sayf al-azal*, which was published in about thirty volumes by the Tunisian Eli'ezer Farḥi of the *Sūq al-Grāna* (the Livornese market) at the printing house of Israel Costa (Livorno, 1885).

In 1861 the first Hebrew press in Tunisia was established, in Tunis, and the first book printed there was *Qānūn al-dawla al-tūnisiyya* (The Constitution of the Kingdom of Tunisia), in Judeo-Arabic. Five years later a Judeo-Arabic story was published for the first time, *Ma'ase sha'ashu'im* (An Amusing Tale). The most effective medium for linguistic communication was the centuries-old vernacular of the Jews of Tunisia, namely, the local form of Judeo-Arabic.[16] The leading activists such as Mas'ūd M'ārek, Daniel Ḥagège, Michel Uzan, and many others worked vigorously to expand maximally education and knowledge among the broader strata of Tunisian Jewry. A striking example of this is Michel Uzan's original novel *Bayn ḥuyūt tūnis* (Within the Walls of Tunis) (Tunis, 1926), in which the author expresses a negative opinion of marriage customs, particularly the high sum of the dowry.[17]

The Role of the *Ḥikāyāt* in Printed Popular Literature

In any event, besides their intense activity with Judeo-Arabic journalism, members of the intelligentsia engaged a great deal in translation into Judeo-Arabic and publication of various stories of an extremely wide range: traditional Hebrew literature, modern and translated Hebrew literature (see Chapter 1), French belles lettres, Jewish history, and a vast amount of folk literature, chiefly tales, many of them love stories. These tales, known as *ḥikāyāt*, reached many hundreds in number. They were printed in small format, usually as booklets of just a few pages, many of them in repeated editions. This printing activity was at its height in the first three decades of the twentieth century in Tunis at printing houses of various scions of the Uzan family. However, in the 1930s Makhlūf Najjār's printing house in Sousse took pride of place and became the almost exclusive printer of *ḥikāyāt*, albeit alongside other genres.

The demand was overwhelming. Many informants have noted that, when these tales were read on various occasions, men and women of the different social strata would gather together. Even the physical state of these booklets, as they came into the possession of booksellers and libraries in Israel, is evidence of the army of readers whose hands had touched them. This of course is also proved by the relatively huge numbers of booklets of this kind that have survived despite their great use. A clear example of this literature is *Qiṣaṣ majnūn laylā* (Stories of Crazy-for-Laila), the well-known tale from early Arabic poetry of the first generations after the rise of Islam.[18] Makhlūf Najjār describes this story in the January 1936 issue of *Tajrīda*, a catalog of hundreds of books printed at his shop, mostly tales.

> It is the tale in which the fabulists' parables are told, and the famous story of the events among men, the story of Qays ibn

> al-Mulawwaḥ, the ardent lover, who loves Laylā, daughter of al-Mahdī, the most beautiful of women, and what he said on the subject of his loving her in the best of the poems, and how he was sorely tried in his love for her day and night, until he went mad for the love of Laylā, and he is known among the people by the name *Majnūn laylā*, a story that reveals pure, unsullied love, which causes the heart to grow faint. Eight pages. Price, two francs.

The cheap price is noteworthy, a result no doubt of the low costs of the extremely poor typography. Be that as it may, it helped to increase sales.

The Negative Attitude of the Djerba Sages to the *Ḥikāyāt* and Their Practical Measures

Hebrew printing in Djerba began only in the first decade of the twentieth century, many years after the establishment of the Hebrew printing houses in the cities of northern Tunisia. Djerba was a traditional and conservative community, which obstinately resisted outside cultural influences, as illustrated by its fierce opposition to the opening of Alliance schools. This press mainly published prayer books and translations of biblical books and various kinds of rabbinic literature. Periodicals were issued that were devoted to questions of religion and the study of halakhic problems and Talmud commentary. The sages of Djerba lacked ideological openness to the surrounding culture, but they displayed profound attachment to the Hebrew language and nationalist Zionist ideas, qualities that did not particularly characterize the communities of the north.

Already in the mid-nineteenth century the rabbis in the North African Jewish communities had begun to voice harsh criticism of the adverse results that might emerge from the readiness to allow in alien culture, both Arab and French. This criticism had begun to take root even in the Jewish quarters in Tunis, and the critics severely condemned those who avidly pursued it (see Chapter 6). Similarly, several editors of anthologies of Hebrew religious poetry prefaced their volumes with apologias, mainly regarding the need to compose Hebrew poems in the spirit of Judaism to counter the influence of Arabic erotic poems. One of these is Eliyahu 'Allūsh of the Constantine community in Algeria; 'Allūsh edited the anthology *'Et la-ledet ve-qol sason* (A Time to Give Birth and the Sound of Gladness) (Tunis, 1911). To counter the Arabic erotic poems that had come to occupy a place at social gatherings of the Jewish communities in North Africa and even in religious celebrations, 'Allūsh presented in his collection not only Hebrew poems but also poems and stories—but not love stories—in Judeo-Arabic, the language understood by all members of the family, not just the men.

Not surprisingly, then, the sages of the Djerba community did not view with favor the exceedingly wide distribution of the profane *ḥikāyāt* literature among the Jewish communities. We first learned about this from Rabbi Asher Ḥaddād,[19] who has devoted his life to the printing of books of the sages of Djerba in particular and Tunisia in general. We asked him if he had in his possession booklets of *ḥikāyāt* that he had no interest in. He let us know his opinion that these booklets were not a respectable kind of literature; he had no interest in them, and in fact the sages of Djerba had proscribed their reading. However, he gave us no written source to substantiate his statement. So we began to search for such documentation ourselves, and indeed, the subject turned up explicitly in the preface by Rabbi Makhlūf Ḥaddād of Djerba to Part 4 ("Pentateuch, Numbers") of his book *Ke-raḥem av* (Djerba, 1957). (In the appendix to this chapter, we give the entire preface, translated from Judeo-Arabic.) On the title page the rabbi states that his book presents "new Torah innovations about the portions from *Bereshit* to *Ve-zot ha-berakha*, all in the Arabic vernacular of our fellow Jews, with several tales and pleasant and nice parables from which the reader will learn good morals and good and upright qualities."

Expressions of this kind are typical of many of the Judeo-Arabic books containing stories printed in Djerba since the 1940s. For example, the rabbis of Djerba, in sanctioning the book *Midrash shelomo* (Djerba, 1948) by Rabbi Khlīfa Ha-Cohen, write: "Part two of the *Midrash shelomo* contains two books, one *Menuḥat yesharim*, the other *Menuḥat shalom*. They are presented in the Arabic language current among us, with tales and stories to go in the right path, the ways of the written and transmitted Torah" ([3]).

It transpires, however, that the complaint of neglect of the rabbinic literature and the clamor for books of tales written in Judeo-Arabic began with the onset of the distribution of these books. Criticism of this kind is contained in Eliyahu 'Allūsh's preface, and it is one of the reasons he gives for including nonprofane stories in Judeo-Arabic in his collection. The person engaged more than all the Djerba sages in the labor of translating the stories into Judeo-Arabic seems to have been Rabbi Mqīqeṣ Hshellī, who immigrated to Israel and lived in the northern town of Shlomi. He frequently translated stories at the request of other sages, and they appended them to their books; or he collated their translations and proofread the printed texts. At times he did this work on his own initiative and under his own name, for example, his book *Midrasho shel shem* (The Midrash of Shem) (Djerba, 1947). In the preface to the first part of this book, he writes:

> I have further printed some moral tales and works of wonder in the Arabic language, sweet and enjoyable things which I translated from precious and rare books, and I have entitled them *Shemen 'arev* (Sweet Oil) because their content is softer than sweet oil to draw the reader's heart and to better his deeds and to go on the good and straight path, the path of Torah and the commandments, and to cling to every good quality to afford satisfaction to our Maker, blessed be He, and to win his soul in the life of the everlasting world to

> come because this is the purpose of every creature. . . . May it be His will that these moral precepts will make an impression and cause an awakening of repentance in the heart of every reader and my part to be among those who win the multitude. Amen.

The typography characteristic of these books is worth noting. Usually the tales are never presented as separate books on their own but, as stated earlier, are sometimes appended at the end of the printed volume, but usually they appear at the bottom of the printed page. The first part of the volume, or at the top of the page, gives the essential element of the essay, which is a rabbinic composition on a certain subject. Other typographic conventions were also used to set off the tales, but we cannot enlarge upon them here.

In any event, Hshellī achieved two goals with his translations. The first was a wider distribution of his book by virtue of the stories, because larger circles would find more interest in them than in the purely rabbinic essay, and the second goal was teaching the moral lesson to the broader public through these tales and thus indirectly getting them away from the *ḥikāyāt*. Detailed comments on this matter, also with respect to the form of printing, were written by one of the Djerba printers, Rabbi Yissakhar Ḥaddād, in his foreword to the book *Yeshu'a ve-raḥamim* (Salvation and Mercy) (Djerba, 1962), the work of his own teacher, Rabbi Yeshu'a Ḥwīta Sofer.

> In order to interest the masses who find it difficult to understand the written sermons in our holy tongue, we have inserted beneath the text stories in Arabic to be clear for all. These stories are historical and true accounts of the renowned saintly righteous man from the town of Mikhalstadt, may his memory be for a blessing. Our Sages said that anyone who occupies himself with the deeds of righteous men, it is as if he is engaged in mystic speculation.

Before us is a clearly religious and moral work, whose concern is not pure enjoyment or expansion of mental horizons and education; its purpose is expressly stated: morality and fear of God. It will therefore be understood why all these stories, which were translated into Judeo-Arabic, were taken from a Jewish source and not from the literature of the Gentiles, whether European Christians or Eastern Muslims. At first the Djerba sage-translators presented tales from ancient sources, such as rabbinic literature, and from later classical sources, such as the praises of Rabbi Isaac Luria and Rabbi Ḥayyim Vital; and example of this is found in the collection *Ma'asim ve-nissim* (Deeds and Miracles), published in three parts as early as 1919 by the printing house of David 'Īdān under the editorship of 'Allūsh 'Īdān, Raḥamim Sofer, and Ya'aqov Bītān. Its subtitle (translated from Judeo-Arabic) is *A collection of very precious tales from which man knew the miracles of the Name, be He blessed, and from which he will get morality and education and fear of the Name, be He blessed.* True, Makhlūf Najjār did not eschew printing collections of this kind in the 1930s, for example, *Ma'ase ṣaddiqim* (The Deed of the Righteous), in four parts, all of it from a Jewish source.

Subsequently the Djerba printers, all of them scholars in Judaism, turned to assemblages of tales from early sources made by recent Ashkenazic sages, such as *Ma'ase ha-gedolim* (The Acts of the Great Ones) by Shelomo Wilf (first printing, Lvov, 1886). This book was translated into Judeo-Arabic by Meir Cohen (Djerba, 1945). The text of the title page (translated from Judeo-Arabic) reads: "It assembles all the famous tales that are referred to throughout the entire Talmud, in clear language, arranged and edited, so that they may be readable by lovers of stories great and small, and through their reading them their heart will be opened to fear of God, be He praised, and they will go on the straight path, and will win life in the world to come which will live for ever."

When these sources dwindled, the Djerba sages did not refrain from approaching Eastern European ultra-religious literature, especially Hassidic works and even Hebrew and Jewish literature printed in various languages in Europe around the turn of the nineteenth century; these works described, by way of morality tales, events in the life of the Jews in Europe. One of the striking examples of this is the collection of stories *Ha-qadosh ba'al ha-shem me'ir mikhalstadt* (The renowned saintly man from the town of Mikhalstadt). This was the collection appended to the book *Yeshu'a ve-raḥamim*. Rabbi Yissakhar Ḥaddād wrote the following in a note on the last page of this book (translated from Judeo-Arabic): "These tales that we mentioned above were published in German in 1853 by Michael Wermesser and were translated into Hebrew in Tel Aviv by Dr. Ḥ. Weizmann. And I, the small servant, translated them into the vernacular Arabic so that they might be printed in a *siddur*[20] by my own master, the late perfect and all-encompassing Wiseman, his honor, our teacher, the R. Ḥwīta Sofer, may . . . in this precious *siddur*, *Yeshu'a ve-raḥamim*." Presumably, this activity of the sages of the Jewish communities of southern Tunisia—namely, establishing an extensive corpus of deeds of the righteous taken from Jewish sources in Judeo-Arabic translation—succeeded in the social respect and certainly contributed to protecting these communities' traditional character more than that of the Jewish communities of northern Tunisia. However, it is questionable to what extent these sages were able to keep potential readers away from the secular *ḥikāyāt* literature. At this stage, without possessing other data, we can only rely on a general impression that arises from fairly close acquaintance with the Jewish communities of southern Tunisia. According to this, the members of those communities never ceased to leaf through the *ḥikāyāt* again and again, and the distribution of the booklets exceeded that of the deeds of the righteous.

Appendix

Translation of the Preface by Rabbi Makhlūf Ḥaddād to His Book *Ke-raḥem av* (Part 4) (Djerba, 1957)

He with understanding will understand and he with intelligence will perceive that the evil inclination always perverts man in everything and sometimes leads him to be drawn to reading books containing nothing that will provide any benefit, especially if they contain matters of villainy and desire for women, which reading them causes the flame to burn in his heart, particularly in men who are of young age and light-headed, with excess spirit who will be snared into great impurity—may it never happen. About them I say the verse "Woe to those who draw iniquity with cords of falsehood" [Isaiah 5:18], that is, they draw iniquities onto themselves with the cord of emptiness, such as the talk and meaningless chatter found in the literature of tales and stories of great passion and little shame. Regarding whomever is trapped in reading those books and in the great excitement for them, let him turn his thoughts from them and undertake complete repentance, because from reading them one is drawn to vile acts, and moreover great punishment derives from this, in this world and the world to come, as is proclaimed and well-known in the statements of our masters in many places.

Now the event is known that occurred in the time of the Holy, our teacher Rabbi Isaac Luria, may his memory be for a blessing, who by virtue of his learning in Kabbalah was knowledgeable in all kinds of transgressions experienced by man. There was a man who was mired in many and great iniquities, and he heard of the power of the above Rabbi Isaac Luria and he thought to himself: "If I go to him and he detects my sins, I will undertake everything he says to me and with his help I will repent a full repentance." He wanted to implement the deed, and he prepared himself for the journey. Just at that time Rabbi Isaac Luria, may his virtue protect us, was learning with his pupils, and the pupils noticed the rabbi chuckling to himself, without knowing about what. One of the pupils asked the reason for his chuckling. He told them, "There is a man in a certain country possessed of great and many sins, and he wishes to come to me to test me if I known his sins or not. He is about to reach us." Right as they heard these things they saw a man of youthful years entering, and greeting the rabbi. At once the rabbi returned his greeting and said to him, "Have you come to me so that I might tell you about your iniquities?" Because he knew what he had come to him for, that man, who intended to repent with his help, was astonished. He fell at the rabbi's feet and said to him, "Reveal to me, my master, everything that you know." The rabbi began to relate to him everything that had passed over his head and the sins he had committed on particular dates. To everything he told him, that man admitted, and struck his own face for the shame and disgrace. Not only that, he even told him that on a certain date he committed a sin with his maidservant on the filth of the privy. He was so bitterly remorseful about this that he denied it, and said, "That I did not do." The rabbi replied, "Will you deny before me or shall we bring her before you?" He at once smote him on the shoulder and his maidservant emerged in her own image and likeness. The man was so terrified and trembling that he fell lifeless before the rabbi and the pupils. After the rabbi and the pupils restored him to life, he sobbed like a little boy and said, "Rabbi, I no longer want life; tell me what I must do in order to atone for my transgressions and I may die. Better than if I continue to live." The rabbi answered him that he had to suffer being burned to be atoned of his iniquities and to go pure into the world to come. He accepted this, and there and then the rabbi sent to buy a piece of lead and a brazier. It would be filled with fire and the lead would be melted in it, and then he would be given that molten lead to swallow and he would die. And so it was. The rabbi blindfolded his eyes and told him to read the confession. He lay on his back to read the confession and waited to be given the lead to swallow. But the rabbi had already prepared a brew of fruits and he took a spoonful of it, and placed it in the man's mouth and said to him: "Your guilt is taken away and your sin forgiven" [Isaiah 6:6]. The man arose, afraid, and shouted, "What have you given me, Rabbi?" The rabbi replied, "Fear no more and I warrant you that you will no longer be in sin, and you will become a perfect righteous one." So he returned to his city glad.

On this account, I, the puny servant, decided to collect from the words of our saintly teachers morals and tales that draw a man's heart to fear of the Name, be He blessed, and to good deeds, and I rendered them into the Arabic language so that people who do not understand the holy tongue will understand them, and be instead of their reading profane books in Arabic which bring upon man sins and transgressions. And as mentioned above, in these collection to which I have added a few Torah innovations to the order of the portions I hope that people will read them and gain the benefit that arises from them, and they will be advantageous for us, I and them, and a little of the virtue of the many will be attributed to me. And we thank the Name, be He blessed, who aided me earlier in the publication of three parts of this: Genesis, Exodus, and Leviticus. Now, in His great loving-kindness He has helped me to complete a fourth part of Numbers and some gleanings of Psalms and Proverbs and more. We wish good to our brothers who with their great assistance through advance payment of the price of the *siddur* I could thus manage until I finished it. I ask of the Lord, be He blessed, that he help me in the future too to complete the text I have on the rest of the Bible.

May it be His will that we and our children are graced always to walk in the way of the Torah and the commandments and good deeds, and to see complete redemption of all Israel in our land, our forefather's heritage, soon and in our time, Amen. I have written and sealed this on 9 Ellul 5716 [1955].

Words of the meager servant of God, Makhlūf, son of the wise and perfect Judge and teacher Khammūs Ḥaddād, may the Lord keep him and resurrect him. Here in Djerba, may the Supreme Being keep it established. Amen.

9

Translation of Daniel Ḥagège's *Circulation of Tunisian Judeo-Arabic Books*

Ever since David Cazès published his *Notes bibliographiques sur la littérature juive tunisienne* in 1893 on rabbinic literature, followed by Eusèbe Vassel's *La littérature populaire des Israélites tunisiens* (1904) relating to Judeo-Arabic literature, the literary works of Tunisian Jewry have been described and given bibliographic listings. Nevertheless, the most important work on Judeo-Arabic literature was written by Daniel Ḥagège, who was himself one of the principal writers in Judeo-Arabic and personally knew most of the authors mentioned in his *Circulation of Tunisian Judeo-Arabic Books* (*Intishār al-ktāyib al-yahūdiyya al-barbariyya al-tūnisiyya*, 1939).[1] Since the publication of Ḥagège's book, however, two comprehensive bibliographies of printed publications in Tunisia have appeared: (1) J. Fraenkel's *L'Imprimerie hébraïque à Djerba* (Paris, 1982; an unpublished doctoral dissertation), which includes Hebrew and Judeo-Arabic material; and (2) Robert Attal's *Ha-sifrut ha-ʿaravit ha-yehudit be-tunisia* (Jerusalem, 2007), which includes Judeo-Arabic material printed only in Livorno, Tunis, and Sousse.

Ḥagège was born in Tunis in 1892 (he died in Paris in 1976), and in his youth he worked at one of the Jewish publishing houses in Tunisia. He continued to be involved with Judeo-Arabic literature ever since then. Therefore it should not surprise us that in his short work *Intishār al-ktāyib al-yahūdiyya al-barbariyya al-tūnisiyya*, published in 1939 by Makhlūf Najjār's printing house in Sousse, he successfully relates a faithful account of the story of Judeo-Arabic literature up until his own time while indulging his readers in a wealth of biographic and bibliographic information regarding scores of writers in the Judeo-Arabic language.[2] Without this work, anyone interested in the history of this new Judeo-Arabic literature in Tunisia would have been groping in the dark, because Ḥagège was the only one to shed light on the personalities of a great many authors. Surprisingly, this important work was ignored by most of the researchers studying Tunisian Jewry, although many years ago (1987) Michal Saraf published an article in which she accurately portrays its importance. In addition, in 1956, Robert Attal prepared a French translation of the work.[3] The high value of Ḥagège's work might be judged by the fact that he lists scores of Judeo-Arabic publications that are not included in Vassel's earlier bibliography (1904, with an addition published in 1907), including some that had appeared before its publication but also some listed in Attal's later bibliography (2007). In some cases, Ḥagège details the names of the authors when that information had not been given by Vassel or Attal.

One may wonder what Ḥagège's motivation was for writing such a book. It seems, just like many other similar works, that what stands behind this deed is the feeling that the language or literature under discussion had reached its final stage and that it was about to disappear or fall into oblivion. Ḥagège, who was then deeply involved with Judeo-Arabic language and literature, felt strongly obligated to document it and to leave a written account of it for the generations to come. Indeed, by the time Ḥagège composed his essay, in the 1930s—an essay composed principally of the written vernacular and to some extent even the spoken vernacular—Judeo-Arabic had ceased to be comprehensible to most modern educated Jews in northern Tunisia, such as in the Jewish communities of Tunis, Nabeul, and Sousse. The shift to French had started at the end of the nineteenth century but had intensified after World War I, when relations between Jews and Arabs steadily grew worse because of the strengthening of nationalistic emotions among the Muslims in Tunisia and their struggle for independence against the French government.[4] So it happened that Ḥagège was, in fact, the last writer of Tunisian Judeo-Arabic in the north, whereas the language continued to flourish in the south, especially in Djerba. Since the printing of Ḥagège's book, Judeo-Arabic publications have not appeared in Tunis and Sousse, except Makhlūf Najjār's newspaper, *al-Najma*. Djerba became the exclusive center of Judeo-Arabic (and Hebrew) printing.

Given these points about the importance of Daniel Ḥagège's 1939 work, we present a full translation of it in this concluding chapter of our treatise on Judeo-Arabic literature in Tunisia. May this translation be an eternal light to his memory and a help to those who study Tunisian Jewry.

The Circulation of Tunisian Judeo-Arabic Books

This is a book concerning a historical episode, important and lofty among Judeo-Arabic literary works. In it is explained the way in which this language began to appear among the Jews,[5] and how it became current everywhere in an orderly matter. It details all the authors and their life histories, as well as their compositions and all the journals and stories they wrote throughout their lives. It goes through from the beginning to the present day, with lucid clarifications and in plain words.

From the lowly servant, Daniel Ḥagège

Printing rights reserved to the Najjār Publishing House
Makhlūf Najjār
Sousse (Tunisia)

Daniel Ḥagège
The well-known writer in the *al-Najma al-waḥīda* newspaper

Preface

Thanks must be given to supreme God, the mighty and the terrible, creator of lands, with the perfection of wholeness, creator of man, and who places him above animals in understanding and language. After this, what will be set forth now is that the *Tunisian Arabic-Berber language*, which our forefathers and even we ourselves have never ceased to speak to the present day,[6] is a language like all the languages scattered all over the world.[7] From the day of its creation until today it has been reinforced by a large number of learned writers, who were able to use this language, and they penned a great many literary compositions and love stories and weekly journals and even daily newspapers. We hope therefore that our historical essay will produce many benefits and will bestow esteem and honor upon our Jewish-Arabic language and renown to all the Tunisian Jewish master writers.

Daniel Ḥagège

The Beginning of the Circulation of the Books

In 1862 a partnership was formed among three Jewish writers, these being Messrs. Mordekhai Tapia, Bīshī Chemama, and Eliyahu Elmāleḥ.[8] They set up a small printing house. The first book that they published in Arabic and with Hebrew script was *Qānūn al-dawla al-tūnisiyya* (The Constitution of the Tunisian State).[9] Five years later, in 1867, Rabbi Eliyahu Guez, father of the printer Ya'aqov Guez in Tunis, published the first popular book in Arabic printed in Hebrew script, titled *Ma'ase sha'ashu'im*, which contained several short stories.[10]

A year after the publication of his first popular book, a Kairouanese storyteller[11] called al-Qarawī arrived in Tunis. He used to work every night in the cafes in Tunis and became very well-known because of this. The first person to be drawn to his stories was Ḥai Ṣarfati, known as Ukhū Bāya (Bāya's brother),[12] who had an excellent talent for memorizing and narrating. Now, he had a tavern,[13] so during the day he would tell his clients the stories he had heard at night from the storyteller. Afterward it occurred to him to write out by hand all the stories he remembered by heart and to rent them out to anyone interested for four and a half riyals[14] a month, payment in advance. In this way he could get much publicity. Soon he had several copyists working under him who would copy out the stories by hand for four riyals for a 100-page booklet. He ended up having a valuable library entirely in handwriting, like the libraries that existed in the fourteenth century.[15]

Ten years later, in 1878, a young man named Abraham Ṭayyib, was bold enough to found the first journal in Tunisia. It was called *al-ʿAmāla al-tūnisiyya*, and he had it printed at the press of Costa in Livorno in Italy. But this paper lasted only a short while.[16] Three years later, after the French entered Tunis, in 1884, Mr. Eliʿezer Farḥi founded a journal called *Ha-Mevasser*, which appeared once a month. Its name was later changed to *al-Mubashshir*, and since then it appeared once a week. A year later, that is, in 1885, a partnership was formed by three people, these being Messrs. Shalom Gwayṭaʿ [Gueta], Eliyahu Sasson, and Abraham Ginisti. They established a journal called *al-Shams*, which was printed in Paris and sold in Tunis.[17] That year too the writer Ṣemaḥ Halevi[18] founded a journal called *Mubashshir al-ḥaqq*, which did not last long. That same year the writer Shalom Flāḥ[19] set up a journal titled *Munawwir al-ḥaqq*, which appeared every ten days and was printed by Uzan and Castro's publishing house in Tunis. A writer for this journal was Yiṣḥaq Cattan,[20] so from the second issue onward it had to move to Finzi's press, as this writer wrote against Michel Uzan.

One year later, in 1886, a journal was founded under the name *Musharriḥ al-aṣdār*. At its head appeared the name Y. S. (Yaʿaqov Chemla),[21] but in truth its actual proprietor was the writer Yiṣḥaq Tammām, who nightly taught the Muslims on al-Dawlatli Street in Tunis. This gentleman founded the journal with the aim of combating Shalom Flāḥ's *Munawwir al-ḥaqq*. About thirty issues of this journal were published, after which it ceased publication. Later that year a journal was established called *al-Badr al-kāmil*, which appeared twice monthly, published by Shalom Flāḥ. But only one issue appeared, and that was in the form of a 24-page book; its aim was to propagate the holy tongue.

A year later, in 1887, the writer Ṣemaḥ Halevi founded a journal called *al-Janān*, but only one issue appeared. That year, Shalom Flāḥ, Yosef Cohen Ganūna,[22] and Yosef Najjār entered into a partnership, and they established a journal titled *Fāḍiḥ al-asrār*. That year also Shalom Flāḥ founded a journal called *al-Mutarjim*, which appeared weekly and survived less than a year. That same year too, when the romance *al-Azaliyya: Sīrat al-malik sayf al-azal*[23] became widely popular in Tunis and throughout Tunisia, the writer Ḥai Ṣarfati Ukhū Bāya first published a romance, called *al-Tījāniyya*, at Uzan and Castro's publishing house;[24] he followed this with the romance *Rīhān* and the stories *Yūsef al-ṣiddīq ma'a zūlēkha* and *Bā nissim al-takārlī*. After his death Ḥai Ṣarfati left several books and stories in manuscript, which his widow sold to the publisher and bookseller Ṣiyyon Uzan. In short, Ḥai Ṣarfati was considered the first of the writers to establish Judeo-Arabic literature in Tunisia, and therefore he has to be thanked and accorded enormous gratitude above all writers who followed him. In that year too the writer Shalom Flāḥ published two books. The first, *Ereṣ ha-ṣvi*, is an account and geographic description of Eretz Yisrael and the second is *al-Tawārīkh al-isra'īliyya*.

In 1888 Ṣemaḥ Halevi published two journals, neither of which lasted more than one issue, the first titled *al-Najma* and the second *Jūrnāl haggin*.[25] That year a partnership was established among the writers Shalom Flāḥ, Yosef Cohen Ganūna, and Ḥai Sitrūk, and they founded a journal that appeared twice a week called *al-Ḥurriyya*;[26] only eight or ten issues appeared. Also that year the writer Ḥai Sitrūk published a journal, of which there was only one issue, titled *al-Maristān*.[27] Likewise, that year the writer Mas'ūd M'ārek[28] started a weekly called *al-Bustān*, which survived until 1887. Five years before that time, his brother-in-law Ya'aqov Chemla was appointed chief editor.

The first daily newspaper founded in Tunisia, covering politics, economics, and news, was *al-Telegraf*, in 1889. This paper was filled with translated cables from the Havas news agency, and its feuilleton was *Les mystères de Paris*.[29] The manager of the paper was Mas'ūd M'ārek, and its chief editor was Yosef Cohen Ganūna. That year too Ṣemaḥ Halevi also founded a paper, which appeared only once, called *Jūrnāl pessaḥ*.

In 1890 Ṣemaḥ Halevi published one issue of the journal *al-Anwār* and then published a weekly called *al-Muḥayyar*.[30] From its eighth issue this journal came under the ownership of an anonymous company, and its feuilleton was titled *Ghuṣn al-bān*.[31]

In 1891 the writer Ya'aqov Cohen[32] published a weekly entitled *al-Naṣra*, which lasted almost a year. Its feuilleton was called *al-Samsūniyya*.

In 1892 Ṣemaḥ Halevi and Ya'aqov Cohen established a partnership and published a journal called *Nāṣir al-muḥayyarīn*, of which only seven issues appeared. The same year Mas'ūd M'ārek, or rather we have to say "Ben Amittai," produced a weekly titled *al-Niḥla*, of which close to twenty-five issues appeared. The chief editor was Abraham Bismūṭ, the owner of the printing house.

In 1893 Shalom Flāḥ published a weekly titled *al-Ittiḥād*, of which twenty-four issues appeared. They contained three feuilletons: *Manām thābit*, *Murūrat al-tamaddun*, and *al-Dans*. Two years later, in 1895, a journal titled *al-Ḥaqīqa* was founded, and its feuilleton was *al-Kasb al-mazrūb*. It appeared weekly under the management of Mas'ūd M'ārek, and its chief writer was Ya'aqov Chemla.

Between 1895 and 1904 no journals were published by Jews in Tunisia, the reason being that the government fixed a deposit; that is, no journal could appear unless its proprietors deposited a large sum of money with the government as a guarantee.[33]

In 1904 Ya'aqov Cohen published a weekly titled *al-Shams*, and its feuilleton was *Nāzlat drayfūs*.[34] Next a daily titled *al-Ṣabāḥ* was founded. This first appeared on November 1, 1904. This daily was printed at the Varius press, which was on al-Tūmī Street in Tunis beside the public water tap; later it was moved to Bāb Sūweiqa Street and then to al-Sharqiyya press on al-Malṭiyya Street. Then it moved to the printing house of ʿAyyūsh Shūshān on al-Dabbāghīn Street and finally to the printing house of Ṣiyyon Castro on al-Malṭiyya Street in Tunis.

Mr. Yaʿaqov Cohen was a famous writer and great scholar in three languages: Arabic, Hebrew, and French. His writing was lucid and composed in original Judeo-Arabic, and he did not insert foreign words,[35] except when absolutely necessary; and in that case he gave their meanings in such a way that the reader could understand what he was reading. This esteemed writer succeeded in maintaining his daily newspaper for ten whole years. Then the poor man died, and he dwells in Eden. When he headed this paper, he published many famous stories of his own, of which we shall present the entire list. After the death of this learned man and his departure from this world, the editing of the paper's feuilleton was assumed by the humble servant Daniel Ḥagège, the writer of this history. But responsibility for editing the political articles and the news reportage in the paper fell to many writers, including Ṣemaḥ Halevi, the anonymous Y. Q., Clement Ḥūrī, Meir Khushkhāsh [Koskas], Yosef Bījāwī, Michel Uzan, Frājī Naqqāsh, and Daniel Ḥagège, the writer of these lines.[36] Recently the paper came under the ownership of Mr. Shimʿon Cohen, the son-in-law of the late Yaʿaqov Cohen.

In 1904, when the government lifted the burden of the deposit from the journals, apart from *al-Shams* and *al-Ṣabāḥ* founded by Yaʿaqov Cohen, some other papers were founded under various names. They were: *al-Ittiḥād*, which appeared twice weekly and was written by the writer Menaḥem Belʿīsh, who several years ago left Tunisia and fixed his abode in the Holy Land together with his entire family; the weekly *al-Bustān*, which was revived that year by the famous writer Masʿūd Mʿārek; *al-Fonograf*, also a weekly established by the famous writer and renowned poet Ṣemaḥ Halevi, with the assistance of his two brothers;

and *al-Barq*, a daily that produced only five issues, written by Ṣemaḥ Halevi.

Two years later, in 1906, a weekly appeared whose purpose was to safeguard the rights of the Jews of Tunisia. It was titled *al-Ḥurriyya*, and it was published by its resolute, courageous, protective, and obdurate owner, Mordekhai Smādja, and his friend Shemu'el Ṣarfati. Also that year *al-Bustān*, belonging to his colleague Mas'ūd M'ārek, which had been a weekly, became a daily.

Two years later, in 1908, our friend Mas'ūd M'ārek, with the assistance of Moshe Katorza, published a new notable journal, called *al-Akhbār*.

In 1909 our diligent friend Naḥum Uzan, the renowned tailor opposite the slope on Bāb Kartājina Street, published a journal called *al-Istiwā*, which appeared once weekly, written by Yosef Bījāwī. In that year, another paper, titled *al-Ikhāwa* was published, written by Ṣemaḥ Halevi. Its manager was Michel Uzan.

In 1910 a dozen papers appeared in Tunisia, as specified below:

1. *al-Niḥla*, a weekly written by Meir Khushkhāsh and David Ḥagège
2. *al-Ḥaqq*, a weekly written by Meir Khushkhāsh and Ṣemaḥ Halevi
3. *al-Kātib*, a weekly, all in rhyme and poetry, written by Ṣemaḥ Halevi
4. *al-Zamān*, an important weekly written by Mas'ūd M'ārek, Abraham Ṣabbān,[37] and Moshe Sitbon
5. *Ḥayāt al-ḍaḥk*, an entertaining paper, appearing once every ten days, the product of the spirit of Yiṣḥaq Berebbi and Edouard Sitrūk
6. *Ḥayāt al-janna*, an entertaining and informative paper published weekly and written by its chief editor, the humble servant Daniel Ḥagège; its manager, Yosef Luīzādā; and the writer of its feuilleton, David Chemama
7. *Khillaṭ millaṭ*, a light, illustrated weekly written by its owner, the writer Ya'aqov Cohen

8. *al-Mughannī*, a journal of poems and songs of which only one issue appeared, written by Meir Cohen and Shelomo Laḥmi[38]
10. *al-Ẓaʿbāl*, a twice monthly, written by Eliyahu Belaḥsen, Victor Ṣabbān, Eliyahu Khriyyef, and Yaʿaqov di Moshe Abrahami, our friend, the famous Zionist speaker in Tunis and Tunisia[39]
11. *al-Nasr*, a weekly written by Eliʿezer Farḥi, Ḥai Belʿīsh,[40] and A. Zarqā
12. *al-ʿĀlam*, a weekly written by Yosef Guez

In 1911 half a dozen journals appeared, and these are their titles:

1. *al-Jarīda*, a daily written by Yosef Bījāwī and several other writers, but no name appeared at the head of the paper
2. *Ḥiss al-khalq*, a weekly written by Meir Khushkhāsh and Felix Būkhobza
3. *al-Ḍaww*, a weekly written by Yosef Bījāwī and Eliyahu Ḥasid
4. *al-Fajr*, a weekly written by Yaʿaqov Chemla and Yosef Bījāwī
5. *al-Jabbār al-tūnisī*, a weekly written by Meir and Yaʿaqov Giurno
6. *Akhbār al-ʿālam*, a weekly written by Edouard Sitrūk and Ḥai Belʿīsh, author of the essay *Ḥayāt bnādam*

Two years later, in 1913, the Society of Aguddat Ṣiyyon [The Association of Zion],[41] whose central office was located on the street of the ice factory, founded a journal in the form of an illustrated booklet that appeared monthly under the title *Qol Ṣiyyon* [Voice of Zion], sponsored by Mr. Felix Barānes.[42] It was written by Victor Khushkhāsh of Nabeul. Its responsible editor was Yosef Bījāwī, who some time later resigned and was replaced by Rabbi Yeshuʿa Sitrūk. In 1914 *al-Fajr* became a daily, under the directorship of Yaʿaqov Chemla and Yosef Bījāwī.

Six years later, in 1920, five new journals were founded in Tunis and all of Tunisia, as follows:

1. *al-Waṭan,*[43] a weekly written by Yosef Bījāwī and Ya'aqov Chemla, and the writer Daniel Ḥagège also joined them, and each week published one article, from issue 57 to issue 70
2. *al-Insāniyya,* a weekly written by Michel Uzan and in the spirit of Yosef Uzan
3. *al-Mukhabbir al-tūnisī,* a weekly written by Eliyahu Guez, Frājī Naqqāsh, and Michel Uzan
4. *al-Tamaddun,* a weekly written by Shelomo Chemama, Yosef Bījāwī, and Ya'aqov Chemla, and the writer Daniel Ḥagège also joined them to write many articles for the benefit of mankind
5. *Najmat al-sāḥel,*[44] a weekly in Sousse written by Makhlūf Najjār and Leon Ṭūviāna

In 1921 a weekly appeared titled *Qol yisrael,* sponsored by Menaḥem Bel'īsh and Eliyahu Levi al-Sūlīmānī. A journal was also founded in Mahdiyya[45] in Arabic and French titled *Ṣadā al-mahdiyya*; it was produced by the writer Natan Djerbī. In 1922 our colleague Yosef Bījāwī founded a weekly called *al-Ḥakīm ghabyūn.*[46] In 1924 too Yosef Bījāwī, assisted by his son-in-law Abraham Khushkhāsh, published a paper titled *Kashshāf al-asrār.* In 1926 a journal appeared titled *al-Tijāra al-tūnisiyya,*[47] published by Yosef Bījāwī and Yosef Uzan. Three years later, in 1929, the Society of Intishār al-ktā'ib al-yahūdiyya [Circulation of the Jewish Books] established the journal *al-Intishār,* whose writers were Yosef Bījāwī and several others.[48] The journal *Najmat al-sāḥel* of Makhlūf Najjār, which had continued to appear irregularly, took the name *al-Najma* on December 13, 1927, and continued in the same way[49] until 1936. But at the end of that year *al-Najma* became a regular paper produced by Makhlūf Najjār, Leon Ṭūviāna, and Felix Bījāwī; and the lowly servant Daniel Ḥagège was a regular writer for it. Also in 1936 a weekly called *al-Yahūdī* was founded by Yosef Bījāwī;[50] its manager was Mordekhai Uzan.

Since the beginning of the establishment of Judeo-Arabic books, the following six daily newspapers have been founded:

1. *al-Telegraf* by Mas'ūd M'ārek
2. *al-Ṣabāḥ* by Ya'aqov Ha-Cohen
3. *al-Barq* by Ṣemaḥ Halevi
4. *al-Bustān* by Mas'ūd M'ārek
5. *al-Jarīda* by Yosef Bījāwī and his partners
6. *al-Fajr* by Ya'aqov Chemla and Yosef Bījāwī

In our estimation, all these writers deserve honor and appreciation above others, as they dared to create daily papers at a time when this was hardest of all, particularly among us, the Jews of Tunisia: one buys, ten read![51]

Six weeklies were founded. After their demise they were revived by other writers. They are:

1. *al-Shams*, founded in 1885 by Shalom Guwayṭa' (Gueta), Eliyahu Sasson, and Abraham Ginisti but revived in 1904 by the famous writer Ya'aqov Ha-Cohen
2. *al-Najma*, founded in 1888 by Ṣemaḥ Halevi and then revived in 1927 and most recently in 1936 by the writer and artist Makhlūf Najjār in Sousse with the aid of the humble servant Daniel Ḥagège and others
3. *al-Niḥla*, founded in 1892 by the writer Mas'ūd M'ārek and revived in 1910 by Meir Khushkhāsh and David Ḥagège
4. *al-Ḥurriyya*, founded in 1888 by Shalom Flāḥ, Yosef Ha-Cohen Ganūna, and Ḥai Sitrūk and revived in 1906 by Mordekhai Smādja and Shemu'el Ṣarfati
5. *al-Ittihād*, founded in 1893 by the writer Shalom Flāḥ and revived in 1904 by the writer Menaḥem Bel'īsh

6. *Fāḍiḥ al-asrār*, founded in 1887 by Shalom Flāḥ, Yosef Cohen Ganūna, and Yosef Najjār and revived in 1924 by Yosef Bījāwī and Abraham Khushkhāsh

Of all the handsome titles that our writers chose and inscribed at the head of their journals are these three splendid names: *al-Ḥurriyya*, *al-Istiwā*, and *al-Ikhāwa*, which are the three principles on which rests the policy of the government of great France, seeker after justice and righteousness, and renowned for them to the ends of the earth.

We have said that the custom of the Tunisians since ancient days is for one to buy and ten to read. This statement of ours is very true and stands upon a true source. As testimony to this, see what was written on the subject in *al-Akhbār*, no. 41:[52]

Tunis, 1 November 1908

> They complain to us out of diffidence, begging us to act as judges for them. This thing is hard for us to undertake, to be judges of the matter. They, the partners [the subscribers] in our journal, have come to complain to us. What is their complaint about? We don't know if they are complaining for themselves or for others. They want to hold back, they are confused, what are they to do? They wish to submit a complaint to the editorial board of the journal, and it will be the judge. One after the next they complain that their journal, before they have read a single letter of it, is already flying around among the hands of borrowers, and on a good day it ends up back in their own. But often it departs never to return. They, the partners, know that the borrowers are people for whom the price of the paper won't make a dent in their pocket, but they are too bashful to send them away empty-handed when they come asking, and they return two or three times until they get it.

> All the readers insist that they greatly desire to read *al-Akhbār*, and can't wait until it appears, but those who pay money know that this custom of one purchaser and ten readers of Jewish journals is harmful to the work and ruinous for the paper. But as we said, they are overcome with embarrassment, and to right this wrong they come to tell us; they want to continue being reticent, and that the paper should deal with the problem for them.
>
> We recall that once one of the journals of our city discussed this matter and wanted to combat the habit with the ancient weapon of "boycott." Such warfare is disgraceful! But decently and politely we shall criticize those people who want to read the paper on loan, while they are not averse to shelling out their money for worthless things. Since the paper is for us, the Jews of Tunisia, if our readers are not its purchasers, this will do nothing but cause gratuitous trouble for the proprietors, with nothing in return. Then it will collapse under the weight of the losses and they will abandon it. We have shown you the problem, and we leave you, the readers, to be the judges of the fault.

We now present a list of 110 writers who wielded the pen, whether in the founding of journals, or whether in writing articles in the pages of the journals, whether stories, or poems, or other writing. These are the names in alphabetical order:[53]

1. Abraham Bismūṭ
2. Abraham Castro
3. Abraham Ginisti
4. Abraham Khushkhāsh
5. Abraham Ṭayyib
6. Abraham Ṣabbān
7. Abraham Uzan
8. A. Zarqā
9. Angelo Farḥi
10. Anonymous Y. Q.
11. Benini Chemama
12. Clement Ḥūrī
13. Daniel Ḥagège
14. David Ḥagège
15. David Chemama
16. Edouard Chemama

17. Edouard Sitrūk
18. Elie'zer Farḥi
19. Eliyahu Elmāleḥ
20. Eliyahu 'Attāl
21. Eliyahu Belaḥsen
22. Eliyahu Bījāwī
23. Eliyahu Cohen
24. Eliyahu Guez
25. Eliyahu Ghānem
26. Eliyahu Ḥai Guez
27. Eliyahu Ḥasid
28. Eliyahu Khriyyef
29. Eliyahu Levi
30. Eliyahu Sasson
31. Felix Barāneṣ
32. Felix Bījāwī
33. Felix Būkhobza
34. Frājī Fittūsī
35. Frājī Naqqāsh
36. Frājī Zētūn
37. Ḥai al-Raccāḥ
38. Ḥai Bel'īsh
39. Ḥai Belaḥsen
40. Ḥai Cohen
41. Ḥai Sitrūk
42. Ḥai Ṣarfati
43. Ḥayyim Bshīrī
44. Ḥayyim Bītān
45. Ḥayyim Bunān
46. Ḥayyim Zarqā
47. Henri M'ārek
48. Leon Ṭūviāna
49. Makhlūf Najjār
50. Mas'ūd M'ārek
51. Meir Cohen
52. Meir Khushkhāsh
53. Menaḥem Bel'īsh
54. Michel Uzan
55. Momo Chemama
56. Mordekhai Luīzādā
57. Mordekhai Smādja
58. Mordekhai Tapia
59. Mordekhai Uzan
60. Moshe Barda'
61. Moshe Dayyan
62. Moshe Katorza
63. Moshe Riāḥī
64. Moshe Chemama
65. Moshe Siṭbon
66. Naḥum Uzan
67. Natan Djerbī
68. Nino Flāḥ
69. Nissim Gershon
70. Refa'el Smādja
71. Semaḥ Halevi
72. Ṣghayyir 'Ashshūsh
73. Shalom Flāḥ
74. Shalom Gwayṭa'
75. Shim'on ben Nissim Cohen
76. Shim'on Cohen
77. Shlomo Baron
78. Shlomo Ḥagège
79. Shlomo Laḥmi
80. Shmu'el Ṣarfati
81. Ṣiyyon Uzan
82. Victor Bel'īsh
83. Victor Khushkhāsh
84. Victor Ṣabbān
85. Ya'aqov Abīḥbūṭ

86. Ya'aqov ben Yiṣḥaq Māmō
87. Ya'aqov Būkhrīṣ
88. Ya'aqov Cohen
89. Ya'aqov di Moshe
90. Ya'aqov Giurno
91. Ya'aqov Chemla
92. Yehuda Sitrūk
93. Yeshu'a S. (Salkamon)
94. Yeshu'a Sitrūk
95. Yiṣḥaq Berebbi
96. Yiṣḥaq Cattān (not he from *al-Ṣabāḥ*)
97. Yiṣḥaq Najjār
98. Yiṣḥaq Tammām
99. Y. Māmō
100. Yom Tov Khalfōn
101. Yosef Elmāleḥ
102. Yosef Brāmī
103. Yosef Bījāwī
104. Yosef Cohen Ganūna
105. Yosef Guez
106. Yosef Luīzādā
107. Yosef Lombrozo
108. Yosef Najjār
109. Yosef Pereṣ
110. Yosef Uzan

This list of ours contains the writers who exposed themselves in print, but to be truthful there are several other writers who used to publish articles in the pages of journals but concealed their names. God knows what secret intent they had in not revealing their names to us and leaving us ignorant of this knowledge. This is the reason that really there have been more than 150 writers in Judeo-Arabic since this unique language was created in Tunisia.

Out of all the writers listed above there are four names of well-known writers with whom the reader is more familiar than the others. What is the reason for this? Why do these four writers excel over the rest? Are they able to write better than the others? No, no, a thousand times no. Heaven save us from favoritism; but painstakingly let us show the reader that on account of these troubled times, out of the great number of Jewish writers only these four remain to us, who continue to write weekly in *al-Najma* and in *al-Yahūdī*. They are Messrs. Makhlūf Najjār, Daniel Ḥagège, Yosef Bījāwī, and Michel Uzan. And whence this dearth? When we examined the situation we discovered various causes. First, readers of Judeo-Arabic did not know the cost of printing and the great expenses and enormous exertion to writers and essayists. This is due to there being one who buys and ten who read. Second, since the writer of the piece or the journal could not live off the income from his articles, and he had a particular occupation from which to make a living, he was unable to devote his time to his writing and therefore was obliged to enter into partnership with another. As is known, partnership is destruction.[54] The Ancients said, If there were a blessing in partnership, two would share a wife.[55] Thus each essay or journal would give up the ghost, this being due to the absence of unity and lack of agreement among the participating writers. On this, the learned poet has expressed himself:[56]

> Times befall a man
> a thing that is not fitting.
> A man who sees the future
> distressful deeds will keep far from him.
> I measured and weighed well
> no one emerges pure.

This means that in this world you can never expect to find a man after your heart, and felicitous language does not attest to purity of heart. The saying goes: You, who are handsome outwardly, what is your condition within?[57] Accordingly, any publishing that was a partnership existed for a short time and then disappeared without a trace.[58]

In the above list we have presented to the esteemed reader 110 writers. The design of our work requires us to include among them a name of a writer who is an important rabbi, writer, and poet, our dear, learned colleague Israel ʿArqī,[59] of Benzert (Bizerte), known by the name Sir Elyachar, renowned in Tunisia and in the other countries for his fine qualities and his forceful defense of, and especially his great determination against anyone who dare humiliate, the religion of Israel. This is because he is stalwart in his belief that it is given by the Lord of the Universe and suffers no change and no contradiction and no amendment. This is the right and immovable thing.

The time has come to present a list of some of the writers who wielded their pen and published valuable stories or compositions in their own name, which were published by them in Tunisia and other countries. We shall note their articles in detail, and set the older ones before the young. These are their names:

1. Ḥai Ṣarfati
2. Ḥai Sitrūk
3. Abraham Ṣabbān
4. Eli'ezer Farḥi
5. Shalom Flāḥ
6. Mas'ūd M'ārek
7. Ya'aqov Chemla
8. Ya'aqov Ha-Cohen
9. Ṣemaḥ Halevi
10. Yosef Bījāwī
11. Meir Khushkhāsh
12. Frājī Naqqāsh
13. Ḥai Bel'īsh
14. Michel Uzan
15. Makhlūf Najjār
16. Daniel Ḥagège

Ḥai Ṣarfati

These are the compositions published by this writer:

1. *Hārūn al-rashīd wa-al-aḥdab*
2. *Hārūn al-rashīd wa-khalīfa al-ṣayyād*
3. *al-Ṣayyād al-maṣrī*
4. *Muḥammad al-saṭṭā'*
5. *Muḥammad al-asīr*
6. *Muḥammad al-dimashqī*
7. *Dalīla al-muḥtāla*
8. *Ḥasan al-khillī'*
9. *Bā nissim al-takārlī*
10. *Ben khamriyya*

11. *al-Sab'a wuzarā aw sindbār*
12. *al-Ḥasaka wa-al-sab'a banāt*
13. *al-Sulṭān brāhīm*
14. *Qaṭr al-zamān*
15. *'Ajīb wa-gharīb*
16. *Ḥayāt al-nufūs*
17. *Yūsef al-ṣiddīq*
18. *al-Tījāniyya*
19. *Rīḥān*
20. *al-Azaliyya* (he[60] who wrote it).

Ḥai Sitrūk

This writer is known among our Jewish brethren as Rabbi Ḥūyā, because he stood at the head of the spacious and modern Talmud Torah on the street of the ice factory in Tunis. It was in the same building of which the Zionist society Aguddat Ṣiyyon purchased a part and which it made its official center. Indeed, this renowned teacher was greatly loved among our brothers of Tunisia, and from his school emerged many pupils too numerous to count. At the same time he was very attentive to the craft of journalism, namely, the writing of articles in Judeo-Arabic journals and composition or translation of beneficial stories. This is the almost full list of stories and essays that flowed from the pen of this late writer, whose stories still today the reader enjoys, and not one of them is missing. Thanks for this is owed to our diligent friend Makhlūf Najjār, who with the agreement of the family of the late Rabbi Ḥūyā has never ceased reviving his stories, which are published every day. Just recently he has restored all these compositions, and they continue to exist after having no trace at all. These are they in detail:

1. *Les mystères de Paris* (a quarter of a story)
2. *Farā'iḍ al-qulūb*[61]
3. *'Uqūbat al-ghaddār*
4. *Robinson crusoe*[62]
5. *Alekhsandrūs mōkdōn*

6. *Flōr dāryān*
7. *al-Bankir alfonse de lūjīk*
8. *Kull ṭammā' khāsir*
9. *al-Mariṣṭān* (single sheet)
10. *Purim al-mabsūṭ wa-al-mazlūṭ wa-bi-al-bāṭin*

Apart from these important stories and essays, Ḥai Sitrūk used to edit and help several Jewish journals with his important articles. Such were *al-Ḥurriyya* of Mordekhai Smādja and *al-Fonograf* of the talented poet and writer Ṣemaḥ ben Natan Halevi. He was also one of the heads of the earlier *al-Ḥurriyya* of Shalom Flāḥ and Yosef Cohen Ganūna. Apart from this he wrote in several journals. It is most distressing that there is no one to recommend that a writer like him be awarded some decoration as a sign of appreciation for his hard-working service for the benefit of the community.

Abraham Ṣabbān

Who of our brothers, the Jews of Tunisia, did not know the late, pious gentleman, the man of understanding, of rational thinking, of insight and awareness, he who was loved by all, our hallowed colleague, Abraham Ṣabbān? This writer had a pure and scrupulous heart. He was a founder and one of the heads of the *Bride and Groom Society*,[63] that dear association established to help poor girls and to facilitate their marriage so that they may not sink into wicked ways and degeneration.[64] In 1906, with the founding of *al-Ḥurriyya*, the daring journal established to defend the rights of the Jews of Tunisia and to demand their inclusion in the family of France,[65] our friend Abraham Ṣabbān was virtually the right hand of the bold journalist, the late Mordekhai Smādja. This was through his important reports and articles that were published in the above journal. Likewise in 1910 an important journal was founded called *al-Zamān*, and one of its best writers was this same journalist Abraham Ṣabbān, who wrote many articles for it successively, all for the benefit of mankind, of value, and of great usefulness. And recently, when the Alliance Israélite was inaugurated in Tunis through the labor and persistence of this worthy person, the society appointed him to the presidency of the Gueddīd Synagogue on Sīdī al-Srīdek Street, then known as Knesset Israel.[66] During his leadership of this important religious domain everything went forward with utter perfection. This esteemed gentleman died at the age of 65 or thereabouts. May the Lord deal kindly with him in the Garden of Eden.

Elie'zer Farḥi

This gentleman was known in the cities and towns as Rabbi Eli'ezer of the Livornese (Grāna) market in Tunis. He was born in our city of Tunis in 1851 to a father who had come here from Jerusalem. He was an expert writer and a fine poet, and above all he was a sworn Zionist. He delivered several speeches at Zionist centers in Tunis in order to plant emotion into the heart of all our Jewish brothers. From 1871 to 1883, in twelve years, Rabbi Eli'ezer made three journeys to the city of Livorno in Italy. He sojourned there for four years with his father's brother, was ordained for the rabbinate, and married. Afterward he returned to Tunis and opened a shop selling both books and fabrics at the same place. This man realized that the Jews of Tunisia were inadequate in those days, and on that account it occurred to him to apply his pen to improve the educational and cultural situation of the Tunisian Jewish people. Therefore in 1884 he founded a journal that appeared monthly called *Ha-Mevasser* and later founded a weekly called *al-Mubashshir*. Then, with the help of the writer Chemama he published a book called *Anīs al-wujūd*, which contains several short stories translated from the holy tongue, a composition of his uncle Yosef Shabbetai Farḥi, who was one of the great scholars.[67] Next he engaged in writing the story *al-Malik sayf al-azal*, which is known as *al-Azaliyya*. The source of this important story was the writer Ḥai Ṣarfati, known as Ukhū Bāya, who heard it from the storyteller and committed it to writing. Thereafter the story came into the hands of Abraham Qaṣenṭīn, and he sold it to Mr. Elie'zer Farḥi for 300 riyals of those days, namely, 180 francs, for by that time the story had won great acclaim. This story has 1,642 pages and is divided into four volumes. Farḥi published it in Livorno, and the work of printing went on for three years. In any event, this important story, although it garnered great success among the Jews of Tunisia, did not reap that won by French and other writers, who sometimes published a single story and got rich of it. An example is *Le Garçon*,[68] which was published in France and brought its author 2 million francs. In short, 500 copies of Farḥi's story were sold, and 500 more were acquired by the printer and bookseller Ṣiyyon Uzan, who had in advance been awarded the publishing rights to the story.

In 1885 Farḥi planned to buy a small press that was up for sale. Having made enormous efforts to obtain the required sum, he learned in the end to his great sorrow that someone had preempted him and all because he had given away the secret. Thereafter he entered into partnership with the printer Varius, and they established a press on al-Tūmī Street, which subsequently was sold to *al-Ṣabāḥ* journal. After long days and years, Rabbi Eli'ezer founded, through his son Angelo Farḥi, a press on al-Sudāniyyāt Street in Tunis, known as Ṣābāt al-Wuṣfān,[69] next to Sīdī al-Srīdek Street. While *al-Azaliyya* was being printed in Livorno, Rabbi Eli'ezer continued working on the publication of the book *Sīrat al-'ānqa* [The Story of Phoenix]. Then Farḥi in his ardor became impatient, thinking day and night, all his thoughts centering on the idea from which benefits of various kinds could be produced. He composed and published a number of stories, all in the form of parables about Tunisians, in order to move them from their corrupt deeds so that they might walk in the path of righteousness; their theme was mutual support, namely, "I am for you and you are for me."[70] Farḥi called the first printing house he set up on al-Tūmī Street Maṭba'at Yerushalayim [Jerusalem Press], and the second, on Ṣābāt al-Wuṣfān, he called Maṭba'at al-Nasr [Eagle Press], and here indeed he founded a journal called *al-Nasr*.

Finally Rabbi Eli'ezer began working with the management of the Charitable Society in Tunis in the post of examiner and supervisor of the sick. He used to visit the sick in the company of the physician Konwirti,[71] and for his good deeds and constancy among the poor and the needy he won over hearts and became loved in the eyes of all. After leaving the Charitable Society fund, he opened a shop selling herbs and medicinal plants on the Livornese Market Street, close to Mūsā Khmīra alley, and lived there for over thirty years. When he grew old and needed rest, I, the humble servant, went in with him and worked with him for some years. This was from 1926 to 1930. Wednesday, January 20, was the day of the death of this scholar and his departure from this world. Here is the list of compositions by this writer:

1. *Ha-Mevasser*, journal
2. *al-Mubashshir*, journal
3. *al-Nasr*, journal
4. *al-Azaliyya*, he was the printer of it
5. *Sīrat al-ʿānqa*
6. *Qiṣṣat al-balʿūt*
7. *Ḥikāyāt zīn al-tmām*
8. *Anīs al-wujūd*
9. *Ḥaṣlat kāmil al-awṣāf*
10. *al-Bint friyyeʿ nashrī*
11. *Naṣrat al-ibnāt*
12. *Kanz al-wazīr*
13. *Bereshit bi-al-ʿarabī*
14. *Tafkīr al-manāmāt*
15. *Shomer piv* for the preservation of health
16. *Wudnīn haman*
17. *Snīn dāʾima*
18. *Gazbar bet ha-ḥayyim*
19. *al-Mishḥāḥ wa-al-karīm*
20. *Iḍḥak yā ḍhū al-ʿīn*[72]

Shalom Flāḥ

This learned gentleman, who was known as Rabbi Shalom Flāḥ, was born in our city of Tunis in 1855. After acquiring advanced knowledge of both the Hebrew and the Arabic languages, he worked as a merchant in 1870, and was married at the age of 20. This was in 1875. Ten years later, in 1885, he opened a school and there began teaching Hebrew to pupils. His colleague Yosef Cohen Ganūna took charge of the French department at this school. At that time Shalom Flāḥ was appointed correspondent of the Hebrew papers *Ha-Maggid* and *Ha-Tsefira* published in Warsaw, a position he held for nine full years. The learned Flāḥ took a step forward and founded an important journal called *Munawwir al-ḥaqq*, but after a short time the journal closed on account of the deposit that the government demanded from journals at a rate of 20,000 riyals. Meanwhile, however, the learned Flāḥ did not remain idle but wrote and published several valuable books for the study of Hebrew, including a book called *Miqra meforash*, for which he received many letters of praise. Among these was a letter from Mr. Parienty, who at that time was the principal of the Alliance schools in Tunisia. This was because it became apparent to him in the clearest possible way that when the pupils of the teacher Flāḥ entered the Alliance schools, they made amazing progress and obtained their French certificate in a short time.

But in 1889, when the government abolished the deposit on the journals, Mr. Shalom Flāḥ was courageous enough to publish a journal called *al-Mutarjim*, whose purpose was to implant the feeling of unity in hearts so that people would help one another. By means of this journal a sense of moral elevation became widespread, and several societies were formed for the purpose noted. At that time the scholar Flāḥ was writing for the journals *al-Ḥurriyya* of Ganūna, *al-Bustān* of M'ārek, and *al-Naṣra* and *Nāṣir al-muḥayyarīn* of Cohen and Halevi. In 1894 he established a new journal called *al-Ittiḥād.* The name attests to the purpose of this paper. He wrote many articles in it, important and effective in instilling unity in the hearts of disparate groups. In this context he considered opening a home for the elderly and first began to collect money for this lofty goal. Praise be to God that such an important institution was brought into being by the saintly, the late Rabbi Abraham Castro, and now stands in the village of Ariana. At this self-same institution of benevolence died the writer Rabbi Shalom Flāḥ, who, as stated, gave counsel and was assiduous in his articles to win over hearts for its foundation.

In 1895 he wrote and published an important story titled *Ben koziva*,[73] and in 1897 he was accepted as a Hebrew teacher at the Alliance schools in Sousse. In 1900 he authored and published the book

Shi'ure ha-ḥinnukh for the study of Hebrew, in which he even wrote in Judeo-Arabic and French. He then went on to write the book *Jadwal mu'abbad*, for knowledge of dates to infinity. He continued, and wrote and published another Hebrew textbook titled *Safa ṭiv'it*, and an excellent book called *Safa berura*. By virtue of the high quality of his work at the Alliance schools in Sousse, the principal recommended him as a recipient of a medal of honor from the government. In 1928 he was appointed chief rabbi of Sousse.

The honorable Shalom Flāḥ was a prolific writer, a fine poet, and one of the best journalists. Apart from the works mentioned, his pen produced several other essays. He was the proprietor of the journals *al-Badr al-kāmil* and *Fāḍiḥ al-asrār*; likewise, he wrote for the journal of our esteemed colleague Meir Khushkhāsh, *al-Ḥaqq*, and for the journal *Najmat al-sāḥil* of our colleague, the famous writer Makhlūf Najjār, which lately has changed its name to *al-Najma al-waḥīda*. True enough, it is the only one in its form, its kind, its innovation, singular in its articles, alone even in its surroundings.[74]

These are all the Arabic books published by the famous writer Shalom Flāḥ:

1. *Ben koziva*
2. *al-Tawārīkh al-isra'īliyyah*
3. *Masārib al-ḥayāh*
4. *Amthāl wa-'abā'ir*
5. *al-Ṣidk anjā*
6. *Ereṣ ha-ṣvi*
7. *al-'Ilm wa-al-amān*
8. *Jadwal mu'abbad*

Apart from his enthusiasm for and his work in Arabic, Rabbi Shalom Flāḥ was also a great scholar in Hebrew, and his eagerness for the propagation of this language was monumental. In 1928 he was appointed chief rabbi of Sousse. On December 4, 1936, in Ariana, he shed the burden imposed on every creature.

Mas'ūd M'ārek

One of the veteran writers in Arabic who won great fame in Tunis, in the city and the country, for their elegant style and their fine writing in the view of all, is Mas'ūd M'ārek, head of the journals *al-Akhbār* and *al-Bustān*. This renowned and important writer was born in 1858, and when he reached adulthood and acquired sufficient knowledge in the three languages, namely, Hebrew, Arabic, and French, he was drawn to the profession of journalism and writing articles in the issues of the journals in Judeo-Arabic. In this way he achieved the greatest acclaim. Our revered colleague Mas'ūd M'ārek always lived with this quality, and not with the quality of a fighter.[75] He was a fluent writer and fine poet, and all readers enjoyed his noble works. This was because they were extremely beneficial for the public, and his lofty counsel was for the most part inspired by the wisdom of Judaism.

At the age of 30, in 1888, the respected writer Mas'ūd M'ārek founded a weekly called *al-Bustān*, which was beyond description, and it was received by all with wonder and joy and great appreciation. It lasted for nine whole years, becoming distributed and well-known in Tunis and all Tunisia. The doyen of writers, Mas'ūd M'ārek was the first who dared, in 1889, to set up a daily newspaper. It was called *al-Telegraf* and was based on translated cables from the Havas news agency. Its feuilleton was titled *Les mystères de Paris*, and the chief editor was the great writer Yosef Cohen Ganūna. In 1892, under the pen name Ben Amittai, our friend Mas'ūd M'ārek founded a weekly called *al-Niḥla*, of which about twenty-five issues appeared. It editor-in-chief was our dear Abraham Bismūṭ, owner of the publishing house, who by a willing agreement reached between him and his wife resided permanently at the Wād al-Jadīd village, where he lived all his life, without regretting it, because, as he said, he had chosen the town of "water and air." In 1895 the worthy writer Mas'ūd M'ārek, together with his relative the writer Ya'aqov Chemla, founded a new journal called *al-Ḥaqīqa*, which appeared weekly; its feuilleton was called *al-Kasb al-mazrūb*. In 1904, after the abolition of the deposit on journals, the writer Mas'ūd M'ārek hastened, before all the other writers, to revive *al-Bustān*, the journal that had already acquired fame in the world of publishing. Indeed, two years later, in 1906, when the writer Mas'ūd M'ārek became aware of the great success of the daily *al-Ṣabāḥ* of the wise writer Ya'aqov Ha-Cohen, he too dared to venture to turn *al-Bustān* from being a weekly into a daily. But after great work and effort for some time, it faltered and disappeared. Finally, two years later, in 1908, the writer Mas'ūd M'ārek, with the help of his friend Moshe Katorza of the publishing house of Rabbi Abraham Castro and Ḥayyim Uzan, founded another new and important journal, called *al-Akhbār*, which indeed became well-known in Tunisia and other countries and was deemed a treasury, in which all its readers would find value thereafter. Apart from this, Mas'ūd M'ārek wrote many articles of extreme importance in the important journal *al-Zamān*, a weekly. He also wrote for the daily *al-Ṣabāḥ*.

The following is the list of the essays and stories from the pen of this prolific writer:

1. *Muḥārabat al-dīn* (he wrote half of it)
2. *al-Ḥubb wa-al-waṭan*[76]
3. *Lallat al-nisā*
4. *Khṣā'il jūḥā*
5. *Janān al-zahw*
6. *Amān al-nisā wa-khiyānathum*
7. *Athmār al-karāma*
8. *Ester al-jamīla*
9. *al-Kasb al-mazrūb*
10. *Ḍulm al-'ibād*
11. *Ḥayya bint al-shammāsh*

Ya'aqov Chemla

One of the excellent writers who became very famous in Tunis and all Tunisia for his lucid style and fine writing is our colleague Ya'aqov Chemla, who was head of the journal *al-Fajr*. This renowned writer was born in 1858, and when he grew up, he wished to enter the profession of journalism and to write successful articles in the pages of journals in Judeo-Arabic. His fame grew still more following the translation and publication of the novel *The Count of Monte Cristo*, which for certain reasons has still not been completed, although only a few issues are left for it to become an important entire novel. We hope that our dear Makhlūf Najjār, who holds rights to the books of Ya'aqov Chemla, will try to complete this important novel, to the delight of all readers.

Our colleague Ya'aqov Chemla was renowned for working in tiles and ancient pottery.[77] At a time when this artistic Tunisian craft was on the verge of utter abandonment, it was he who acted with the fullest energy and acumen and physical effort to revitalize this important branch, to the point where the government several times granted him important awards, such as Chevalier du Legion d'Honneur, Commandant of the Medal of Grandeur, and Chevalier de l'Académie. Our colleague Ya'aqov Chemla was greatly admired by all, this being by virtue of his important articles, which were published on the pages of the journals. These were his own or those of others who wished him to write for them because he was a fluent writer and fine poet. He wrote many articles regularly for the journals *al-Tamaddun* and *al-Ḥurriyya*. He was the director of *al-Fajr*, which was regarded as the best-known and esteemed journal in Tunis. He was of balanced outlook and was even-tempered. He spent more than fifty years in publishing, and was known among the press workers as Mr. Director. Eventually he served for many years as a pleader at the Rabbinic Court on al-Dabbāghīn Street in Tunis, and in this field too he earned a fine reputation and great acclaim. This important writer, one of the veteran writers, acted as director or editor of the papers listed here: *al-Ḥaqīqa*, *al-Bustān*, *Musharriḥ al-aṣdār*, *al-Istiwā*, *al-Ḥurriyya* (the first and the second), *al-Fajr*, *al-Waṭan*, *al-Tamaddun*, and others.

But, man is made of dust and to dust he will return. Thus July 30, 1938, was the day on which the soul of this scholar was extinguished and on which he departed this world. And indeed, this is a great loss, which causes anguish and sorrow in the heart of all citizens of Tunis who enjoyed the work of this famous writer. On the death of this revered writer the journal *al-Usbūʿ al-yahūdī* published an important article written in praise and appreciation on the life of the renowned writer Yaʿaqov Chemla. Among other things it mentioned that he wrote for most of the Jewish journals many hundreds, even thousands, of useful pieces and wrote serious and lovely stories. But, "all these benefits are dispersed, and not a trace remains in reality!"[78] We may say that our colleague who produced this statement is mistaken, for many people are to be found for whom the pen of Yaʿaqov Chemla is dear in their eyes and who desire his writing, who have not ceased gathering his compositions and the compositions of others. I am one of them, the humble servant Daniel Ḥagège of the younger writers of the journal *al-Najma al-waḥīda*, which has useful news reports and well-written articles.

Our colleague Yaʿaqov Chemla knew four languages—Hebrew, Arabic, French, and Italian. He was so well versed in them that when he sat with the religious leaders, he was able to converse with them and discuss with them, so much so that you might say that Yaʿaqov Chemla was a brilliant rabbi and scholar. This applied likewise when he was in the company of the younger generation, who are free in their opinions and advanced in the sciences, languages, and education. His discourse and his sagacity were much appreciated by them and were regarded with great esteem. This fine manner of his was also well liked by the courageous journalist Mordekhai Smādja, and it brought him close to Yaʿaqov Chemla and caused him to select him for the post of writer for his journal *al-Ḥurriyya*; he felt that the thinking of the two of them was compatible. Indeed, Yaʿaqov Chemla was a man of his time, and was liberal in his views. This freedom of thought led him to the path of demanding of the religious leaders, through his articles, "amendments in religion, without religion being undermined."[79] But there were several people—how can we put it? zealously religious—who opposed this and charged him with lack of adherence to the faith.[80] But we who really knew the ways of Ya'aqov Chemla, with his God and his people, can attest that the guilt which a few simpletons lay on him has no foundation. Ya'aqov Chemla was one of the purest of men that could be, and he possessed wisdom, learning, and artistic qualities.

Al-Najma al-waḥīda, issue no. 95, of August 5, 1938, published on its front page an important and solemn article by our colleague Makhlūf Najjār, filled with sorrow and pain at the loss of our dear departed. So as not to deprive members of our community, we present what our friend Mr. Najjār wrote word for word:

Ya'aqov Chemla Is Dead

The tongue is weary, the pen confused.
    the poet of poets is dead.
Over him we shall deluge tears of pain
    with an abundance of weeping and laments.
They say: There is none who goes forth from death whole.
    but it behooved death to pass by.
The gate of comforting—no one knows.
    woe, woe, and again, woe.
Ya'aqov Chemla is dead!

Dead is that man, great in wisdom, master of the fine word and the pen!

Dead, and we so utterly in need of his like!

And today, where is he, the fluent writer who will depict this stunning loss? Where is he, the great poet who will rhyme his trembling verses?

It is hard for me to write words describing the man, who is beyond all description, and my pen cannot show what agony and misery lies on my soul.

What can I say and what shall I tell? I shall say that he was a person of grace, a person of humility and purity of heart; I shall say that he was a person to be cherished and respected, a man of grandeur and loftiness; I shall say that he was the knight of the writers, and their king, father of the people of letters, and their elder; I shall say that he was alone in his golden pen, and after him the writer of literature is lost and gone.

On the Sabbath, 30 July, this pure soul was extinguished, in the midst of his family, in his eightieth year, and on Sunday the bier of the departed was accompanied by a large multitude of relatives and citizens, all weeping and mourning over this enormous loss.

Who is there of the Jews of Tunisia and abroad who does not know and hear and speak with words of praise and gratitude of this mighty writer Ya'aqov Chemla? Who is there of the Jews who has not perused his successive articles in the many journals of which he was the director and chief editor? Who is there among the Jews who has not raised the name of Ya'aqov Chemla above all names, knowing that he is the writer of such wonderful works as *The Count of Monte Cristo*, *al-Yahūd fī ispānyā*, *Ṣudūr al-aḥrār qubūr al-asrār*, *al-Ḥīla wa-al-'ishq*, and *'Ishq wa-hajrān wa-mukhālafat al-adyān*?

Ya'aqov Chemla is dead, but his name will flourish forever, as long as the sun shall illumine the world.

Ya'aqov Chemla is dead, but his name remains and will remain alive throughout the days and the years. It will remain alive in the heart of every Jew who knows his lofty works and his compositions, whose like there are not. And above all, his memory will stay among the people of the pen, editors of journals, and writers of books. For when they reflect on the talent and daring that nature bestowed on him in the quality of his pristine writing, they will realize that the loss of Ya'aqov Chemla will be considered the greatest of losses.

O, our colleague Ya'aqov! You who captured our hearts! By what word shall we remember you? By what pen shall we

> thank you? And By what blessing shall we bless you. Life—the Creator, may He be praised, granted you in plenty; respect—you have received it, to the highest degree of human honors, as you hold the Chevalier du Legion d'Honneur, Commandant of the Medal of Grandeur, and Chevalier l'Académie. Were I to make mention of your good name and the great loyalty that you exercised all your days, there may not be sufficient pages for it.
>
> Today, you have departed from us; the earth has called you to dwell with our ancient masters. You have gone from us and have left us like your children, weeping and grieving.
>
> And now we must raise our eyes to Heaven and beg mercy and comfort: mercy for the departed, as he merits it, and comfort for his children and all his relatives and all the mourners. Finally, we may beg comfort for all the Jewish writers and those who wield the pen in Tunisian Arabic, particularly the adherents of our *al-Najma al-sāḥiliyya.*
>
> May God have mercy upon you, our colleague Ya'aqov!

In issue 98 of *al-Najma* a dignified article appeared among the others. It was written by our fellow learned writer, friend of the love of progress, Mr. R. Khammūs Arīs, known among the community of Sūq al-Khamīs (Thursday Market).[81] By an oversight on our part, we did not include his name in the list of all the Tunisian writers who take pains to write books in Judeo-Arabic. But he is to be numbered among the writers, and his fine work evokes respect and consideration.[82] His heart likewise melted at the loss of the late Ya'aqov. He concluded his article with the following verses:

> It is proper for them, the masters of the pen
> to share in this great loss
> The eyes of the hearts weep in anguish
> over the master of essays and translations
> He opened our eyes with books of narrative

with his poems of deep formulation
With his pen of gold he added, and wrote, and commanded
We saw his fear of heaven and the greatness of his wisdom
We saw the sea of knowledge, and he was its anchor
Wise, kind, pure, flawless
His death has touched countless hearts
and writers who there are, who seek progress
His children will have a support in the World to Come,
and he will seek for them victory and life
May God send Elijah speedily
And let the Son of David come to us soon as our Prince.

The following is the list of books written by the late Ya'aqov Chemla, most of which have been reissued and have recently become available through the good offices of Mr. Makhlūf Najjār:

1. *al-Conti di monte cristo*
2. *al-Yahūd fī ispānyā*
3. *Ṣudūr al-aḥrār qubūr al-asrār*
4. *al-Ḥīla wa-al-'ishq*
5. *'Ishk wa-hajrān wa-mukhālafat al-adyān*

Ya'aqov Ha-Cohen

This esteemed gentleman, who was the director and editor of the only Jewish daily newspaper in Tunisia, called *al-Ṣabāḥ*, and who became very famous throughout Tunisia as a masterly writer and one of the most distinguished of authors, was born in our city of Tunis on November 9, 1872. At the age of 7 years he entered the sea of Hebrew studies to learn, and at the age when he put on the phylacteries[83] he entered the sea of French studies. Barely had he reached the age of 17 years when he received his matriculation certificate, which was among the highest certificates in the above studies. This was in 1891, when he too became enamored by the art of journalism, and he began the work of editing with Jewish journals. He founded a weekly called *al-Naṣra*, which existed for two whole years. At the end of that period he joined his saintly friend Ṣemaḥ Halevi, owner of the journal *al-Muḥayyar*, and together they founded a new journal called *Nāṣir al-muḥayyarīn*. In 1892, when he was 20, he began work as a teacher of French at the schools of the Alliance Israélite Universelle in Tunis and continued to do so for a full five years. Thereafter he worked for a year with his prospective father-in-law, the well-known merchant Rabbi Sha'ul al-Ḥūrī, and in 1896 Mr. Ya'aqov Ha-Cohen married Miss Thérèse al-Ḥūrī. In 1898 he resumed his work as a teacher at the Alliance, continuing until 1903.

In 1898, with his return to work as a teacher with the Alliance, that very year he was awarded the high certificate in Arabic studies, and at that time too he received a high certificate in accountancy. He likewise worked as a writer and translator in Arabic and French for the governors of Mateur.[84] In 1904 he founded the great weekly called *al-Shams*, of which forty-one issues appeared, and then he closed it to establish in its stead a daily paper called *al-Ṣabāḥ*. He succeeded in maintaining that paper for a long period, ten whole years. But around the Sukkot festival in 1913 the journalist Cohen had to travel to towns in Tunisia, as was his custom, to deal with matters regarding his work. First he stopped in Sousse, and on a visit he made to the house of one of his friends it was necessary for him to remain with him for a longer time than expected, and he could not take his leave until late at night. From there he walked to the hotel where he was lodging in order to sleep, but on arrival he did not feel well, and the following morning he was obliged to take the train back to Tunis even though he had not completed the matters for which he was making the journey. On his return he called the doctor, who saw his ill state and diagnosed that he was suffering from pneumonia. He began treating him as required by science and medicine. But our friend Cohen, though ill and under medical care, did not agree to withhold publication of the paper, and with great suffering he daily prepared his articles while on his sickbed. This went on to the point where his condition worsened, and he had to stop publication of the paper for about five weeks. Afterward, when he felt better, he resolved to return to work at *al-Ṣabāḥ*, so he printed large notices that were posted throughout the city, stating: "All of you, read the newspaper *al-Ṣabāḥ*." And sure enough, on the evening of that day, December 25, 1913, the famous paper *al-Ṣabāḥ* came out. In it we found an excellent article written in fine style, expressing thanks to God for the beginning of his restoration to vigor, and thanks to the readers and others for their expression of sorrow at his illness. This is what he wrote in the aforementioned article:

> To the dear readers. Whom shall I thank, and whom shall I mention among the writers of letters and postcards that we have received from every city, from our friends and from our subscribers, friends, and readers of *al-Ṣabāḥ*? They evinced their feelings of friendship to us, and the greatness of their sorrow over our poor health throughout that period in which the light of *al-Ṣabāḥ*, illuminating and lively with ideas, was concealed from them.
>
> Letters and postcards in their hundreds. May the good God reward all those who contacted us, by letter or postcard, for this shows the purity of their thoughts for us, and their closeness to us and their desire for *al-Ṣabāḥ*, which has been their companion these ten years. Our many thanks are sent to the writers of these letters and missives, are sent to everyone who visited us personally, from Tunis and from the [other] cities when they learned of our illness and of our poor state of health. They are sent to everyone who felt sorrow for our condition and expressed this in asking after us or in some other way. Our great thanks are also sent to the one who wrote those lines in the journal *al-Ḥurriyya*, wishing us restoration to strength soon and the reappearance of *al-Ṣabāḥ*.

> My fellow readers! I am still bodily weak and cannot [return] to work fully, but with the agreement of the physician I have received permission to rise from my bed for several hours in the day. And because our subscribers long to read *al-Ṣabāḥ* regularly, God willing, and because of my longing also to remain close to the journal of "the Morning"[85] with my brother readers and the dear subscribers, I have put my fate in God's hands, and I have decided to begin work insofar as my weakness and poor health allow. I trust in God that he will facilitate the work for me and will succor us with Divine help to continue our work in the future, as we have done in the ten years that have gone by, in preparing, properly and consistently, the appearance of *al-Ṣabāḥ*.
>
> We are quite certain in our heart that our brother subscribers will not blame us for the recent interruption because—praise God—the Lord saved us from the jaws of death, and it is they who throughout our illness showed us feelings of love. This is the victorious proof. And praise be to God the generous and the protector!
>
> The Editor

Afterward, the respected editor continued with the work of *al-Ṣabāḥ* for three and a half months, until the week of Passover in 1914. Throughout this period of his illness, namely, from Sukkot to Passover, he did not leave his house, even though he continued the work of his newspaper. The doctor visited him periodically to check his condition. But two days before Passover the gentleman went out to go around the city, and everyone he met was happy to see him and congratulated him on his deliverance from the serious illness. On the first night of the intermediary days of Passover he went to the Théâtre Municipale and saw the play *Ṣafāwat al-maḥabba* of David Ḥagège and his company, and after midnight he returned from the theater in a carriage and arrived at his place healthy and very content. The next morning likewise he rose well and without feeling any ailment.

But, on the first day after Passover, April 19, 1914, he took ill and retired to bed. Such a relapse by a person after recovering from an illness is hard. This is the reason why despite all the treatments and despite all the consultations, the invalid's condition became grave. The finest physicians in Tunis could give no happy tidings as to the patient's state, and they made it clear to the family that his condition was dangerous. The foreboding of the doctors came to pass, and Friday, May 8, 1914, was the day when the life's breath of this sage failed and on it he departed this world. All the citizens—Jews, Muslims, and Christians—grieved greatly over the huge loss, because the deceased was renowned and much loved by all. The first journal to publish the painful announcement was *al-Fajr* in its 277th issue, penned by the sensitive writer Ya'aqov Chemla. This is what he wrote:

> At five o'clock this morning we were shocked by the sad news, news that stultified minds and melted hearts, because we realized that with the publication of this news all our brother Jews of Tunis would suffer pain and mourning, and tears would stream from their eyes. Namely: Woe to treacherous time, O how great is it among the agonies! In truth, all the Jews, dwellers in Tunisia, mourn the loss of our friend Ya'aqov Ha-Cohen!
>
> The morning descended howling on our friend, the editor of *al-Ṣabāḥ*! The departed was famous as a great master of the pen, a fluent writer, a poet of pure tongue, but the departed was stalwart in his course, which forced our paper to oppose his articles. Yet politics did not obliterate our friendship that resided in our hearts and that will not be erased ever from our thoughts. Quite the reverse: his love is in our hearts eternally, and the mourning over him shall lodge in our memory all the days.

> We shall bid our last farewell to our friend through our journal and we shall curse treasonous, cunning time, which carried no favor, and we shall share in the mourning of this bereft family, which, on account of his death, will exist for ever and always in grim anguish. We shall share in the grief with his brothers and relatives, with his brothers-in-law and his dear ones, with the orphan his only daughter, with his widow his helpmate, and mostly with his mother and his father, who will never find solace for the flower of the family, plucked off in his prime and gone from his glory and his stature into the grave.
>
> O vicious, treacherous time—it has no covenant, nor trust—has betrayed always and will ever betray in the world of tribulation, the world of agony. Nothing remains for us but to beg the greatest consolation from the good God, to cause the soul of our dear friend to dwell in Heaven.
>
> The Editor

When news of the death of the editor of *al-Ṣabāḥ* spread, most journals published long or short articles on this event. These included *La tunisie française* (no. 3150), *L'Unioni* (on May 8, 1914), *La dépêche tunisienne* [no. 8652], *Le courrier tunisi* (no. 3440), *La tunisie française* (a second time, no. 3151), *al-Fajr* (a second time, by Ya'aqov di Moshe Abrahami and by George Naqqāsh), *La tunisie française* (a third time, on Friday, May 15, 1914), *La tunisie française* (a fourth time, on Sunday, May 17, 1914, by Yasal Lombrozo, a friend of the late Ya'aqov Ha-Cohen), *Les republicains* (no. 748), *La petite tunisi* (no. 1297), and other articles published in *al-Ṣabāḥ*, etc., etc. If we wished to publish them as they are, we would require a gigantic book of many hundreds of pages. What we have related is but an outline of the life of the deceased from the day of his birth to the day of his death.

Recently we read what was written about him by our colleague Mr. Makhlūf Najjār in his composition *Kitāb snāwī* [yearbook] for 1918, page 37, Part III, speaking of his friend, the deceased:

> He was the renowned and good man, possessor of wisdom and master of the lucid pen, the great and learned expert writer, pleasant and holy, the late Mr. Ya'aqov Ha-Cohen, may his soul rest in peace. Indeed, the name of this person has etched in the heart of the Jews of Tunisia the deepest impression, in the heart of anyone who was in his presence, even for a short time, because up to now, or rather forever, that esteem and those thoughts about the departed will not be expunged from our memory.

The writer Cohen was known as Kiki [Ya'aqov] Cohen of *al-Ṣabāḥ*, and apart from being loved by the entire population, without distinction of community and religion, he was loved by the heads of the charitable societies and even by the government, which awarded him the Medal of Honor with the rank of Officer. He would enter the office of the Embassy of France at any time, like a man entering his home. Apart from his extensive knowledge and the important certificates he won in the Hebrew and French languages, he was versed in and enthusiastic about the arts and music and was a specialist in the art of the violin and the piano. Most virtuosi were his friends, among them the great Fallo, the personal oud player of the Bey, Nissim Jāwī; Asher Mizraḥi, the famous Egyptian oud player;[86] Mrīdekh Salāma, the *qānūn* player; and others, who used to gather constantly at his home. Through his great love of art he came to write a *malzūma*[87] titled *Khṣūmat al-ma'lūf wa-al-maṣrī*;[88] he wrote a poem called *'Arḍūnī zūj ṣbāya*, another titled *Mā aḥlā limmat al-ibnāt*, and more.

The pen of Ya'aqov Ha-Cohen produced many important essays; among them he studiously worked at preparing a French-Hebrew dictionary, but treacherous time did not allow him the freedom to complete this important work. The story *al-Nasr al-aḥmar*, which won great renown in Tunisia, first appeared as a feuilleton in *al-Ṣabāḥ*[89] at the instigation of Ya'aqov Ha-Cohen, although he did not write it. In addition, in 1892 he published a *malzūma* called *Khṣūmat pessaḥ wa-al-sukkah*, and afterward *Malzūmāt līlat al-ghalṭa*. In 1897 he wrote *Qiṣṣat yūsef* and *Qiṣṣat shimshon* in verse, and an amusing book titled *Nuzhat al-zamān*. He likewise wrote a *malzūma* about Purim called *B'ūth al-ṣīniyya*. Apart from the journals that we listed earlier, he also published a journal called *Khillaṭ-millaṭ*.

After having detailed the essence of all the important works written by the famous writer Ya'aqov Ha-Cohen, it is time to present all the stories penned by this notable writer, as they are an important possession for one who holds them. They are:

1. *Nāzlat drayfūs*
2. *al-Ṣiyyonism*
3. *al-Nasr al-aḥmar* (he published it)
4. *al-Bint al-muḥdiyya*
5. *Jabal al-sūd*
6. *Lahīb al-gharām fī 'āliyīn al-maqām*
7. *Irghām al-gharām*
8. *al-Fāris al-maḥrūm*
9. *al-Ḥīla wa-al-sulūk fī 'ishq al-mulūk*
10. *Ṣani' al-zamān fī al-'ishq wa-al-amān*
11. *Makārem al-akhlāq*
12. *Ghawāmiḍ lundrā wa-asrārhā*
13. *al-Mujāhada fī sabīl al-ḥubb*
14. *Zuhrat al-falak wa-bint al-malik*
15. *al-Iḥtiyāl fī taḥṣīl al-māl*

Ṣemaḥ Halevi

This great writer was born in our city of Tunis in 1868 to a respected family that originally came from Gibraltar after they had lived for a long period in Austria, now under the rule of Hitler. This writer was the son of Natan Halevi, who died in 1904, and Najma Ṣarfati, who died in 1906. A cousin of Ṣemaḥ's father was the millionaire Rabbi Natan Halevi, one of whose daughters married Mr. Joseph

Valensi, who was Vice-Consul of Austria in Tunis. He was the father of the lawyer Alfred Valensi, who was president of the Agud-dat Ṣiyyon Society in Tunis, and the well-known lawyer Théodore Valensi, a member of the parliament in Paris.[90] Yet this millionaire Rabbi Natan Halevi was a great Hebrew language scholar, and he wrote several books in Hebrew that became very well-known, and in them several problems that perplexed the rabbis of that era were resolved.[91]

Our learned colleague and friend Ṣemaḥ ben Natan Halevi was from childhood very diligent in academic subjects and began learning and acquiring deep knowledge of Hebrew and Arabic. When he became an adult, he married a lady of the Livornese Bueno family, who bore him five children. At the same time he invested a good part of his money in learning French and Italian. He became so profound in his knowledge of Hebrew that he reached the point of writing a number of books in the field of Talmud. He was also the right hand of the famous rabbi Yehuda Jarmon,[92] who loved him greatly because he was aware of the vastness of his deep knowledge and his great comprehension of the Hebrew language.

The great renown won by Ṣemaḥ Halevi caused several people to emulate him and to compete with him, in keeping with the saying "Compete with others, don't wish them ill."[93] But not one of them was able to reach his excellence or to equal him because he was a fluent writer, a silver-tongued poet. The pen in his hand, particularly in the domain of poetry, he would knead as one kneads candies, so that most, if not all, of the *qinot*[94] published in Tunisia were from his pen, and the poetry was as if created by it. In his leisure time he wrote a book of *ghinā* and *'urūbiyyāt* titled *Riyāqat al-nufūs*.[95]

In 1877 the writer Ṣemaḥ Halevi founded a weekly called *al-Janān* and in 1888 another journal called *al-Najma*. In 1889 he established a third one, called *al-Anwār*, in 1891 a fourth called *al-Muḥayyar*, in 1892 a fifth called *Nāṣir al-muḥayyarīn* together with his important and wise soul mate Ya'aqov Ha-Cohen. In 1904 he founded a sixth paper, a daily called *al-Barq*, and finally he created a weekly that became famous all over the world called *al-Fonograf.*

How was it that *al-Fonograf* won worldwide renown? It was not just because most of its many articles and fine pieces were good and excellent; it also contained poems and funny stories, anecdotes and puzzles, fables and sayings, historical accounts, and articles in French by Vehel[96] and others. This marvelous paper lasted four whole years. In the end, after Ṣemaḥ Halevi made a great effort and acquired his own press at Nahj al-Nakhla close to Nahj Sīdī Mardūm in Tunis, he changed the format of the paper and designed it as a sixteen-page illustrated magazine; twenty-three issues appeared. To highlight the importance of this paper, we need only point out that the people who wrote for it were the following: Ṣemaḥ Halevi, editor; his brother Zuwīkī Levi, who was manager of Finci printers; Mr. Halevi's father, who today serves as principal of the Alliance school in Sousse; and his brother, Victor Levi, known as Vehel, who was the chief writer for the *La petite tunisie* paper and in charge of the section of articles in *al-Fonograf* in French; Eusèbe Vassel; Louis Nicola; Zadoq Kahn; the great Yosef Cohen Ganūna; Emil M'ārek; Ḥai Sitrūk; Ḥai Bel'īsh; Israel 'Arqī (Sir Elyachar) of Benzert; Refa'el Smādja; and Nino Flāḥ, who worked for *Dépêche tunisienne*; and others.

Ṣemaḥ Halevi was the proprietor of these journals: *Mubashshir al-ḥaqq*, *al-Firdaws*, *al-Ikhāwa*, *al-Kātib*, *Jūrnāl pessaḥ*, *Jūrnāl haggin*, and more. Eventually he worked for several years as a writer for the daily *al-Ṣabāḥ*, and he also composed many *malzūmāt*. These included *Nawbat al-dīl* (The Mode Dīl) (*ma'lūf*[97]), *Khzānat al-gharām* (poems), *Lisān al-'āshiq* (poems), *Ṣawt al-taghrīd* (elegies), *Khlā'at purim*, *Sakrat purim*, *Purim al-ma'shūq*, *Purim jadīd*, *Malzūmāt haman*, *Nuzhat al-qulūb*, *Tadgīz al-amūrī*, and *al-yahūd fī Cōrfū*. He also wrote and published a number of books of religion in the holy tongue and in Arabic, such as *Minḥat 'erev*, *Lel shimmurim*, *Bet ha-levi*, *Berit 'olam*, and *'Et li-vkot*.

Apart from all we have mentioned in this section, we now list the important published books and essays written by this famous writer:

1. *Muḥārabat al-dīn* (half)
2. *Les mystères de Paris* (quarter)
3. *Ohole ṣaddiqim* (half)
4. *Sayf al-mulūk wa-badī'at al-jamāl*
5. *Flōr māria and sara*
6. *Shaykh al-qaṭāṭīs*
7. *Ḥamīda bin 'uthmān*
8. *Sī ḥaḍba al-khabbāz*
9. *Zīn al-ḥimār*
10. *Ghzālat al-ahbāb*
11. *Far' al-'anbar fī jabal al-dhahab*
12. *al-'Anbara*
13. *al-Ṭifla diāmanṭa*
14. *Far' al-diyāmanṭ*
15. *Ḥabīb wald al-sulṭān*
16. *Isidor lavoranti*
17. *al-Khāyūṭ*
18. *al-Ward fī al-akmām*
19. *Yūsef al-marhūn*
20. *al-Sirriyya*
21. *Kharrāfat al-kadhb*
22. *Juli bint al-milord*
23. *al-'Arabiyya*
24. *al-Ṣābra al-mabkhūtha*
25. *Ghadrat al-ẓālim wa-ḥasrat al-sālim*
26. *al-Khayr bi-al-khayr*
27. *Khalāṣ al-jamīla min al-khaḍ' wa-al-ḥīla*

Yosef Bījāwī

This excellent writer, best known in the journal *al-Yahūdī*, was born in Tunis on January 15, 1890. When he was grown, he took up the tailoring profession and at the same time showed great interest in the field of journalism. Through his reading of stories and journals with great diligence, he succeeded in acquiring extensive knowledge, which won him the reputation of a great journalist among the journalists of Tunisia, and in the course of time he managed to write for eleven journals. These are *al-Istiwā*, *al-Jarīda*, *al-Ḍaww*, *al-Fajr*, *al-Waṭan*, *al-Ḥakīm ghabyūn*, *Kashshāf al-asrār*, *al-Tijāra al-tūnisiyya*, *al-Intishār*, *al-Ṣabāḥ*, and most recently *al-Yahūdī*. The writer Bījāwī was engaged in publishing first-rate stories, these being *al-Ṣāḥib al-maghdūr* and *al-Waṭan wa-al-dīn*, but unfortunately they were not finished.

This is the list of published stories written by our dear brother Yosef di Abraham Bījāwī:

1. *al-Khāyūṭ al-faqīr*
2. *al-Khāyūṭ al-muṣaṭṭak*

3. *al-Zīna al-zīnawiyya*
4. *Zudār ibn ʿumar*
5. *al-Aḥdab*
6. *Khṣāʾil al-nemmīla*
7. *Muḥammad al-ʿajzān*
8. *Wa-kān fī ayyām ḥukm al-ḥākimīn*
9. *ʿIlm al-falak*
10. *al-Manām wa-tafsīrhu*
11. *al-Kasb yajlib*
12. *Bint al-markīz*
13. *al-Rbāya wa-al-adab*

Meir Khushkhāsh [Koskas]

This gentleman was born in our city of Tunis in 1888. As soon as he was grown up, he began to study the profession of tailoring, and at the same time his heart's desire was for the art of writing in journals, and he began to engage in this important field, which he entered with great vigor and energy. In the days of the second *al-Ḥurriyya* of the late journalist Mordekhai Smādja, our friend Meir Khushkhāsh was appointed by that gentleman to the section of translations from the *Le Justice*, which appeared in French, for publication in *al-Ḥurriyya*, which appeared in [Judeo-]Arabic. Both journals belonged to the late Mordekhai Smādja, who founded them with the goal of bringing the Jews of Tunis into the French family and of removing them entirely from Tunisian jurisdiction. The journalist Meir Khushkhāsh founded three journals in his own name, which lasted for some time, and then stopped. These were *al-Niḥla*, *al-Ḥaqq*, and *Ḥiss al-khalq*. In addition, our dear Meir Khushkhāsh wrote many articles for various papers, such as *al-Istiwā*, *Akhbār al -ʿālam*, *al-Fajr*, and particularly *al-Ṣabāḥ*, for which he wrote for several years after the death of its owner. In short, Meir Khushkhāsh occupied a very important position in the editing branch of the Judeo-Arabic newspaper. But now he has ceased this pursuit entirely and has devoted himself to reading French journals exclusively.

Frājī Naqqāsh

This gentleman was born in our city of Tunis in 1893, and when was grown, he chose the printing trade, which he greatly desired, and began working at the presses of Castro and Ṣiyyon Uzan. His reading of the Jewish journals awakened a powerful urge in his heart and his wits and fortified his spirit to compose a small feature to appear periodically titled *Janān al-faraḥ*, which contained amusements and funny stories. During World War I our friend Frājī Naqqāsh published a small pamphlet in the form of a book that appeared occasionally titled *al-Kitāb al-tūnisī* (The Tunisian Book). Afterward he participated with his friend Eliyahu Guez in publishing a weekly called *al-Mukhabbir al-tūnisī*, which lasted for some time. This writer wrote a number of articles in the journals *al-Fajr* and *al-Ṣabāḥ* and also published several *qinot* and diverse poems.

This is the list of the three essays that he published:

1. *Taṣʿībāt al-aḥwāl wa-bulūgh al-āmāl*
2. *ʿUqūbat al-fāsīq wa-naṣrat al-ʿāshiq*
3. *al-Marʾa al-khāʾina*

Ḥai Belʿīsh

This gentleman was born in our city of Tunis in 1885, and when he was grown, he started work at the printing houses in Tunis and learned the bookbinding trade and the field of the art of etching and painting. He was talented in these and became well-known in this art, so much so that when the late Yaʿaqov Ha-Cohen, when he was alive, founded a weekly called *Khillaṭ-millaṭ*, which appeared with pictures, our friend Ḥai Belʿīsh occupied a respectable position and was in charge of the pictures section. These showed the reader of that era the life of the Jews of Tunisia. The journalist Ḥai Belʿīsh wished to edit stories and articles in journals, and accordingly he initiated publication of the feature *Jadwal ṣiyyon* with pictures, which continued for six years. He also published the feature *Ḥayāt bnādam*, which contained the story *Firqat al-ḥayā*. Likewise, he published three short illustrated stories, *Qiṣṣat yehuda vi-yehudit*, *Brīka u-brāmīno*, and *al-Malik ʿamrūn*. In addition, our friend Ḥai Belʿīsh wrote several excellent articles in the journals *al-Nasr*, *Akhbār al-ʿālam*, and *al-Mukhabbir al-tūnisī*. It is sad that a writer such as this has entirely abandoned the pursuit of editing in the Judeo-Arabic papers.

Michel Uzan

The year 1890 witnessed the birth of the writer Michel Uzan, who for many years now has made his home in the village of Ariana. There he founded a journal called *L'Echo de l'ariana* in French, of which nineteen issues appeared before it ceased publication. In 1937 he was appointed correspondent at the branch of the Spio Company in Ariana and was also made provisional manager of the Initshār al- ktā'ib al-yahūdiyya Company, which likewise was abandoned through lack of unity. He was also the editor of *al-Ikhāwa* and head of the political section for the journals *al-Insāniyya* and *al-Mukhabbir al-tūnisī*. He similarly participated in the journals *al-Fajr*, *al-Ṣabāḥ*, *al-Ḍaww*, *al-Jarīda*, *al-Waṭan*, *Kashshāf al-asrār*, *al-Istiwa*, *Ḥiss tūnis*, and *Ḥayāt al-ḍaḥk*. But in recent years our friend Michel Uzan has continued to write occasionally in *al-Najma* and sometimes in *al-Yahūdī*, and he has been singularly notable for his articles *Akhbār wa-afkār*. We wish him success, advancement, and continued strength.

This is the list of all works published so far, written by our colleague Michel Uzan:

1. *al-Ḥarb fī ūrōppā* (verses on the war of 1914)
2. *Maʿase ḥanukka*
3. *Maʿase purim*
4. *Maʿase pessaḥ*
5. *Maʿase shavuʿot*
6. *Maʿase ruth*
7. *Bayn ḥuyūṭ tūnis*

Makhlūf Najjār

A knight among the creative and sensitive writers who became celebrated through their important pen is our dear brother Makhlūf Najjār, whose name is known in all countries; he is the director of al-Sāḥil Press in Sousse and editor of the famous journal, praised throughout Tunisia, *al-Najma al-waḥīda*, which became renowned for its useful articles and well-written reports.

Makhlūf Najjār was born in the town of al-Moknīn[98] on Wednesday, 24 Kislev 5649 (November 28, 1888). From the age of 13 he chose to live in Sousse at the home of his grandfather, the sage and perfect in honor, Rabbi Mordekhai al-Guez, of blessed memory, whose name was famous among the great sages. He liked the art of journalism and reading Arabic journals and books.

At the same time, the journalist Makhlūf Najjār was leader of the artistic drama company known as the Najjār Troupe, which became well-known in Tunisia and Algeria. Members of this company were young men and women who presented famous plays on the stages of large theaters, performing in flawless Arabic. Often, the audience at these theaters included important people of rank and stature, and they enjoyed with great admiration the talent in the presentation and the exemplary skill of the acting, so much so that one might imagine that Mr. Najjār and his disciples were graduates of Egyptian troupes on account of the beauty of their Arabic. The first play presented by the Najjār Troupe at the Sousse Theater was *Yūsef al-ṣiddīq*; this was on February 15, 1913. The following is the complete list of plays performed by this marvelous group: *Yūsef al-ṣiddīq*, *Esther ha-malka*, *David and Goliath* (in the holy tongue), *Moshe rabbenu*, *al-Ṭbīb al-maghṣūb*, *Nākir al-jamīl*, *Maḥāsin al-ṣadaf*, *Romeo and Juliet*, *Charlotte*, *'Āqibat al-baghy*, *al-Ḥakīm al-ṭayyār*, *Hārūn al-rashīd ma'a khalīfa al-ṣayyād*, *al-Sāḥir al-'ajīb*, *Ghīrat barboy*, *al-Zūj ṭrash*, *Jamā'at al-surrāq*, *al-Juhalā' al-mid'iyyin bi-al-'ilm*, *Kāmil effendi*, *La Georgienne* (in French), etc. The names of the cities where the group played are these: Sousse, Sfax, Tunis, Nabeul, Ḥalq al-Wād, Mārsa, Mahdiyya, Moknīn, Kairouan, Bizerte, and

Monastir. In Algeria the cities were Algiers, Constantin, 'Unāba, Qālima [Guelma], 'Ayn al-Bayḍa, Settīf, Blīda, Bejāya, Khinshla, and Sūq Harās.

Our friend Makhlūf Najjār, the director of this excellent artistic group, always donated income from many performances to charitable institutions, and many are the societies that enjoyed the artistic evenings with the help of considerable sums. The first person who was drawn to the artistry of the Najjār Troupe and who made known his opinion in favor of its advancement in the Arabic language was the dear and upright man, the respected and courteous the late al-Bashīr Ṣafar, who was the governor of Sousse and who died in 1917 at age 54.

We have related all this summary in our collection in order to inform readers of the advanced level and interest possessed by our brother, the journalist Makhlūf Najjār, in the Arabic language. Furthermore, although he was not involved in the printing branch and had no knowledge of printing matters, when he read in one of the journals that Mr. Ṣemaḥ Halevi was offering his press for sale, our friend Mr. Najjār was bold enough to purchase all the printing tools and equipment from Mr. Halevi. This was in 1917. Our friend Mr. Najjār entered the printing branch and its operations and began distributing books in Judeo-Arabic, to the extent that we really must praise him wholeheartedly. Through him, and by his many efforts and diligence, he was able to convey to the lovers of this art a huge and great collection of books, which, if he had not invested his energy in them, would have disappeared into thin air like dust, and by now not a trace of them would have remained. In addition, he was at pains, and never stopped even for a day, to publish and print books in Judeo-Arabic. For this it is said, "May God bless you,"[99] Mr. Najjār, director of al-Sāḥiliyya Press.

This is the full list of all the essays, books, stories, and tales that have been published to date at the Najjār Printers, whether as the composition of Mr. Najjār or his translation, or works for which he received permission to publish them and the rights passed to him:

1. *Abū al-ḥasan ma'a shajarat al-durr*
2. *Abūqīr wa-abūṣīr*
3. *Ibrāhīm wa-jamīla*
4. *Edison* (a tale)
5. *al-Ab al-ḍālim*
6. *al-Ayyām al-sābiqa*
7. *al-Bankīr*
8. *al-Bakkūsha*
9. *al-Ḥīla wa-al- 'ishq*
10. *al-Yahūdī al-ḥā'ir*
11. *al-Yahūd fī ispānyā*
12. *al-Conti di monte cristo* (in press)
13. *Alexandrūs mōqdōn*
14. *al-Kharūf* (a tale)
15. *al-Liṣṣ al-sharīf* (*Qātilat ṭiflahā*)
16. *al- Mar'a al-makhnūqa fī al- ti'atrō*
17. *al-Sindbād al-baḥrī*
18. *al-'āshiq al-'ajīb*
19. *al-'Ilm wa-al-amān*
20. *al-'Ishq wa-al-ḥubb mā fīhim tibb*
21. *Alf ḍaḥka wa-ḍaḥka*
22. *al-Ṣāḥib al-ghaddār*
23. *al-Ṣāḥib wa-nisf*
24. *al-Shābb al-baghdādī*
25. *al-Shābb al-'āshiq*
26. *al-Tājir 'alī al-maṣrī*
27. *al-Taggāz al-ḥassāb*
28. *al-Turjamān al-frānṣāwī bi-al-'arabī*
29. *Anīs al-jalīs ma'a al-zūj wuzarā*
30. *Intishār al-ktā'ib al-yahūdiyya*
31. *Budūr bint al-jawharī*
32. *Bustenai* (a tale)
33. *Bet pereṣ*
34. *Ghānim ibn ayyūb*
35. *Ghawāmiḍ barr al-yaman*
36. *Goralot aḥitofel*
37. *Geza' david* (a tale)
38. *Hārūn al-rashīd ma'a muḥammad al-jawharī*
39. *Ziwḥe toda*
40. *Zīn al-mawāṣif*
41. *Ḥadīth al-ḥayawān*
42. *Ḥayāt shelomo ha-melekh*
43. *Ṭbīb al-dār*
44. *Yehudit al-shajī'a*
45. *Yūsef al-ṣiddīq* (theater [play])
46. *Kīd al-nīsā al-'aẓīma*
47. *Kasb al-māl wa-bulūgh al-āmāl*
48. *Kharāb massina*
49. *Kitāb snāwī*
50. *Majnūn laylā*
51. *Muḥammad al-kaslān*
52. *Miyāt ḥikāya wa-ḥikāya*
53. *Malkat sheva ma'a shelomo ha-melekh*
54. *Manāḍir al-tawārīkh al-yahūdiyya*
55. *Menuḥat shalom*, part I
56. *Menuḥat shalom*, part II
57. *Menuḥat shalom*, part III, illustrated
58. *Menuḥat shalom*, part IV
59. *Menuḥat shalom*, part V

60. *Mistēre pārīz* (in press)
61. *Ma'rūf al-iskhāfī*
62. *Ma'ase avraham avinu*
63. *Ma'ase eldad al-dānī*
64. *Ma'ase moshe rabbenu*
65. *Ma'ase 'āhid al-bint*
66. *Ma'ase ṣaddiqim*
67. *Marat al-sū*
68. *Nes purim al-kabīr*
69. *Sayf al-mulūk wa-badī'at al-jamāl*
70. *'Abd allah al-barrī ma'a 'ābd allah al-baḥrī*
71. *'Alī nūr al-dīn*
72. *'Uqūbat al-ghaddār*
73. *'Ishq wa-hajrān wa-mukhālafat al-adyān*
74. *Fadlekāt jūḥā al-kubrā*
75. *Flōr dāryān*
76. *Ṣudūr al-aḥrār qubūr al-asrār*
77. *Qur'at al-atmār fī kashf al-iḍmār*
78. *Robinson crusoe*
79. *Sha'ul ve-david*
80. *Charlotte*

Daniel Ḥagège

The journalist Daniel Ḥagège, who has written for the journal *al-Najma al-waḥīda* since its revival, was born in our city of Tunis on July 15, 1892. After completing his schooling, a graduate of three grades in basic studies, he began working at the printing house with the revered writer the late Ya'aqov Ha-Cohen on the weekly *al-Shams* and the daily *al-Ṣabāḥ*. This was in 1904. On October 21, 1910, this writer was appointed chief editor of the weekly *Ḥayāt al-janna*, which lasted for several months. On August 1, 1913, he founded a magazine called *al-Nuzha al-tūnisiyya*, which continued to appear until the end of 1915. It was revived in 1933, when seven issues were published. Thereafter it closed by order of the government. In 1914 he published an important book titled *Anwār tūnis*, which contained the account *Sabab takwīn ḥarb ūrūppā* and the story *al-'Ishq wa-al-ḥubb mā fīhim ṭibb* and several stirring Arabic articles and amusing tales.

December 24, 1919, was the wedding day of this journalist, with Miss Fartūnī Cohen, and from April 1924 he began to work for one year as a mixer of medicines at the pharmacy of the Greek opposite Sinigalia on the square. From 1926 to 1930 he worked at the Sūq al-Grāna with the late Rabbi Eli'ezer Farḥi, the pharmacist famous for his wisdom in plants and essences. Afterward he himself opened a shop at 4 Sīdī al-Srīdek Street in Tunis. This shop became well-known to everyone, as they came to learn of its great usefulness.

This journalist was still better known among the community through his pieces in various journals, for which he wrote articles useful for the benefit of the community, especially on the protection of the rights of the poor and the deprived. He planted the feeling of unity between the individual and the commonalty, of calm between the elements and the communities, and of affection by the citizens for France forever; this was apart from many hundreds of articles he wrote for the daily *al-Ṣabāḥ*, all for the good of the people. For many years he also helped with his pen as editor for the journals *al-Egalité*, *al-Tamaddun*, *al-Waṭan*, *al-Mukhabbir al-tūnisī*, *al-Yahūdī*, *al-Najma*, and more. After the death of the late director of *al-Ṣabāḥ*, the writer Ḥagège produced many works and compositions that appeared every day in the above paper in the form of a feuilleton from 1914 to 1926.

The following is the complete list of stories written by him:[100]

1. *Lā hurūb min al-maktūb* (80)
2. *Bint al-dallāl wa-rizq al-ḥalāl* (326)
3. *Ṣidq al-aṣḥāb fī al-awqāt al-ṣi'āb* (200)
4. *al-Ḥubb wa-al-intiqām* (140)
5. *Mashaqqat al-barrī* (120)
6. *Ṣafāwat al-maḥabba* (125)
7. *al-'Amm al-ghaddār* (105)
8. *Fawz al-ḥabīb* (124)
9. *al-Bahhālīn* (93)
10. *Nawā'ib al-'ushshāq* (121)
11. *al-Ṣāḥib al-ghaddār* (50)
12. *Mukāfāt al-af'āl* (150)
13. *'Awāqib al-khaṭṭār* (125)
14. *Najāḥ al-muthābbibīn* (105)
15. *Jināḥ al-muthābbibīn* (95)
16. *Kasb al-māl wa-bulūgh al-āmāl* (115)
17. *'Uqūbat al-muḥtāl* (125)
18. *'Ishq al-jamāl* (150)
19. *al-Bniyya al-matlūfa* (183)
20. *al-Hajjāla al-ṣghīra wa-al-'āzib fī ḥīra* (144)
21. *al-Ḥabīb al-awwal* (200)
22. *Ṭbīb maskīn* (240)
23. *al-Zīna al-musrāra* (190)
24. *al-Ḥakīm simanof* (855)
25. *Maṣāyib al-maḥabba* (142)
26. *al-Raḍī' al-wārith* (128)
27. *al-Khaddām al-ḥarīṣ* (844)
28. *Surūr al-'afw* (150)

29. *Zawāj bi-al-maḥabba* (100)
30. *al-ʿIshq wa-al-ḥubb mā fīhim ṭibb* (56)
31. *Ṣāniʿ al-ḥajjām* (58)

To our brother the reader: of the first story in this list, *Lā hurūb min al-maktūb*, the late Yaʿaqov Ha-Cohen wrote the first six chapters. After the poor man died, the story was completed by the author of this book, Mr. Daniel Ḥagège. Finally, it should be noted that this book, titled *Intishār al-ktāʾib al-yahūdiyya*, is the work of the journalist Daniel Ḥagège, writer of the stories enumerated, and he is one of the writers for the periodical of the journalist Mr. Najjār, namely, *al-Najma al-waḥīda*, known throughout Tunisia and other countries.

Yaʿaqov di Moshe Abrahami

We will be counted among the greatest of fools if we do not speak of the life of our friend the journalist Yaʿaqov di Moshe Abrahami. This gentleman, whose age today is approaching 55 years, is one of the founders of the Aguddat Ṣiyyon society in Tunis, which was established in 1911. In that year, out of the abundance of sublime and natural feeling that flowed in his veins for the proliferation of the Zionist movement through Tunisia, he published, out of his own pocket, at the press of Rabbi Eliʿezer Farḥi, the Jewish Zionist anthem "Hatikvah" and distributed it free of charge to Zionists and to non-Zionists. It was received among them with great joy and delight. The gentleman YDMA (Yaʿaqov di Moshe Abrahami), apart from being a writer in Jewish journals, and whose articles are all for the benefit of the people, had the courage to lecture at all times in Tunis and the other cities of the country to plant Zionist feelings and love of the homeland in the heart of all our fellow Jews, until he was appointed chairman of the Jewish National Fund from 1913 to 1926. He delivered ninety-four political, religious, and national speeches in Tunis and throughout the country. He also planted this feeling in the heart of his daughter Rachelle, and she made several Zionist speeches. In 1926, in a speech delivered by Mr. YDMA in the presence of the city governor on the love of Eretz Yisrael and France, and Tunis, he was awarded the title Chevalier d'Honneur, and in 1936 he was awarded the title Honorary Officer.

Works of Various Writers

By Ṣiyyon Uzan, or through his good offices: *Pirqe avot* in Arabic, *Shavua' ṭov* in Arabic, *al-Maghdūr wa-'āqibat al-ghāddārīn*, *al-Zīr abū laylā al-muhalhil*

By Abraham Uzan: *Nawbat al-ḥasīn*[101]

By Mordekhai Uzan, who was at one time director of *al-Fajr*: *Zahw al-aṣḥāb*, *Ṣawt al-mughannī*

At the press of Ṣiyyon Uzan: *al-Ḥaṭṭāb wa-bint al-sulṭān*, *Ḥikāya fī sabab qatl al-barāmika*, *Ma'asiyyot fī shān ḥokhmat shelomo ha-melekh*, *'Alī bin bakkār ma'a shams al-nahār*, *Qra'āt aḥitofel*, etc.

By Rabbi Eliyahu Ghānim through Makhlūf Najjār: *Kippur be-'aravi* (Arabic)

By Ḥai Cohen: *Ḥibbur nuzhat al-zamān*, *al-Samsūniyya*, *al-Intiqām li-bulūg al-marām*

By Y. Mamo: *Karīm al-dahrīn*, *Jāsim al-istanbūlī*, *al-Ḥammāl wa-al-ghassāl wa-al-takārlī*

By Ya'aqov Abīḥbūṭ: *al-Kadhdhāb wa-al-sāriq wa-al-bal'ūṭ*

By Rabbi Ḥai Belaḥsen: *Ohole ṣaddiqim* in Arabic (half), *Minḥat 'erev* in Arabic (half)

By David Chemama: *al-Amērīkān*

By the journalist Menaḥem Bel'īsh, who has now settled in Eretz Yisrael: *Qiṣṣat ispāniā wi-yrushalayim aw ibn 'ezra wa-bint r. yehuda ha-levi*, which was published as a feuilleton of seventy episodes in the journal *Qol yisrael*

By Ḥayyim Zarqā: *al-Lord jōzēf*

By Moshe Riāḥī: *al-Avoqāt ghiyūm*, *al-Arba'a aṣḥāb*

By Ḥayyim Bshīrī: *'Alī al-baghdādī*

By Yiṣḥaq Berebbi: *Rāshu a'lā min grāna*

By Edouard Chemama: *al-'Ishq al-khafīf*

By Abraham Castro: *Mistēre pārīz* (quarter)

By Nino Flāḥ: *Mistēre pārīz* (quarter)
By Shelomo Baron: *Yūsef al-ṣiddīq* in verse
By Mordekhai Luīzādā: *Lel shimmurim* in Arabic (half)
By Frājī Fittūsī: *'Īsā wa-al-jamjama*
By Abraham Ṭayyib: *Haggadat purim bi-al-taṣāwir*
By Benini Chemama: *Malzūmāt 'awj al-waqt wa-sūq pārīs*
By Yosef Elmāleḥ: *Arshīr ibn al-malik yūzdār*

We have likewise learned that Mr. Abraham Ṣabbān, of whom we told at the beginning of this collection, is he who translated the stories of *'Alf layla w-layla*, which also have become very popular, even though the printing has not been completed. Our glorious government, which recognized the insights and the fine leadership of this gentlemen, appointed him Elder of the Jews[102] in Tunis and gave him the task of collecting taxes and recently awarded him the title of Honorary Officer.

So, our dear brothers and our fellow writers and journalists, we declare to you that after all these clarifications, explanations, and information, we cannot boast that we have achieved the pinnacle of perfection, because perhaps such a thing is beyond reach. And we shall say, No! A thousand times, No! For every man is subject to error and forgetfulness, and there is no one who does not err, except the Maker, may His name be praised. Therefore, it is possible that we have erred in several matters in this book, and several names of writers of essays and stories have been interchanged. If indeed this has happened, we beg forgiveness from the possessors of kindness.

And peace is the seal.
Daniel Ḥagège
The book was completed on February 10, 1939.

Important Notice

There are people who have commented on the section we published concerning the journalist Mr. Makhlūf Najjār.[103] To them the matter of eighty books we mentioned seems excessive. To those simple folk who read and do not understand, and to the wise who err and do not know, we reconfirm once more before them that the list of eighty works is composed of essays and translations, and those whose rights he holds, and those which without the devotion and diligence of the journalist Makhlūf Najjār would not have been published for the readers of Tunisia and the other countries. And now, after this clear explanation, whoever has a stone can cast it in the well.[104]

Daniel Ḥagège

Appendix 1

Judeo-Arabic Journals and Other Periodicals

The following list of journals and other periodicals in Judeo-Arabic has been compiled from Ḥagège's *Circulation of Tunisian Judeo-Arabic Books* compared to Attal (2007).

TITLE IN ARABIC[a]	TRANSLATION	FOUNDERS, OWNERS, OR WRITERS
Al Akhbār [1180]	The News	Mas'ūd M'ārek, Moshe Katorza
Akhbār al-'ālam [1181]	World News	Edouard Sitrūk, Meir Khushkhāsh, Ḥai Bel'īsh
al-'Alam [1231]	The Standard	Yosef Guez
Al Anwār[b]	Flowers	Ṣemaḥ Halevi
Anwār tūnis[b]	Flowers of Tunis	Daniel Ḥagège
al-Badr al-kāmil[b]	The Full Crescent	Shalom Flāḥ
al-Barq [1190]	Lightening	Ṣemaḥ Halevi
al-Bustān [1189]	The Garden	Mas'ūd M'ārek, Ya'aqov Chemla, Shalom Flāḥ
al-Ḍaww [1243]	The Light	Yosef Bījāwī, Eliyahu Ḥasid, Michel Uzan
al-Egalité[b]	Equality	Daniel Ḥagège
Ereṣ ha-ṣvi [1356]	The Beloved Land	Shalom Flāḥ

Fāḍiḥ al-asrār [1235]	Revealer of Secrets	Shalom Flāḥ, Yosef Cohen Ganūna, Yosef Najjār
al-Fajr [1237]	The Dawn	Yaʿaqov Chemla, Yosef Bījāwī, Meir Khushkhāsh, Frājī Naqqāsh, Michel Uzan, Abraham Uzan
al-Firdaws[b]	Orchard	Ṣemaḥ Halevi
al-Fonograf [1238]	The Phonograph	Ṣemaḥ Halevi
al-Ḥakīm ghabyūn [1201]	Gebioun the Wise	Yosef Bījāwī
al-Ḥaqīqa [1205]	Truth	Masʿūd Mʿārek, Yaʿaqov Chemla
al-Ḥaqq [1204]	Truth	Meir Khushkhāsh, Ṣemaḥ Halevi, Shalom Flāḥ
Ḥayāt al-ḍaḥk [1198]	Life of Laughter	Yiṣḥaq Berebbi, Edouard Sitrūk, Michel Uzan
Ḥayāt al-janna [1197]	Life of the Garden of Eden	Daniel Ḥagège, Yosef Luīzāda, David Chemama
Ḥiss al-khalq [1220]	The Voice of the People	Meir Khushkhāsh, Felix Būkhobza
Ḥiss tūnis [1203]	The Voice of Tunis	Michel Uzan
al-Ḥurriyya [1206]	Freedom	Shalom Flāḥ, Yosef Cohen Ganūna, Ḥai Sitrūk, Yaʿaqov Chemla
al-Ḥurriyya [1207]	Freedom	Mordekhai Smādja, Shemu'el Ṣarfati, Abraham Ṣabbān, Yaʿaqov Chemla, Meir Khushkhāsh
al-Ikhāwa [1179]	Fraternity	Ṣemaḥ Halevi, Michel Uzan

al-Insāniyya [1183]	Humanity	Michel and Yosef Uzan
al-Intishār [1184]	Circulation	Makhlūf Najjār, Yosef Bījāwī
al-Istiwā [1185]	Equality	Naḥum Uzan, Yosef Bījāwī, Ya'aqov Chemla, Meir Khushkhāsh, Michel Uzan
al-Ittiḥād [1186]	Unity	Shalom Flāḥ
al-Ittiḥād [1187]	Unity	Menaḥem Bel'īsh
al-Jabbār al-tūnisī[b]	The Tunisian Hero	Meir and Ya'aqov Giurno
Jadwal ṣiyyon [1322]	Calendar of Zion	Ḥai Bel'īsh
al-Janān [1191]	The Garden	Ṣemaḥ Halevi
Janān al-faraḥ [694]	Pleasure Garden	Frājī Naqqāsh
al-Jarīda [1193]	The Journal	Yosef Bījāwī, Michel Uzan
Jūrnāl haggin [480]	Journal of Lamentations (9 of Av)	Ṣemaḥ Halevi
Jūrnāl pessaḥ [481]	Passover Journal	Ṣemaḥ Halevi
Kashshāf al-asrār [1209]	Revealer of Secrets	Yosef Bījāwī, Abraham Khushkhāsh, Michel Uzan
al-Kātib[b]	The Writer	Ṣemaḥ Halevi
Khillaṭ-millaṭ [1210]	Stir and Mix	Ya'aqov Ha-Cohen, Ḥai Bel'īsh
al-Mariṣṭān [456]	The Madhouse	Ḥai Sitrūk
Ha-Mevasser [1212]	The Herald	Eli'ezer Farḥi
al-Mubashshir [1214]	Herald	Eli'ezer Farḥi
Mubashshir al-ḥaqq[b]	Herald of Truth	Ṣemaḥ Halevi
al-Mughannī[b]	The Singer	Meir Cohen, Shelomo Laḥmi

al-Muḥayyar [1217]	The Perplexed	Ṣemaḥ Halevi
al-Mukhabbir al-tūnisī[b]	The Tunisian Herald	Eliyahu Guez, Frājī Naqqāsh, Michel Uzan, Ḥai Belʿīsh, Daniel Ḥagège
Munawwir al-ḥaqq [1218]	Illuminator of Truth	Shalom Flāḥ
Musharriḥ al-aṣdār [1219]	Cheerer of Hearts	Yiṣḥaq Tammām, Yaʿaqov Chemla
al-Mutarjim [1220]	The Translator	Shalom Flāḥ
al-Najma [1222]	The Star	Ṣemaḥ Halevi
al-Najma [1223]	The Star	Makhlūf Najjār, Leon Ṭūviāna, Felix Bījāwī, Daniel Ḥagège, Michel Uzan
al-Najma al-waḥīda[b]	The Unique Star	Makhlūf Najjār, Daniel Ḥagège
Najmat al-Sāḥel (*al-Najma al-sāḥiliyya*) [1224]	The Coast Star	Najjār Makhlūf, Leon Ṭūviāna, Shalom Flāḥ
Nāṣir al-muḥayyarīn [1221]	Supporter of the Perplexed	Ṣemaḥ Halevi, Yaʿaqov Ha-Cohen
al-Nasr [1228]	The Eagle	Eliʿezer Farḥi, Ḥai Belʿīsh, A. Zarqā
al-Naṣra [1230]	Victory	Yaʿaqov Ha-Cohen
al-Niḥla [1226]	Opinion	Ben Amittai [Masʿūd Mʿārek], Abraham Bismūṭ
al-Niḥla [1227]	Opinion	Meir Khushkhāsh (Koskas), David Hagège
al-Nuzha al-tūnisiyya [1225]	Tunisian Pastime	Daniel Ḥagège

Qol siyyon [1245]	The Voice of Zion	Felix Barānes, Victor Khushkhāsh, Yosef Bījāwī, Yeshuʿa Sitrūk
Qol yisrael [1244]	The Voice of Israel	Menaḥem Belʿīsh, Eliyahu Levi al-Sūlīmānī
al-Ṣabāḥ [1240]	The Morning	Yaʿaqov Ha-Cohen, Masʿūd Mʿārek, Ṣemaḥ Halevi, Yosef Bījāwī, Meir Khushkhāsh, Frājī Naqqāsh, Michel Uzan, Daniel Ḥagège
Ṣadā al-mahdiyyah [1242]	Mahdiyya Echo	Natan Djerbī
al-Shams [1246]	Sun	Shalom Gueta, Eliyyahu Sasson, Abraham Ginisti, Yaʿaqov Ha-Cohen, Daniel Ḥagège
al-Shams [1247]	Sun	Yaʿaqov Ha-Cohen
al-Tamaddun [1251]	Progress	Shelomo Chemama, Yosef Bījāwī, Yaʿaqov Chemla, Daniel Ḥagège
al-Tawārīkh al-israʾīliyya [463]	History of the Jews	Shalom Flāḥ
al-Telegraf [1250]	The Telegraph	Masʿūd Mʿārek, Yosef Cohen Ganūna
al-Tijāra al-tūnisiyya [1248]	Tunisian Trade	Yosef Bījāwī, Yosef Uzan
al-Usbūʿ al-yahūdī	The Jewish Week (see *al-Yahūdī*)	
al-Waṭan [1194]	Homeland	Yosef Bījāwī, Yaʿaqov Chemla, Daniel Ḥagège, Michel Uzan
al-Yahūdī [1208]	The Jew	Yosef Bījāwī, Mordekhai Uzan, Michel Uzan, Daniel Ḥagège

al-Zaʿbal [1196]	The Entertainer	Eliyahu Belaḥsen, Victor Ṣabbān, Eliyahu Khriyyef, Yaʿaqov di Moshe Abrahami
al-Zamān [1195]	Times	Masʿūd Mʿārek, Abraham Ṣabbān, Moshe Siṭbon

Notes

a. The numbers after the titles refer to their numbers in Attal (2007).

b. Not included in Attal (2007).

Appendix 2

Judeo-Arabic Books

The following list of books in Judeo-Arabic has been compiled from Ḥagège's *Circulation of Tunisian Judeo-Arabic Books*, Attal (2007), and other sources.

TITLE IN ARABIC[a]	TRANSLATION	WRITER(S)
al-Ab al-ḍālim, ḥikāyat (497)	The Abuser Father	Makhlūf Najjār
ʿAbd allah al-barrī maʿa ʿabd allah al-baḥrī, ḥikāyat (648)	ʿAbd Allah the Land Man and ʿAbd Allah the Sailor Man	Makhlūf Najjār
Abū al-ḥasan maʿa shajarat al-durr, ḥikāyat (493)	Abū al-Ḥasan with the Abundance Tree	Makhlūf Najjār
Abūqīr wa-abūṣīr, ḥikāyat (494)	Abūqīr and Abūṣīr	Makhlūf Najjār
al-Aḥdab, ḥikāyat (499)	The Hunchback	Yosef Bījāwī
ʿĀhid al-bint, maʿase (750)	He Who Promised the Girl (Marriage)	Makhlūf Najjār
ʿAjīb wa-gharīb, ḥikāyat (649, 650)	Strange and Bizarre	Ḥai Ṣarfati
Alexandrūs mōqdōn, sīrat (767, 768)	Alexander of Macedon	Ḥai Sitrūk
Alf ḍaḥka wa-ḍaḥka, kitāb (688)	Thousand Laugh and Laugh	Makhlūf Najjār
ʿAlī al-baghdādī, ḥikāyat (651)	ʿAlī of Baghdad	Ḥayyim Bshīrī
ʿAlī bin bakkār maʿa shams al-nahār, ḥikāyat (652)	ʿAlī the Son of Bakkār and the (Girl) Day's Sun	Ṣiyyon Uzan

ʿAlī nūr al-dīn, ḥikāyat (653)	ʿAlī Nūr al-Dīn	Makhlūf Najjār
Amān al-nisā wa-khiyānathum, ḥikāyat (569)	Women's Confidence and Their Treachery	Masʿūd Mʿārek
al-Amērīkān (442)	The Americans	David Chemama
al-ʿAmm al-ghaddār[b]	The Treacherous Uncle	Daniel Ḥagège
Amthāl wa-ʿabāʾir (464)	Proverbs and Sayings	Shalom Flāḥ
al-ʿAnbara, ḥikāyat (557)	The Earring	Ṣemaḥ Halevi
al-Anīs al-jalīs maʿa al-zūj wuzarā, ḥikāyat (571)	The Companion Anīs and the Two Viziers	Makhlūf Najjār
Anīs al-wujūd, kitāb (691)	The Existence Companion	Eliʿezer Farḥi, David Chemama
al-ʿĀnqa, sīrat (769)	The Story of Phoenix	Eliʿezer Farḥi
ʿĀqibat al-baghy[b]	The Result of Adultery	Makhlūf Najjār
al-ʿArabiyyah[b]	The Arab (Girl?)	Ṣemaḥ Halevi
al-arbaʿa aṣḥāb, ḥikāyat (503, 504)	The Four Buddies	Moshe Riāḥī
ʿArḍūnī zūj ṣbāya, ghnāyat (977, 1036, 1167)	Two Young Girls Came Across with Me	Yaʿaqov Ha-Cohen
Arshīr ibn al-malik yūzdār, ḥikāyat (573, 574)	Arshīr, the Son of King Yuzdār	Yosef Elmāleḥ
al-ʿĀshiq al-ʿajīb, qiṣṣat (803)	The Wondrous Lover	Makhlūf Najjār
Athmār al-karāma, qiṣṣat (806, 870)	The Fruits of Benevolence	Masʿūd Mʿārek
al-Avoqāt ghiyūm, ḥikāyat (498)	The Lawyer Guilluame	Moshe Riāḥī
Avraham avinu, maʿase (724)	Abraham Our Forefather	Makhlūf Najjār
ʿAwāqib al-khaṭṭār[b]	The Consequences of the Solicitor	Daniel Ḥagège

ʿAwj al-waqt wa-sūq pārīs, malzūmat (1108)	The Distortion of (Our) Time and Paris's Market	Benīnī Chemama
al-Ayyām al-sābiqa, kitāb (685)	The Earlier Days	Makhlūf Najjār
Azaliyya	See *al-Malik sayf al-azal*	
Bā nissim al-takārlī, ḥikāyat (573, 576–81, 759)	Father Nissim, the Hashish Smoker	Ḥai Ṣarfati
al-Bahhālīn[b]	Rope Dancers	Daniel Ḥagège
al-Bakkūsha, ḥikāyat (507)	The Dumb (Woman)	Makhlūf Najjār
al-Balʿūt, qiṣṣat (508)	The Tale of the Boaster	Eliʿezer Farḥi
al-Bankir alfonse de lūjīk, ḥikāyat (505, 506)	The Banker Alfonse de Logique	Ḥai Sitrūk
Bayn ḥuyūṭ tūnis (474)	Between the Walls of Tunis	Michel Uzan
Ben khamriyya, ḥikāyat (585–88, 670)	Khamriyya's Son	Ḥai Ṣarfati
Ben koziva (476, 477)	Koziva's Son (Bar Kokhva)	Shalom Flāḥ
Bereshīt muʿarrab (1)	Translation of Genesis	Eliʿezer Farḥi
Berit ʿolam (75)	Eternal Covenant (laws of circumcision)	Ṣemaḥ Halevi
Bet ha-levi (74)	The House of Levi (laws of ritual slaughter)	Ṣemaḥ Halevi
Bet pereṣ, maʿase (734–736)	The House of Pereṣ	Makhlūf Najjār
Bint al-dallāl wa-rizq al-ḥalāl[b]	The Auctioneer's Daughter and Honestly Achieved Livelihood	Daniel Ḥagège
Bint al-markīz, ḥikāyat (589)	The Marquis's Daughter	Yosef Bījāwī

al-Bint al-muḥḍiyya (466)	The Preferred Daughter	Ya'aqov Ha-Cohen
al-Bint friyye' nashrī, ḥikāyat (510, 511)	The Girl (Whose Name Is) the Rose's Bud	Eli'ezer Farḥi
Bint ribbi yehuda ha-levi w-ribbi abraham ibn 'ezra, ḥikāyat (591, 906)	Rabbi Yehuda Ha-Levi's Daughter and Rabbi Ibn Ezra	Menaḥem Bel'īsh
al-Bniyya al-matlūfa, ḥikāyat (509, 835)	The Lost Girl	Daniel Ḥagège
Brīka u-brāmīno wa-malik 'amrūn[b]	Brīka and Brāmīno and King 'Amrūn	Ḥai Bel'īsh
Budūr bint al-jawharī, ḥikāyat (582, 583)	Budūr the Daughter of al-Jawharī	Makhlūf Najjār
Bustenai, ma'ase (34, 731–33)	Bustenai	Makhlūf Najjār
B'ūth al-ṣīniyya (184)	The Sending of the Tray	Ya'aqov Ha-Cohen
Charlot, ḥikāyat (671, 831, 908)	Charlotte	Makhlūf Najjār
al-Cunti di monte cristo (451, 452, 679, 879, 1321)	*The Count of Monte Cristo* by Alexandre Dumas	Ya'aqov Chemla
Dalīla al-muḥtāla, ḥikāyat (596, 597)	Cunning Dalīla	Ḥai Ṣarfati
Dans (836)	Impurity	(unknown)
David ve-Goliath[b]	David and Goliath	Makhlūf Najjār
Ḍulm al-'ibād	Mistreatment of Human Beings	Mas'ūd M'ārek
Edison, ma'ase (725)	Edison	Makhlūf Najjār
Eldad al-dānī, ma'ase (726)	Eldad Ha-Dani	Makhlūf Najjār
Ester al-jamīla, qiṣṣat (469, 805, 868)	Esther the Beauty	Mas'ūd M'ārek
Ester ha-malka[b]	Queen Esther	Makhlūf Najjār
'Et li-vkot (86)	Time for Weeping (Arabic translation of the haftarah for 9 of Av)	Ṣemaḥ Halevi

Fadlekāt jūḥā al-kubrā (787)	The Great (Collection of) Juḥa Jokes	Makhlūf Najjār
Far' al-'anbar fī jabal al-dhahab, kharrāfat (683)	The Ambar's Branch in the Golden Mountain	Ṣemaḥ Halevi
Far' al-diāmanṭ (662)	The Diamond's Branch	Ṣemaḥ Halevi
Farā'iḍ al-qulūb[b]	Duties of the Hearts (Tunisian Judeo-Arabic translation of Baḥya ibn Paqūda's book)	Ḥai Sitrūk
al-Fāris al-maḥrūm[b]	The Deprived Cavalier	Ya'aqov Ha-Cohen
Fawz al-ḥabīb[b]	The Beloved's Success	Daniel Ḥagège
Firqat al-ḥayā[c]	Departure of Life	Ḥai Bel'īsh
Flōr dāryān, ḥikāyat (658–60)[d]	The Flowers of Ariana	Ḥai Sitrūk
Flōr māria wa-sāra (894)[e]	The Flower of Maria and Sara	Ṣemaḥ Halevi
La Georgienne (French)	*La Georgienne* (Of Georgia)	Makhlūf Najjār
Gazbar bet ha-ḥayyim, ḥikāyat (594)	The Cemetery's Treasurer	Eli'ezer Farḥi
Geza' David, ma'ase (737, 738)	David's Trunk	Makhlūf Najjār
Ghadrat al-ẓālim wa-ḥasrat al-sālim[b]	The Exploiter's Betrayal and the Decent's Disaster	Ṣemaḥ Halevi
Ghānim ibn ayyūb, ḥikāyat (592, 593)	Ghānim, the Son of Ayyūb	Makhlūf Najjār
Ghawāmiḍ barr al-yaman (740)	The Mysteries of the Land of Yemen	Makhlūf Najjār
Ghawāmiḍ lundrā wa-asrārhā (875)	The Mysteries of London and Its Secrets	Ya'aqov Ha-Cohen
Ghīrat barboy[b]	The Envy of Barboy	Makhlūf Najjār
Ghuṣn al-bān, ḥikāyat (877)	The Ban Tree	Ṣemaḥ Halevi

Goralot aḥitofel	See *Qrā'āt Aḥitofel*	
Ghzālat al-aḥbāb[b]	The Buddis' Doe	Ṣemaḥ Halevi
al-Ḥabīb al-awwal (841)	The First Lover	Daniel Ḥagège
Ḥabīb wald al-sulṭān, ḥikāyat (610)	Ḥabīb, the Sultan's Son	Ṣemaḥ Halevi
Ḥadīth al-ḥayawān, kitāb (696)	*The Talk of the Animals* (translation of Jean de La Fontaine's book)	Makhlūf Najjār
Haggadat purim bi-al-taṣāwir (568)	The Purim Haggadah in Pictures	Ṣemaḥ Halevi, Abraham Ṭayyib
al-Hajjāla al-ṣghīra wa-al-'āzib fī ḥīra, ḥikāyat (837)	The Young Widow and the Perplexed Bachelor	Daniel Ḥagège
al-Ḥakīm al-ṭayyār	The Flying Judge	Makhlūf Najjār
al-Ḥakīm simanof[b]	Judge Simanof	Daniel Ḥagège
al-Ḥarb fī ūrōppā, ghnāyat (941)	The War in Europe	Michel Uzan
Ḥasan al-khillī', ḥikāyat (615)	Stupid Ḥasan	Ḥai Ṣarfati
Haman, malzūmat[b]	The *Malzūma* of Haman	Ṣemaḥ Halevi
Ḥamīda bin 'uthmān, ḥikāyat (614)	Ḥamīda, the Son of 'Uthmān	Ṣemaḥ Halevi
al-Ḥammāl wa-al-ghassāl wa-al-takārlī	The Porter, the Washer, and the Hashish Smoker	Y. Māmō
Ḥanukka, ma'ase[b]	Hanukkah	Michel Uzan
Hārūn al-rashīd ma'a khalīfa al-ṣayyād, ḥikāyat (602–604)	Hārūn al-Rashīd and Khalīfa the Fisherman	Ḥai Ṣarfati
Hārūn al-Rashīd ma'a muḥammad al-Jawharī, ḥikāyat (605)	Hārūn al-Rashīd and Muḥammad al-Jawharī	Makhlūf Najjār
Hārūn al-Rashīd wa-al-aḥdab, ḥikāyat (599–601)	Hārūn al-Rashīd and the Hunchback	Ḥai Ṣarfati
al-Ḥasaka wa-al-sab'a banāt, ḥikāyat (605)	The Oil Lamp and the Seven Daughters	Ḥai Ṣarfati

Ḥasde avot (24, 26, 28)	Favors of the Fathers (Arabic translation of *Pirqe Avot*)	Ṣiyyon Uzan
Ḥaṣlat kāmil al-awṣāf (676,677)	Embarrassment of He Who Has Perfect Qualities	Eliʿezer Farḥi
al-Ḥaṭṭāb wa-bint al-sulṭān, ḥikāyat (519, 520)	The Woodchopper and the Sultan's Daughter	(unknown)
Ḥayāt al-nufūs, ḥikāyat (612)	The Soul's Life	Ḥai Ṣarfati
Ḥayāt shelomo ha-melekh (490)	The Life of King Solomon	Makhlūf Najjār
Ḥayya bint al-shammāsh, ḥikāyat (613, 876)	Ḥayya the Beadle's Daughter	Masʿūd Mʿārek
Ḥayāt bnādam (489)	The Human Being's Life	Ḥai Belʿīsh
al-Ḥīla wa-al-ʿishq (459, 460)	Trickery and Lust	Yaʿaqov Chemla
al-Ḥīla wa-al-sulūk fī ʿishq al-mulūk[b]	Trickery and Behaving with the King's Lust	Yaʿaqov Ha-Cohen
al-Ḥubb wa-al-intiqām[b]	Love and Vengeance	Daniel Ḥagège
al-Ḥubb wa-al-waṭan, ḥikāyat (518, 687, 839)	Love and Homeland (translation of *Ahavat zion* by Abraham Mapu)	Masʿūd Mʿārek
ibn ʿezra wa-bint ribbi yehuda ha-levi	See *Bint ribbi yehuda ha-levi w-ribbi abraham Ibn ʿezra*	
Ibrāhīm wa-Jamīla, ḥikāyat (495)	Ibrāhīm and Jamīla	Makhlūf Najjār
ʿIḍḥak yā ḍhū al-ʿīn, qiṣṣat (820, 821)	Laugh, O Eyesight	Eliʿezer Farḥi
al-Iḥtiyāl fī taḥṣīl al-māl[b]	Deception for the Sake of Achieving Fortune	Yaʿaqov Ha-Cohen

ʿIlm al-falak (1379)	The Science of Orbit (translation of *Reʾashim u-reʿamim* by Shelomo Azard)	Yosef Bījāwī
al-ʿIlm wa-al-amān, ḥikāyat (556)	Enlightenment and Confidence	Shalom Flāḥ
al-Intiqām li-bulūg al-marām, ḥikāyat (501)	Punishment to Get an Objective	Ḥai Cohen
al-ktāyib al-barbariyya al tūnisiyya	The Circulation of Tunisian Judeo-Arabic Books	Daniel Ḥagège
Irghām al-gharām[b]	Coercion of Love	Yaʿaqov Ha-Cohen
ʿĪsā wa-al-jamjama, qiṣṣat (827)	Jesus and the Skull	Frājī Fittūsī
ʿIshq al-jamāl, ḥikāyat (468, 866)	Lust of Beauty	Daniel Ḥagège
al-ʿIshq wa-al-ḥubb mā fīhim ṭibb, ḥikāyat (559, 560)	There Is No Remedy in Lust and Love	Daniel Ḥagège
ʿIshq wa-hajrān wa-mukhālafat al-adyān (893)	Lust and Abandonment and Conversion	Yaʿaqov Chemla
Isidor lavoranti, ḥikāyat (496)	Isidor Lavoranti	Ṣemaḥ Halevi
Ispāniā vi-yrushalayim	See *Bint ribbi yehuda ha-levi*	
Jabal al-sūd (478, 873)	The Black Mountain	Yaʿaqov Ha-Cohen
Jadwal muʾabbad (1333)	Eternal Calendar	Shalom Flāḥ
al-Jahala al-mudʿiyyin bi-al-ʿilm[b]	The Ignorants Who Seem to Be Scholars	Makhlūf Najjār
Jamāʿat al-surrāq[b]	The Burglars' Band	Makhlūf Najjār
Janān al-zahw (479)	Garden of Entertainment	Masʿūd Mʿārek
Jāsim al-istanbūlī[b]	Jāsim of Istanbul	Y. Māmō
Jināḥ al-muthābbibīn[b]	The Wing of the Beloveds	Daniel Ḥagège
Jūlī bint al-milord, ḥikāyat (590)	Julie, Milord's Daughter	Ṣemaḥ Halevi

al-Kadhdhāb wa-al-sāriq wa-al-balʿūṭ[b]	The Liar, the Thief, and the Deceptions	Yaʿaqov Abīḥbūṭ
Kāmil effendi[b]	Kāmil Effendi	Makhlūf Najjār
Kanz al-wazīr, ḥikāyat (620)	The Vizier's Treasure	Eliʿezer Farḥi
Karīm al-dahrīn[b]	The Most Precious of the Worlds	Y. Māmō
Kasb al-māl wa-bulūgh al-'āmāl, ḥikāyat (621, 881)	Gaining Fortune and Realizing Hopes	Daniel Ḥagège
al-Kasb al-mazrūb, ḥikāyat (528)	The Infected Profit	Masʿūd Mʿārek
al-Kasb yajlib (453)	Profit Pulls	Yosef Bījāwī
al-Khaddām al-ḥarīṣ (848)	The Industrious Servant	Daniel Ḥagège
Khalāṣ al-jamīla min al-khaḍʿ wa-al-ḥīla[b]	The Rescue of the Beauty from Submissiveness and Trickery	Ṣemaḥ Halevi
Kharāb Messina, ḥikāyat (623)	The Destruction of Messina	Makhlūf Najjār
Kharrāfat al-kadhb (682)	The Legend of Deceit	Ṣemaḥ Halevi
al-Kharūf, ḥikāyat (530, 531)	The Lamb	Makhlūf Najjār
al-Khayr bi-al-khayr (850)	The Best in Exchange of the Best	Ṣemaḥ Halevi
al-Khāyūṭ al-faqīr, ḥikāyat (526)	The Poor Porcelain's Mender	Yosef Bījāwī
al-Khāyūṭ al-muṣaṭṭak, ḥikāyat (524)	The Stupid Porcelain's Mender	Yosef Bījāwī
al-Khāyūṭ, ḥikāyat (525)	The Porcelain's Mender	Ṣemaḥ Halevi
Khlāʿat purim (681)	Purim's Licentiousness	Ṣemaḥ Halevi
Khṣā'il al-nemmīla, ḥikāyat (622)	The Virtues of the Ants	Yosef Bījāwī
Khṣā'il jūḥā, kitāb (699)	The Virtues of Jūḥā	Masʿūd Mʿārek

Khṣūmat al-ma'lūf wa-al-maṣrī, qinat (289)[f]	The Quarrel Between the *Ma'lūf* and the Egyptian	Ya'aqov Ha-Cohen
Khṣūmat Pessaḥ wa-al-Sukkah (289)	The Quarrel Between Passover and Sukkot	Ya'aqov Ha-Cohen
Khzānat al-gharām (680, 1072–1076)	Love Treasure	Ṣemaḥ Halevi
Kīd al-nīsā al-'aẓīma, ḥikāyat (618)	The Intrigues of the High-Ranked Women	Makhlūf Najjār
Kippur be-'aravi[b]	Yom Kippur Prayers in Arabic	Eliyyahu Ghānim
Kitāb snāwī (1347)	Yearbook (1918/19)	Makhlūf Najjār
Kull 'ṭammā' khāsir, ḥikāyat (619)	Every Miser Loses	Ḥai Sitrūk
Lā hurūb min al-maktūb, ḥikāyat (624, 882)	No Escape from What Is Written (Fate)	Ya'aqov Ha-Cohen, Daniel Ḥagège
Lahīb al-gharām fī 'āliyīn al-maqām (716)	The Fire of Love at the Highest Class	Ya'aqov Ha-Cohen
Lallat al-nisā, ḥikāyat (625 626)	The Women's Lady	Mas'ūd M'ārek
Lel shimmurim (126)	Guarded Night (liturgy for the first night of Passover)	Ṣemaḥ Halevi, Mordekhai Luīzādā
Līlat al-ghalṭa (798)	The Mistake Night	Ya'aqov Ha-Cohen
Lisān al-'āshiq (1086)	The Lover's Tongue	Ṣemaḥ Halevi
al-Liṣṣ al-sharīf (qātilat ṭiflahā), ḥikāyat (533 561, 562)	The Respected Thief (The Killer of Her Daughter)	Makhlūf Najjār
al-Lord jōzēf, ḥikāyat (532)	Lord Joseph	Ḥayyim Zarqā
Ma'ase ṣadqiqim (751)	Tales of the Just	Makhlūf Najjār
Ma'ase sha'ashu'im (781)	Pastimes	Eliyahu Guez
Ma'asiyyot fī shān ḥokhmat shelomo ha-melekh (755)	Tales About King Solomon's Wisdom	(unknown)

al-Maghdūr wa-ʿāqibat al-ghāddārīn, ḥikāyat (536, 537)	The Betrayed and the End of the Betrayers	(unknown)
Maḥāsin al-ṣadaf [b]	The Virtues of Concurrence	Makhlūf Najjār
Majnūn laylā, qiṣṣat (712)	Majnūn of Laylā	Makhlūf Najjār
Makārem al-akhlāq [b]	The Benevolent Human Beings	Yaʿaqov Ha-Cohen
al-Malik ʿamrūn, ḥikāyat (538)	King ʿAmrūn	Ḥai Belʿīsh
al-Malik sayf al-azal, sīrat (534, 763)	The King Eternity's Sword	Eliʿezer Farḥi
Malkat sheva maʿa she-lomo ha-melekh, ḥikāyat (637–639)	The Queen of Sheba and King Solomon	Makhlūf Najjār
Manāḍir al-tawārīkh al-yahūdiyya (1372)	Scenes of Jewish History	Makhlūf Najjār
Manām thābit (885)	A True Dream	(unknown)
al-Manām tafsīrhu, kitāb (1364)	The Dream and Its Meaning	Yosef Bījāwī
al-Mar'a	See *al-Mar'a al-khāʾina*	
al-Mar'a al-khāʾina (455)	The Treacherous Woman	Frājī Naqqāsh
al-Mar'a al-makhnūqa fī al-ti'atrū, ḥikāyat (539, 540)	The Strangled Woman in the Theater	Makhlūf Najjār
Maʿrūf al-iskhāfī (640)	Stupid Maʿrūf	Makhlūf Najjār
Masārib al-ḥayāh (756)	Paths of Life	Shalom Flāḥ
Maṣāyib al-maḥabba [b]	The Disasters of Love	Daniel Ḥagège
Mashaqqat al-barrī [b]	The Landman's Distress	Daniel Ḥagège
Menuḥat shalom [b]	Peaceful Rest (translation of Psalms)	Shelomo Zarqā
Minḥat ʿerev (81)	Evening's Offering (translation of the afternoon and evening services)	Ṣemaḥ Halevi, Ḥai Belaḥsen

Miqra meforash (1376)	The Bible Explained	Shalom Flāḥ
al-Mishḥāḥ wa-al-karīm[b]	The Miser and the Benevolent	Eli'ezer Farḥi
Mistēre pārīz (707, 886)	Judeo-Arabic translation of Sue Eugène's *Les Mystères de Paris*	Ḥai Sitrūk, Ṣemaḥ Halevi, Abraham Castro, Nino Flāḥ
Miyāt ḥikāya wa-ḥikāya (705, 706)	Hundred Story and a Story	Makhlūf Najjār
Moshe rabbenu, ma'ase (744, 745)	Moses Our Master	Makhlūf Najjār
Mrat al-sū, qiṣṣat (811)	The Wicked Woman	Makhlūf Najjār
Muḥammad al-'ajzān, ḥikāyat (636)	Lazy Muḥammad	Eliyahu Bījāwī[g]
Muḥammad al-asīr, ḥikāyat (627–629)	Prisoner Muḥammad	Ḥai Ṣarfati
Muḥammad al-dimashqī, ḥikāyat (630, 631, 759)	Muḥammad of Damascus	Ḥai Ṣarfati
Muḥammad al-kaslān, ḥikāyat (632, 633)	Lazy Muḥammad	Makhlūf Najjār
Muḥammad al-saṭṭā', ḥikāyat (634, 635)	Shining Muḥammad	Ḥai Ṣarfati
Muḥārabat al-dīn (704, 884)	Anti-Religion War	Mas'ūd M'ārek, Ṣemaḥ Halevi
al-Mujāhada fī sabīl al-ḥubb[b]	Exertions for the Sake of Love	Ya'aqov Ha-Cohen
Mukāfāt, al-af'āl[b]	The Reward of Deeds	Daniel Ḥagège
Murūrat al-tamaddun (887)	The Bitterness of Progress	Ḥai Sitrūk
Najāḥ al-muthābbibīn[b]	The Triumph of the Beloved (plural)	Daniel Ḥagège
Nākir al-jamīl[b]	Handsome Nākir	Makhlūf Najjār
al-Nasr al-aḥmar (457, 854)	The Red Eagle	Ya'aqov Ha-Cohen
Naṣrat al-ibnāt, ḥikāyat (644)	The Girls' Victory	Eli'ezer Farḥi

Nawāʾib al-ʿushshāq[b]	The Lovers' Calamities	Daniel Ḥagège
Nawbat al-ḥasīn (1135)	(Songs in) the Ḥasīn Mode	Abraham Uzan
Nāzlat drayfūs (888)	The Dreyfus Case	Yaʿaqov Ha-Cohen
Nes purim al-kabīr, maʿase (746)	The Great Miracle of Purim	Makhlūf Najjār
Nuwwār riāna	See *Flōr dāryān*	
Nuzhat al-qulūb, kitāb (708)	Pastime for Hearts	Ṣemaḥ Halevi
Nuzhat al-zamān (757, 758)	Pastime	Yaʿaqov Ha-Cohen
Nuzhat al-zamān, ta'līf[b]	Pastime	Ḥai Cohen
Ohole ṣaddiqim (778)	Tents of the Righteous	Ṣemaḥ Halevi, Ḥai Belaḥsen
Pessaḥ, maʿase (760)	Passover	Michel Uzan
Pirqe avot	See *Ḥasde Avot*	
Purim, maʿase[b]	Purim	Michel Uzan
Purim al-mabsūṭ wa-al-mazlūṭ wa-bi-al-bātin (791)	Happy Purim, the Penniless, and What Is in Between	Ḥai Sitrūk
Purim al-maʿshūq (790)	Beloved Purim	Ṣemaḥ Halevi
Purim jdīd[b]	New Purim	Ṣemaḥ Halevi
Qānūn al-dawla al-tūnisiyya (790)	The Constitution of the Tunisian State	Mordekhai Tapia, Bīshī Chemama, Eliyahu Elmāleḥ
Qamr al-zamān, ḥikāyat (674)	The Moon of the Time	Ḥai Ṣarfati
Qraʿāt aḥitofel (1358–1360, 1365)	*Goralot Aḥitofel* (Aḥithophel's Lots)	Shalom Bekāsh
Qurʿat al-atmār fī kashf al-iḍmār (829)	Lot of Dates for Revealing the Undisclosed	Makhlūf Najjār
al-Raḍīʿ al-wārith[b]	The Baby Inheritor	Daniel Ḥagège
Rāshu aʿlā min grāna[b]	His Head Is Higher than a Livornese	Yiṣḥaq Berebbi
al-Rbāya wa-al-adab (863)	Education and Etiquette	Yosef Bījāwī

Rīhān, sīrat (777)	Rīḥān	Ḥai Ṣarfati
Riyāqat al-nufūs, kitāb (714)	The Pleasure of Souls	Ṣemaḥ Halevi
Robinson crusoe, ḥikāyat (666, 667)	Judeo-Arabic translation of Daniel Defoe's *Robinson Crusoe*	Ḥai Sitrūk
Romeo w-juliet, ḥikāyat (666 667)	Judeo-Arabic translation of William Shakespeare's *Romeo and Juliet*	Makhlūf Najjār
Ruth, ma'ase[b]	Ruth	Michel Uzan
al-Sab'a wuzarā aw sindbār, ḥikāyat (543–545)	The Seven Viziers or Sindbar	Ḥai Ṣarfati
Sabab qatl al-barāmika, ḥikāya fī (656, 657)	The Cause of the Killing of the Barmakids	(unknown)
Sabab takwīn ḥarb ūrūppā	Causes of the Development of the European War	Daniel Ḥagège
al-Ṣābra al-mabkhūtha (859)	The Lucky Patient	Ṣemaḥ Halevi
Safa berura[b]	Eloquent Tongue (manual for Hebrew)	Shalom Flāḥ
Safa ṭiv'it[b]	Natural Tongue (manual for Hebrew)	Shalom Flāḥ
Ṣafāwat al-maḥabba (899)	The Purity of Love	Daniel Ḥagège
al-Ṣāḥib al-ghaddār, ḥikāyat (563, 862)	The Betraying Friend	Makhlūf Najjār
al-Ṣāḥib al-maghdūr, ḥikāyat (458)	The Betrayed Friend	Yosef Bījāwī
al-Ṣāḥib wa-nisf (730)	The Friend and a Half	Makhlūf Najjār
al-Sāḥir al-'ajīb[b]	The Wondrous Wizard	Makhlūf Najjār
Sakrat purim[b]	Purim's Drunkenness	Ṣemaḥ Halevi

al-Samsūniyya, ḥikāya (551, 856)	The Samsonite	Ḥai Cohen
Ṣāniʿ al-ḥajjām (812, 895)	The Barber's Apprentice	Daniel Ḥagège
Ṣanīʿ al-zamān fī al-ʿishq wa-al-amān[b]	The Trainee of Time in Lust and Confidence	Yaʿaqov Ha-Cohen
Ṣawt al-mughannī (1153–1168)	The Singer's Voice	Mordekhai Uzan
Ṣawt al-taghrīd[b]	The Voice of Cooing	Ṣemaḥ Halevi
Sayf al-mulūk wa-badīʿat al-jamāl (646, 647)	The King's Sword and the Beauty's Breathtaking	Ṣemaḥ Halevi
al-Ṣayyād al-maṣrī, ḥikāyat (564, 565)	The Egyptian Hunter	Ḥai Ṣarfati
al-Shābb al-ʿāshiq, ḥikāyat (567)	The Loving Youngster	Makhlūf Najjār
al-Shābb al-baghdādī, ḥikāyat (566)	The Youngster of Baghdad	Makhlūf Najjār
Sha'ul w-david, qiṣṣat (711, 904)	Saul and David	Makhlūf Najjār
Shavuaʿ ṭov bi-al-ʿarabī (97–100)	Good Week (Arabic translation of the Saturday night liturgy)	Ṣiyyon Uzan
Shavuʿot, maʿase (832)	Shavuot	Michel Uzan
Shaykh al-qaṭāṭīs, ḥikāyat (672 673)	The Cats' Chief	Ṣemaḥ Halevi
Shimshon, qiṣṣat[b]	Samson	Yaʿaqov Ha-Cohen
Shiʿure ha-ḥinnukh (1378)	Educational Lessons (manual for Hebrew)	Shalom Flāḥ
Shomer piv (1378)	He Who Keeps His Mouth (daily prayers and liturgy)	Eliʿezer Farḥi
al-ʿIshq al-khafīf[b]	Gentle Lust	Edouard Chemama
Sī ḥadba al-khabbāz, ḥikāyat (645)	Mr. Ḥadba the Baker	Ṣemaḥ Halevi
al-Ṣidk anjā, qiṣṣat (804 860)	Truth Saves More	Shalom Flāḥ

Ṣidq al-aṣḥāb fī al-awqāt al-ṣiʿāb, ḥikāyat (663, 897)	Friends' Amity During Hard Times	Daniel Ḥagège
Sindbād al-baḥrī, ḥikāyat (552, 553)	Sindbād the Sailor Man	Makhlūf Najjār
al-Sīrat malik sayf al-azal	See *al-Malik sayf al-azal*	
al-Sirriyya, ḥikāyat (554, 628)	The Sirriyya	Ṣemaḥ Halevi
al-Ṣiyyonism (1351, 1352)	Zionism	Alfred Valensi, Yaʿaqov Ha-Cohen, Yosef Brāmī
Snīn dāʾima (1373)	Lasting Years (liturgy for Rosh Hashanah and Yom Kippur)	Eliʿezer Farḥi
Ṣudūr al-aḥrār qubūr al-asrār, ḥikāyat (664, 896)	The Hearts of the Liberated are the Graves of Secrets	Yaʿaqov Chemla
al-Sulṭān brāhīm, ḥikāyat (546–550)	The Sultan Ibrāhīm	Ḥai Ṣarfati
Surūr al-ʿafw [b]	The Delight of Pardoning	Daniel Ḥagège
Tadgīz al-amūrī (761)	Sorcery of Love	Ṣemaḥ Halevi
Tafkīr al-manāmāt [b]	Remembering the Dreams	Eliʿezer Farḥi
al-Taggāz al-hassāb [b]	The Foreseeing Sorcerer	Makhlūf Najjār
al-Tājir ʿalī al-maṣrī, ḥikāyat (568)	The Merchant ʿAlī al-Maṣrī	Makhlūf Najjār
Taṣʿībāt al-aḥwāl wa-bulūgh al-ʾāmāl [b]	Hardness of (Life) Conditions and Realizing Hopes	Frājī Naqqāsh
Ṭbīb al-dār, kitāb (1366)	The Home Doctor	Makhlūf Najjār
al-Ṭbīb al-maghṣūb [b]	The Coerced Doctor	Makhlūf Najjār
Ṭbīb maskīn [b]	A Poor Doctor	Daniel Ḥagège
al-Ṭifla diāmanṭa, qiṣṣat (557)	The Young Girl Diamanṭa	Ṣemaḥ Halevi
al-Tījāniyya, sīrat (773)	The Crown	Ḥai Ṣarfati

al-Turjamān al-frānṣāwī bi-al-ʿarabī (1353)	The French Translator in Arabic (manual for French)	Makhlūf Najjār
ʿUqūbat al-fāsīq wa-naṣrat al-ʿāshiq (890)	The Punishment of the Licentious and the Lover's Victory	Frājī Naqqāsh
ʿUqūbat al-ghaddār (709, 710)	The Punishment of the Traitor	Ḥai Sitrūk
ʿUqūbat al-muḥtāl[b]	The Punishment of the Trickster	Daniel Ḥagège
Wa-kān fī ayyām ḥukm al-ḥākimīn[b]	Once upon a Time When the Judges Judged	Yosef Bījāwī
al-Ward fī al-akmām, ḥikāyat (513, 514, 522)	The Rose in the Sleeves	Ṣemaḥ Halevi
al-Waṭan wa-al-dīn, ḥikāyat (838)	Homeland and Religion	Yosef Bījāwī
al-Zīr abū laylā al-muhalhil, qiṣṣat (817)	The Wooer Abū Laylā al-Muhalhil	Ṣiyyon Uzan
Wudnīn haman (695)	Haman's Ears	Eliʿezer Farḥi
Yā mā aḥlā limmat al-ibnāt, ghnāyat (1163)	How Nice Is the Girl's Assemblance	Yaʿaqov Ha-Cohen
al-Yahūd fī ispānyā (450, 818, 847)	The Jews of Spain	Yaʿaqov Chemla
al-Yahūd fī cōrfū (449)	The Jews of Corfu	Ṣemaḥ Halevi
al-Yahūdī al-ḥāʾir, maʿase (727)	The Perplexed Jew	Makhlūf Najjār
Yehuda vi-yehudit, qiṣṣat[b]	Judah and Judith	Ḥai Belʿīsh
Yehudit al-shajīʿa[b]	Judith the Heroine	Makhlūf Najjār
Yūsef, qiṣṣat (224)	Joseph	Yaʿaqov Ha-Cohen
Yūsef al-marhūn, ḥikāyat (616)	Pawned Joseph	Ṣemaḥ Halevi
Yūsef al-ṣiddīq (ti'atro) (713)	Joseph the Just (theater) (play)	Makhlūf Najjār
Yūsef al-ṣiddīq, qiṣṣat (222)	Joseph the Just (in verse)	Shelomo Baron

Yūsef al-ṣiddīq ma'a zūlēkha (741, 742, 824–826)	Joseph the Just and Zūlēkha	Ḥai Ṣarfati
Zahw al-aṣḥāb (1049–1068)	The Friends' Entertainment	Mordekhai Uzan
Zawāj bi-al-maḥabba[b]	Getting Married with Love	Daniel Ḥagège
Zīn al-ḥimār, sīrat (774)	The Donkey's Prettiness	Ṣemaḥ Halevi
Zīn al-mawāṣif, ḥikāyat (607)	The Beauty of the Virtues	Makhlūf Najjār
Zīn al-tmām, sīrat (775)	The Perfect Beauty	Eli'ezer Farḥi
al-Zīna al-musrāra, ghnāyat (1017)	The Amusing Beauty	Ṣemaḥ Halevi
al-Zīna al-zīnawiyya, ḥikāyat (515, 516, 759)	The Beautiful Beauty	Yosef Bījāwī
Ziv̇he toda	Sacrifices of Gratitude (ritual slaughter)	Makhlūf Najjār
Zudār ibn 'umar, ḥikāyat (606)	Zudār, the Son of 'Umar	Yosef Bījāwī
Zuhrat al-falak wa-bint al-malik[b]	Zodiac's Venus and the King's Daughter	Ya'aqov Ha-Cohen
al-Zūj ṭrash[b]	The Deaf Couple	Makhlūf Najjār

Notes

a. The numbers after the titles refer to their numbers in Attal (2007).

b. Not included in Attal (2007).

c. Included in *Ḥayāt bnādam.*

d. As indicated by Vassel (1904: 77–78), the title on the face of the book is *Nuwwār riāna,* which is the Arabic translation of the French title on the title page of the book.

e. A mistake in Attal (2007): *wa-ṭara.*

f. Daniel Ḥagège defines it as a *malzūma.*

g. As stated on the title page; Ḥagège, however, ascribes it to Yosef Bījāwī.

Notes

Chapter 1

1. On the history of Judeo-Arabic, see Blau (1981) and Tobi (2010c).
2. On poems and *maqāmāt* written in Arabic by Jewish poets in the Middle Ages, see Stern (1963), Ratzahbi (1980; 1997), and Sadan (1996).
3. Moreh (1974; 1978: 60–68).
4. Vassel (1904); Ḥagège (1939); Attal (1980b; 1996; 2007).
5. Fraenkel (1982) discussed the Hebrew press in Djerba (about 600 entries, many of them Judeo-Arabic); and Sharabāni (1969) wrote on the Judeo-Arabic literature of the Jews of Iraq.
6. Avishur (1988; 1998); Chetrit (1980b; 1981; 1989; 1994); Ḥazan (1987); Ilan (1993; 1996); Saraf (1979; 1987); and Zafrani (1980).
7. For Judeo-Arabic publications printed in the Hebrew presses in the countries of Islam, see Attal and Harosh (1986/87) for Algiers; Marciano (1989) for Morocco; Harosh (1984) for Tripoli; and Ya'ari (1937/40) for India, Aden, Iraq, Syria, and Egypt.
8. See Y. Tobi (1991; 2008).
9. See Abitbol (1986), Attal (1980b), Chetrit (1990), Laskier (1991), and Stillman (1991).
10. See Chetrit (1986; 1991).
11. See Chapter 9.
12. See Cazès (1888: 149–58) and Hirschberg (1965, 2: 145–47, 306–12).
13. For a general review, see Ettinger (1981/86).
14. Attal (1980b; 2007).
15. Elmāleḥ (1946); Ḥazan (1984); Chetrit (1983; 1999: 317–94); Naḥum (1925).
16. Ya'ari (1932); Verses (1989: 43).
17. Attal (1975b).
18. On Shelomo Twena, see Avishur (2003).
19. On the Grāna community in Tunisia and its relations with the old established Jewish inhabitants, see Elmāleḥ (1928), Avrahami (1980), and Tsur (1986).
20. Attal (1975a); Marciano (1989: 39, 50, 53).
21. See Attal (1980b; 2007).
22. For a comprehensive list of the Judeo-Arabic publications in Tunis and Sousse, see Attal (2007).
23. Vajda (1978).

24. Abraham Laredo, *Dat yehudit* (Livorno, 1827). This book focuses on religious commandments of special relevance to women.
25. See Chapter 9.
26. See Chapter 8.
27. See Attal (1983).
28. See Attal (1996).
29. See Attal (1960).
30. For the objection of rabbis of Djerba to the passionate stories and the substitute they wished to disseminate instead among the Jewish communities, see Chapter 8.
31. Abraham, in the dialect of the Jewish Judeo-Arabic speakers of Tunis.
32. The Members' handkerchief refers to the collection of money in a handkerchief for the members of the Burial Society (*Ḥevra qaddisha*), nicknamed the Members by the Jews of Tunis.
33. Bertha, as pronounced by French speakers.
34. The right to make matzot was taken from the members of the community for religious reasons and given to a factory supervised by the Beth Din.
35. Making dishes kosher by immersion in boiling water.
36. The tanners street.
37. A porger cuts away the forbidden fat and veins in kosher meat.
38. The quarter of the old city where many Jews lived.
39. The nickname for Lag la-'Omer (the thirty-third day of the counting of the Omer) by the Jews of Tunis, after Rabbi Shimʿon Bar Yoḥai, who is celebrated on that day.
40. That is, the search for *ḥametz*, or leavened bread.
41. A small-pot coal-burning hearth for cooking or incense.
42. The incense burning is done by placing crystals of resinous perfumes on the coals.
43. Robert, as pronounced by French speakers.
44. A pet name for Yiṣḥaq (Isaac) by the Jews of Tunis.
45. According to Halakha, the seder participants lean to the left as they drink the cup of wine.
46. "Let me get drunk, Jew!" a Judeo-Arabic song commonly sung after the reading of the Haggadah. It is given in translation in Chapter 2.
47. On the second night of Passover it was customary to read the Haggadah with the *sharḥ*, its Judeo-Arabic translation.

Chapter 2

1. The Arabic poems of Frājī Shawwāṭ were published by Saraf (1984). One of the poems is in the *maṭrūz* structure, that is, a mix of Hebrew and Arabic verses. Noteworthy early sources for this structure are two laments for 9 Av written in the nineteenth century: (1) "Aḥnān alladhī lāzim nkūnū ḥazīnīn," in the book *Allon bakhut* by Rabbi Ḥayyim Ha-Cohen (Livorno, 1883: 44a–45a); and (2) "Ah nthạrr qalbī w-hājat nārhū," in the book *Qol bikhyi* by Rabbi Raḥamim

Būkhrīs (Livorno, 1894: 114). One poem, "Arsal yā wāḥid waḥdānī," was also copied in Yemeni manuscripts. See Tobi (1982: 331, no. 1114).

2. See, for example, the comments of Adādī (1976): "On the day of the Feast of Weeks it was customary to study reading the Ten Commandments, every commandment in the translation attributed to Yonatan ben 'Uzziel, and then the Arabic commentary . . . gathered from our Sages of blessed memory and from the *midrashim*. So it is in Tunis and Algeria: they study the Ten Commandments in the Arabic language. I recall that I saw that the first version of this Arabic is by R. Sa'adia Gaon, but each of these three cities had it in its dialect" (sec. 34.19: 127). Note that Zuareṣ and Ṭayyār, the editors of *Se'u zimra*, still saw fit to insert the "Ten Commandments with the translation of R. Sa'adia Gaon, of blessed memory, which it was customary to read on the day of the Feast of Weeks" (209–33). The late Rafael Ginnīsh of Jerusalem informed us that the Ten Commandments in Arabic translation was read not at the time of the reading of the Torah on the morning of 9 Av but in the afternoon, unconnected to the reading of the Torah. He likewise told us that it was customary in the synagogue to read the *piyyut* "Bar yoḥai" with its Arabic translation. This *piyyut* with its Arabic translation was indeed printed at the end of each of the two volumes of the book of Psalms *Nora tehillot* (including an Arabic rendering and the commentaries *Dumiyya tehilla* and *Qodesh hillulim*) (Djerba, 1925/26). So much for the Tripoli custom. For the reading of the Ten Commandments in Arabic translation in Djerba, see *Divre shalom* (Djerba, 1946: [4A]). As regards reciting Arabic lamentations on the eve of 9 Av in the Djerba custom, see the books mentioned in the previous note: *Allon bakhut* (44–66) and *Qol bikhyi* (116–24).
3. It was apparently the custom to recite poems during the reading of the Song of the Sea just before the verse *Mi kamokha*. This was also the case with the poem *Mi kamokha* by Yehuda Halevi, which was said on Shabbat Zakhor before Purim. See Adādī (1976): "On Sabbath of *Zakhor*, with the recital of *Mi kamokha*, their custom was to say it in the Song of Sea, as it was with the other poems in the prayer-books and with the poems" (sec. 34.17: 125). On the poems of the *Mi kamokha* genre, see Hazan and Ḥitin (2012). On the custom of the Jews of Morocco saying *Mi kamokha*, see also Bar-Tiqva (1988: 60). The custom of composing *Mi kamokha piyyutim* in Judeo-Arabic as songs of thanksgiving for deliverance from harsh decrees continued to World War II. These poems were published by Saraf (1988: 7–51).
4. See Hirschberg (1965: 2: 178–79).
5. On Rabbi Abraham Khalfōn, see Saraf (1986).
6. Hirschberg (1965: 2: 180).
7. Ha-Cohen (1979: 101–7, 199–200, 270); Elmāleḥ (1929: 127–34); Slouschz (1943: 47–58); Hirschberg (1965: 179–83); Zuareṣ et al. (1960: 42–52, 69). Slouschz is almost the only modern scholar who had before him not only Khalfōn's poem *Mi kamokha* but also its other sources. Slouschz also uses European sources to describe the events, namely, accounts by foreign consuls and travelers.

8. The poem was recorded by Davidson (1923: א, 2247). Slouschz (1943: 57) writes that the poem was first printed by the author in Livorno in 1800. I do not know which book he refers to. In any event, it seems that that publication, which has not come down to us, is alluded to by Avraham Adādī in his introduction to the poem published by Ya'aqov Raccāḥ in his *Qeshurim le-ya'aqov* (Livorno, 1858): "This has been in print for several years" (5). Slouschz also had the original manuscript of the author and his introduction to the poem, which is not found anywhere else. Slouschz published it in 1943 (on p. 57). In the anthologies of prayers and poems, the poem was regularly printed after the poem of the *Mi kamokha* genre "Avo bi-gvurot adonai elohim" by Rabbi Shabbetai Ṭayyār, which relates the miracle of Purim al-Sharīf. See, for example, Y. Raccāḥ (1878: 2–11) and also Y. Raccāḥ (1963: 20–32); *Derekh ha-ḥayyim* (Tripoli, 1923: 13–18); and Zuareṣ and Ṭayyār (1972: 191–206). Both poems were published in their entirety by Elmāleḥ (1929) and Zuareṣ et al. (1960).
9. Friedberg (1952: 2: 598, no. 1671) calls the book *Mayim ḥayyim.*
10. On Rabbi Ḥai Mīmūn, see Zuareṣ et al. (1960: 70). Zuareṣ gives his dates as 1800–1847, but his son Ḥai Mīmūn notes in his preface to *Mayim ḥayyim* (2a) that his father died in 1847 at the age of 38. Hence, the father's year of birth would be about 1809. Zuareṣ mentions the two books and erroneously attributes them to Ya'aqov Mīmūn; nor is Zuareṣ precise in his description of them: "*Mayim ḥayyim* is about the kabbalah, *Derekh ḥayyim* expounds the Torah." He does not mention the poem by Isaac Luzon either. Perhaps he wrote from hearsay only. See later discussion on the content of the two compositions and their authors. On Ḥai Mīmūn (1847–1885), see Zuareṣ et al. (1960: 72–73).
11. Rabbi Ḥ. Y. D. Azulai was revered by the rabbis of Tripoli. On his ties with Rabbi Abraham Khalfōn since 1781, see Benayahu (1959b: 178–80). *Yosef tehillot* is a commentary by Azulai on the book of Psalms, first published in his lifetime in Livorno in 1801. On p. 138b appears *Bet menuḥa*, which is the service alluded to by Ḥai Mīmūn and Ya'aqov Raccāḥ. This service was published as a separate book, *Bet menuḥa*, in Livorno in 1802. See Benayahu (1959a: 221). Benayahu did not include *Derekh ha-ḥayyim* among the list of prayer books according to the compilations of Azulai that he published (1959a: 253–58). It is interesting that Ya'aqov Mīmūn and Ya'aqov Raccāḥ do not mention *Bet menuḥa*, in which the service is set forth in its entirety, but they do mention *Yosef tehillot*, in which only references to biblical chapters from the rabbinic literature and from the *Zohar* are given.
12. On Ya'aqov Raccāḥ (1800–1886), see Zuareṣ et al. (1960: 73–74).
13. See, for example, the booklet *19–29 Tevet, A Booklet Devoted to the Memorial Days of Our Teachers and Our Masters the Great Ribbi Moshe Al-Srūsī, of Blessed Memory . . . R. Ḥwāto Luzon, of Blessed Memory, Ten Years After He Left Us (29 Tevet 1954)* (Tel Aviv, 1954).
14. G. Raccāḥ (1945); *The Rabbis of Libya*, in Zuareṣ et al. (1960: 65–91).

15. In general, we were able to decipher the amended text; there were two exceptions: lines 3 and 142. Nor could Tripoli natives help us here.
16. The forces of ʿAlī Burghul that besieged the city were few, but he managed to trick the citizens into believing that they were many, so the city fell without a fight.
17. Aḥmad and Yūsuf, the sons of the previous ruler ʿAlī Pāshā Kārāmanlī.
18. ʿAlī Burghul.
19. Ḥai Dodon was a Tunisian Jew who made firearms and ammunition.
20. ʿAlī Burghul suspected Ḥai Dodon of supporting the sons of the previous ruler, Aḥmad and Yūsuf, after hearing false information about him.
21. An English source reports that Ḥai Dodon's legs were bound to a sack filled with lead to increase his agony. See Hirschberg (1965: 2: 181).
22. Hirschberg (1965: 2: 180n): "A gold coin then legal tender in the Maghreb and Egypt. It was worth about as much as a Venetian ducat or a florentini."
23. ʿAlī Burghul wished to abduct Jewish children and bring them up as Muslims, in the manner of the Mamluks. Rabbi Khalfōn also writes in *Se'u zimra*: "Wicked men continued in their wickedness / Babes of our master's house they tore from their Torah / and took them to offer their services" (Zuareṣ and Ṭayyār, 1972: 201).
24. Physical labor for the regime.
25. Joseph Ha-Cohen was a Jew who wished to restore Aḥmad and Yūsuf, the sons of the previous ruler, to power.
26. A Muslim of European extraction.
27. David Khalfōn (the son of Rabbi Khalfōn and the president of the community) and Joseph Ha-Cohen and perhaps some others were partners in the deed.
28. For ʿAlī Burghul.
29. In Tunisia.
30. Ḥamūda Pāshā, the Bey of Tunisia, who did not view ʿAlī Burghul's expansion favorably.
31. The community's president.
32. From the forces of ʿAlī Burghul.
33. A coastal town about 50 miles west of Tripoli.
34. In the city.
35. A neighborhood in Tripoli.
36. Instead of Rabbi Abraham Khalfōn.
37. On Rabbi Shelomo ben Shalom Zarqā, see B. R. Cohen (1986: 165).
38. Malachi 3:23.
39. On the Ḥayyūn family in the Tunis community, see B. R. Cohen (1986: 166).
40. On Rabbi Eliyahu and his writings, see B. R. Cohen (1986: 141–42).
41. The threshing floor, where Shimʿon Bar Yoḥai and his colleagues assembled before he passed away. The text in the *Zohar* depicting this gathering is called *Iddera*, and it is recited at different social events.
42. A kabbalistic nickname for the devil.

43. Ḥazan (1976); Saraf (1984).
44. Ḥazan (1976: 267–72).
45. Ṣemaḥ Halevi, one of the most important writers in Judeo-Arabic also published the poem and wrote on its pattern a Judeo-Arabic poem in honor of Rabbi Yeshuʿa Besīs (d. 1860) with a similar opening: "Yā ilāhanā yā ilāhanā / zkhut al-ribbi ykūn maʿānā." See Halevi (n.d.).
46. In the original the Hebrew word *gizbar* was used. *Gizbar* (promounced: gazbar) serves in this sense in the Arabic dialect of the Jews of Tunisia.
47. The sultan's Muslim sentry stationed on the highway.
48. The title of the ruler in Tunisia.
49. This is the town where the grave of Rabbi Frājī Shawwāṭ is located.
50. The place of origin of Rabbi Frājī Shawwāṭ in Morocco.
51. A town in northern Tunisia, about 200 km west of the capital, Tunis, not far from the Algerian border.
52. Rabbi Moshe is a legendary figure who arrived in Tunisia from Fes in Morocco. Nothing is known about him, and he is not mentioned in any source other than this poem.
53. A metonym for the bar mitzvah celebration.
54. A metonym for the joy of marriage.
55. See Najjār (1919: 3: 63).
56. "Yah go'ali ṣarim ʿalay noʿadu" can be found in Davidson (1923: י, 813); "Reṣe le-shire qehal ʿadathekha" in Davidson (1923: ר, 1022); and "Deleni mi-yad ha-zari" in Davidson (1923: ד, 252).

Chapter 3

1. Some explanations for this noun have been given, but none seems acceptable. See, for example, Marçais and Guiga (1960: 7: 3620–21).
2. On Muslim Tunisian folk poetry, see Marzūqī (1967: 86), where there is a short notice on the malzūma; see also Turkī (1967).
3. We do not include the *ghnāya* genre, which we consider in Chapter 5.
4. See Chapter 2.
5. On the theater, see Chapter 7; on the theoretical and propagandistic literature, see Chapter 6.
6. For more on the leaflet ballads, see Bold (1979: 66–82), Friedman (1961; 1982), and Preminger and Brogan (1993: 148–49).
7. S. Yaniv (1986: 25–26).
8. S. Yaniv (1999: 38).
9. For brief comments on the lament, see Vassel (1904: 62–63) and Attal (1979: 205–6). Vassel (1908) also published "al-Qina al-zarbiyya" with a French translation. This lament was first published by Eliʿezer Farḥi (Tunis, n.d.). For another publication of the lament with a Hebrew translation, see Slouschz (1918: 83–89).
10. For an account of the atmosphere of preparations for Passover in Michel Wazan's novel *Bayn ḥuyūt tūnis*, see Chapter 1.

11. We were unable to ascertain who this Rabbi Nissim was. In the oral and written traditions he is mentioned under the name "R. Nissim al-Maṣrī" (Rabbi Nissim the Egyptian) and always in connection with Passover. He may be no other than a metonym for the miracles (*nissim* in Hebrew means "miracles"), needed at the time of preparations for the festival. Thus, for example, we have the tale about the prophet Elijah who appeared as a human being with the name of R. Nissim the Egyptian to a poor person in Jerusalem on the eve of Passover. This happened after the person was forgotten by the rabbi of the community, and his wife and the members of his family urged him to get out and look for the needed expenses for the festival. This tale is told by Sukkari (1882): 40a–42b; for a Judeo-Persian enlarged adaptation of the tale, see Ḥakham (1906): 40a–42b.
12. *Indiāna* was a kind of material.
13. *Qadīd* is a desiccated meat, and *mergēz* is a sausage.
14. *Zigzag* is a strip of material; both zigzag and lace are used for decorating cloths.
15. The search for *ḥametz* (leavened bread) the evening before Passover.
16. A mixture of finely chopped fruit, nuts, and honey eaten on Passover night.
17. The Tunisian legal tender; at that time 1 *riyāl* was equivalent to 1 English pound.
18. One *qanṭar* is equivalent to about 45 kg.
19. On Ṣemaḥ Halevi, see what Daniel Ḥagège has to say in Chapter 9.
20. *al-Fonograf* (The Phonograph) was a Judeo-Arabic weekly that appeared in Tunis between 1904 and 1908; it was edited by Ṣemaḥ Halevi. See Attal (1986: 55) and later discussion in Chapter 9.
21. The funds of the community.
22. One *raṭl* equals about 450 grams.
23. On the legendary figure of Rabbi Nissim, see note 11.
24. For a discussion of Ḥai Ṣarfati's place in Judeo-Arabic literature and his works, as compiled by Ḥagège, also see Chapter 9.
25. We are indebted to our dear friend, the late Robert Attal, who was kind enough to provide us with a photocopy of the printed version of the *malzūma*.
26. A 5-franc coin.
27. The following is the master's response.
28. Meaning, "If you have changed your mind about working in my house."
29. The words of the author of the poem.
30. The Hebrew word in the original is *avir* (air).
31. On this hospital, see Karmi (1986: 106) and Najjār (1919, 3: 26).
32. Dār al-Pāshā seems to be a structure that belonged to one of the Pāshās who ruled in Tunis.
33. A kind of fine cloth.
34. Two well-to-do suburbs of Tunis.
35. A neighborhood in Tunis.
36. The Alliance Israélite Universelle.
37. A low price; an insulting offer.
38. A kind of jasmine.

Chapter 4

1. For more about the *qina* and its relation to the *malzūma*, see Chapter 3.
2. Bḥēra is a neighborhood in Tunis built on a spit of land in the sea that had dried out.
3. A penny.
4. *Filla* in the original, after a perfume plant.
5. The trousseau and copper refers to bedding, towels, copper utensils, and the like that the bride prepares in readiness for marriage.
6. Al-Wād is a neighborhood in Tunis near the river estuary, a center of entertainment and amusements.
7. A sexual metaphor for a woman.
8. A phrase meaning a made-up young girl.
9. Probably 200 *soldi*, the legal Tunisian currency. In 1927, US$1 bought 19 Italian lire.
10. *Shaqshūqa* and *maghmūma* are vegetable dishes, the first with eggs.
11. A cheap fish.
12. The Ten Commandments.
13. On Yosef Bījāwī, see what Daniel Ḥagège wrote, in Chapter 9. But in the list of Judeo-Arabic writers in Tunisia in modern times Ḥagège (see Chapter 9) gives several more names with the initials Y. B.: Yosef Brāmī, Isaac Beribbī, and Jacob Būkhrīṣ.
14. The Capitol and the Royale were names of cinemas in Tunis.
15. His wife.
16. A 5-franc coin.
17. A football team.
18. The Empire Hotel was apparently not a respectable place for decent people.
19. Emptied of money.
20. We were told by Ḥasana Twātī of Manuba University in Tunis that two poems of lament for Ḥabiba Messica were written by Muslims immediately after the poet's death.
21. See Shokeid and Deshen (1977).
22. Several books about Ḥabiba Messica were published. Two, in French, were published in Paris in 1997: J. F. d'Arcier, *Habiba Messica: La brulûre du péché* (a novel); and J. Riahi, *Cantique pour Habiba* (a biography). See more in Y. Tobi (2010b). The noun *msīka* is the feminine diminutive form of the masculine noun *misk*, a common form in the Arabic dialect of the Jews of Tunis. See D. Cohen (1964/75: 2: 124–48) and Bar-Asher (1986). In the pronunciation of the Jews of Tunisia the short vowel at the beginning of the word and the diphthong in the middle are elided: *musayka* → *msīka*.
23. Moshe Cohen died in 1974; he was the father of Tsivia Tobi.
24. See, for example, the booklet *Shuva yisrael* ("Return, O, Israel") (Livorno, 1886), which is a joint declaration (*haskama*) of the rabbis of Tunis that censures and fiercely condemns the pursuit of the alien culture, that is, European culture, which began to take root in the Jewish quarters of Tunis. Also

see the booklets *Neṣaḥ yisrael* (The Eternal of Israel) (Tunis, 1888) and *Ba zeman ha-yeshuʿa* (The Time of Salvation Has Come) (Tunis, n.d.), excerpts from which are given in Chapter 6. See also Tsur (1988; 1990) and Cazès (1888: 149–67).

25. See Brown (1974), Ganiage (1968), and Cohen Hadria (1976).
26. For pictures of Jews from the turn of the nineteenth century wearing on their heads the black tasseled red Turkish fez (*kabbūsh stambūlī*) or a simple red fez without the tassel (*kabbūsh*), see *Mi-qartago li-yerushalayim* (1986: 124).
27. On the effects of European modernism on Judaism, see Chapter 1.
28. According to tradition, Ḥabiba Messica was born in Egypt and as a child migrated with her parents to Tunis. This difference in birthplace seems to be one detail in the myth that grew up around her image as a singer, because Egypt, particularly Cairo, was the center of Arab music and song, where internationally renowned male and female singers from the Arab peoples were active.
29. That modern Jews of Tunisia chose European names and eschewed Arabic names, even though they identified with Tunisian Westernization, can be ascribed to the fact that the Arabic names actually signified conservatism. Incidentally, this process, so typical of the Jewish communities in northern Tunisia as early as the late nineteenth century, occurred quite later in the conservative Jewish communities in southern Tunisia, such as Gābes, Djerba, Zarzīs, Taṭāwīn, and Mednīn. For example, in the long lists of donors' names and those memorialized (men and women) in the prefaces of books published in Djerba, even as late as the 1940s and 1950s, most of the women's names are Arabic and only a few are Hebrew, whereas European names are hardly to be found at all.
30. The Sfez family was well-known in Tunisia; the Bato Sfez episode is named after them. Bato Sfez was a Jew executed at the order of the Muslim shariʿa court in 1857 after he was accused by a Muslim of besmirching the religion of Islam. See Bar-Ḥen (1988: 162–72), Hirschberg (1965: 2: 145), and Attal (1993: 658, s.v. Sfez, Bato [Samuel]).
31. Like his famous brother, Muḥammad Bourguiba was born in Monastir (1894) and was trained as a lawyer.
32. Ḥabib Bourguiba's favorable attitude toward the Jews is well-known. Emigrants from Tunisia attest that in his speeches he frequently used Hebrew words. See also Ḥadad (1965).
33. On the participation of Ḥabiba Messica, and of the Jews in general, in theater in modern Tunisia, see Chapter 7.
34. See Allali (1988), Hoummous (1987), "Habibat Al-kul" (three pages from an unidentified French periodical, n.d.), and Chanhaz (1962). Because these accounts are short and because many details in them are repeated, we do not give references for all the details set out in the text, unless for a specific purpose. We thank Yaʿaqov Assal, grandson of the poet and *paytan* Asher

Mizraḥi, a native of Jerusalem, who was adulated by the Jews of Tunisia, for making available to us the accounts from the French press.

35. The Tunisian cinema dealt with a Jewish theme in at least four films; it was always sympathetic to the Jewish characters and took an approach of fraternity of religions.
36. We offer our heartfelt thanks to Ms. Baccar for her great courtesy to us at our meetings when she was in Israel in October 1996 for the Mediterranean film festival, in which her film was screened.
37. The exhibition was held under the auspices of the Association des Tradition Populaires des Juifs de Tunisie; its curator was Bernard Allali. Our thanks go to Prof. Amnon Shiloah, who gave us this information.
38. See Allali (1988: 31). On the unique person of Sarah Bernhardt, a Jewish actress of Alsatian origin who was a major figure in French theater at the end of the nineteenth century and early twentieth century, see Pronier (1942). On a famous Swiss Jewish singer, Rachel, who became a star of the Comédie Française at the end of the nineteenth century, see *Encyclopaedia Judaica*, s.v. Rachel (Jerusalem, 1972), 13: 1492–93; cf. Attal (1980c).
39. Under the influence of the era, in her film Salma Baccar developed the character of the singer as both a feminist heroine and a national heroine struggling against French rule in Tunisia.
40. See Allali (1988: 31). We have not discovered the meaning of the word *souzat.*
41. See Hoummous (1987: 50).
42. According to Ines Fiorentino, a native of Tunis. The chief rabbi of the Tunis community in 1930 was Rabbi Yosef Guez (1928–1934). The head of the Grāna community (originating in Livorno) was Rabbi Jacob Abūqāra (1914–1941). On them, see B. R. Cohen (1986: 81, 142, 387, 388).
43. On Sūlīka Ḥatchuel, see Vance (2011) and Hassine (2012). Sūlīka Ḥatchuel won great fame, and various literary works were written about her, such as poems and also dramas. See Attal (1993: lxxvii, s.v. Hachouel, Sol). On a Judeo-Arabic poem about her, see Fleischer (1864); on Frēḥa, see Chetrit (1980a); on Diamanṭa, see Chapter 3. The Judeo-Arabic folk literature throughout North Africa, not just Tunisia, gave rise to many long poems, a kind of ballad and lament, on these figures. The poems were preserved through an oral tradition, committed to writing in manuscript form, and even published by special Hebrew printers or as single sheets. See David ʿAmmār, *Qina wa-qiṣṣa dī lālā* [lady] *sūlīqā al-ṣaddīqa dī . . . fās awīlī bi-al-wīl ʿalā mā zrālī* [Fes, n.d.], single sheet (in the collection of the Ben-Zvi Institute, Jerusalem); and Shalom Ṭayyār, *Ghnāyat Būshāyef: Aʿṭū al-ṣdaqa waqt al-ḍīqa ṣarrfū al-ʿawon* [Tripoli, n.d.], single sheet (in the Tobi collection).
44. Babylonian Talmud, *Megilla* 15a.
45. This seems to be the person Daniel Ḥagège mentions among the Judeo-Arabic writers in Tunisia (see Chapter 9).
46. This booklet is rare; we first found a flawed copy (the second page is missing) of it in the collection of Pinḥas Cohen of Lod. We offer him heartfelt

thanks for so kindly lending it to us. Later we obtained a complete copy of the booklet for our private collection.

47. See D. Cohen (1964/75: 1: 121–25).
48. These versions were recorded by Tsivia Tobi from her mother Varda Cohen (Gābes), from Mennāna Gābsī (Gābes), and from Koka Uzan (Nabeul).
49. Our esteemed friend, the late Robert Attal, the renowned scholar of North African Jewry and possessor of the largest collection of Judeo-Arabic literature in Tunisia, which contains a copy of this *qina*, was kind enough to make a photocopy of it for us. He was also good enough to tell us that, shortly before the death of Daniel Ḥagège, who wrote the history of Judeo-Arabic literature in Tunisia (translated in Chapter 9), he asked him about the identity of Datan. Ḥagège replied that Datan was indeed Makhlūf Najjār, owner of the printing house in Sousse. Rabbi Meir Māzūz also told us that this was the nickname of Makhlūf Najjār.
50. We are indebted to Joseph Chetrit for this information.
51. Prof. Joseph Chetrit has conducted extensive research on this matter. See Chetrit (1994: 375). On Judeo-Arabic poetry in Yemen, see Gamli'eli (1979), Ratzahbi (1986), Y. Tobi (1986: 30), and Kapeliouq (1963).
52. See Chapter 8.
53. Many editions of the story of Hannah and her seven sons were published by Hebrew printers in the East and in North Africa. They appeared in different Arabic dialects.
54. See Ibn ʿAbd Rabbihi (1928: 158–62) and Levin (1973: 81–94).
55. An oral testimony provided by Mennāna Gābsī.
56. An oral testimony provided by Varda Cohen.
57. We have been helped in compiling this descriptive image of Ḥabiba Messica by the following bearers of tradition: (1) Koka Uzan, born in Nabeul ca. 1925 and immigrated to Israel in 1952; (2) Varda Cohen, born in Gābes in 1912, immigrated to Israel in 1951, and died in Jerusalem in 1997; (3) Moshe Cohen, born in Gābes in 1900, immigrated to Israel in 1951, and died in Jerusalem in 1973 (Cohen was an eyewitness to Messica's performances in Tunis); (4) Mr. Sitruq, the caretaker of the Rabbi Ḥai Ṭayyeb synagogue in Beersheba (based on the Archives of Jewish Art at the Hebrew University in Jerusalem); (5) Ines Fiorentino, born in Tunis (we conducted an interview with her in 1993; her deceased husband, Moshe Fiorentino, who was also born in Tunis and who passed away in Jerusalem in 1992, headed the Grāna community in Tunis); and (6) Mennāna Gābsī, born in Gābes ca. 1920, immigrated to Israel in 1956, and died in Jerusalem in 1996.
58. This Torah scroll was displayed in an exhibition on Tunisian Jewry held in the Bet Ha-Tefuṣot in Tel Aviv, in 1986. See B. Yaniv (1994: 110).
59. Several years ago, a number of compact discs came out bearing Ḥabiba Messica's songs. According to Paul Fenton (Yosef Yinnon) of the Sorbonne in Paris, Viviane Lesselbaum, a painter who now lives in Israel and whose

parents had been friends with Messica, has produced a painting of Messica and even collects anecdotes about her life.

Chapter 5

1. See Slouschz (1918: 81–82).
2. In fact, for centuries Jews had dominated as musicians and singers in North Africa and Andalusia.
3. See Chapter 8.
4. See Chapter 8.
5. On Ṣemaḥ Halevi, see Chapter 9.
6. The use of Arabic script by Jews creates a rather thorny problem from the viewpoint of Islam, a matter that apparently prevented Jewish printers from printing in this script. Furthermore, they themselves were undoubtedly not expert in it.
7. At this stage we have no information whether these writings were published in their time in Arabic script also, or later by our contemporary scholars.
8. Victor Halevi is the brother of Ṣemaḥ Halevi. He is mentioned by Daniel Ḥagège (see Chapter 9).
9. Ḥalq al-Wād is a seaside resort close to Tunis. Its French name is La Goullette.
10. For other poems about the German occupation of the Jews of Tunisia, see Attal (1986) and Saraf (1988).
11. "Ghnāyat Khammūs Jānā" was published in Tunis, in about 1945. The *ghnāya* was reprinted with a Hebrew translation by Saraf (1988: 74–85).
12. A sheikh is a chief; the *qā'id* is the leader of the community.
13. The name of a coin.
14. The Sanctuary and the Ark.
15. In the original, "Our spittle was dry."
16. President Truman was the first to recognize the State of Israel after its establishment.
17. The reference is to the Irgun Zvai Leumi (Also referred to as Etzel).
18. A metaphor for the powerful enemy.
19. The main underground organization of the Jewish settlement in the Land of Israel.
20. A call to send immigrants to Israel.

Chapter 6

1. On *'Ahd al-amān*, see Tsur (2010).
2. The ruler of Tunis from 1859 to 1882.
3. Rabbi Abraham Ḥajjāj served as head of the court of Tunisian Jewry from 1874 to 1881. On him, see B. R. Cohen (1986: 167–69).
4. That is, the outer protecting shell.
5. An expression meaning, "I bless you that you may succeed in what I have bidden you to do."

6. ʿAlī Pāshā Bey was the brother and successor of Muḥammad al-Ṣādiq; he ruled Tunis from 1882 to 1902.
7. The date is being referred to as the Bible verse read for that week.
8. Rabbi David Ben ʿAṭṭār was the head of the rabbinical court in Tunisia after the death of Rabbi Abraham Ḥajjāj. On him, see B. R. Cohen (1986: 128); on the other signatories to the statement, see B. R. Cohen (1986) under their respective entries.
9. Our thanks go to the late Robert Attal, who was kind enough to provide us with a photocopy of the booklet.
10. The formulation of the title page to Part II is identical.
11. Reuven Asher Brodes was an important Hebrew writer at the end of the Haskalah and the beginning of the Revival period in Eastern Europe (1851–1903).
12. The parenthetical comment is in the original.

Chapter 7

1. For the Jewish theater Les Escholiers (later called Ha-Qol [The Voice]) (1942–1961), all of the performances of which were in French, see Tobi (2013c).
2. On the *qaraqoz* in general, see Landau (1958: 1–47), Moreh (1987; 1992), and Moreh and Sadgrove (1996: 33–34); on the *qaraqoz* in Tunisia from the sixteenth to the twentieth century, see Landau (1958: 39–45) and Ben Halima (1974: 22–24). In this traditional theater in Tunisia the Jew was presented as a negative character.
3. See Landau (1958: 49–55).
4. See Ben Halima (1974: 16). Apart from Ben Halima's book in French, two books in Arabic on Arab theater in Tunisia have been published: Idrīs (1993) and Sharaf al-Dīn (1997). See also Maume (1970). For a review on this work, see Mettrop (1971).
5. Moreh and Sadgrove (1996: 34).
6. Ben Halima (1974: 16).
7. Avrahami (1980). On the Grāna community and its relations with the long-standing community, see Avrahami (1986), Tsur (1990), and Attal (1982).
8. The translation itself is lost, and only the opening poem remains. It was published by Cassuto (1936). For an English translation of the play, see Rojas (2009); for a Hebrew translation of the opening poem, see Rojas (1963: 163–64).
9. On Yehuda Somo's life, writings, and activity in theater and on the publication of *Ṣaḥut bedihūta de-qiddushin*, see Schirmann (1946) (the introduction is also published in Schirmann [1980: 115–24]).
10. Schirmann (1980: 44–160).
11. On Zacut and his plays, see Melkman (1966) and Schirmann (1980: 126–32); on Franco Mendes, see Melkman (1951); on Luzatto and his plays, see David (1972) and Schirmann (1980: 161–75).
12. On this play, see Schirmann (1980: 176–83) and Moreh and Sadgrove (1996: 7). By Schirmann's reckoning, Palache lived in the early eighteenth

century. The play has survived in manuscript only. Note that drama as a literary medium, for expressing discussions between people of different views on philosophical and moral subjects, usually in the form of allegory, was common in rabbinic Hebrew literature until the twentieth century. See, for example, Alkalay (1884). This genre deserves a study of its own.

13. Moreh and Sadgrove (1996: 9–10).
14. The main source on the Italian influence on Tunisian theater is an article by Darmon (1951). Darmon was undoubtedly a Tunisian Jew of the Livorno community. Because this publication was not available to us, we rely mainly on Ben Halima (1974: 17–19).
15. Ben Halima (1974: 17).
16. Ben Halima (1974: 17).
17. For members of the Tapia family in Tunis, see Attal and Avivi (1989: 308).
18. The Cohen-Tanuji family is a famous dynasty of rabbis from Tunis. See B. R. Cohen (1986: 183–90).
19. Ben Halima (1974: 92). On Sarah Bernhardt and her enormous admiration in France even after her death, see Pronier (1942).
20. Ben Halima (1974: 18–20) (citing Darmon [1951]).
21. Ben Halima (1974: 22) notes the visit to Tunis in 1890 of Yaʿaqov Ṣanūʿ, an important Egyptian Jewish writer and journalist who was also active in theater (he wrote thirty plays); but his lectures in the city had nothing to do with his theater activity (Ben Halima disregards his being Jewish). Therefore one cannot infer from this a connection of the Jews to Tunisia to theater at that time. On Ṣanūʿ (1839–1912), also known as Abū Naẓẓāra (the man with glasses), one of the central figures in the national awakening in Egypt at the end of the nineteenth century, see Landau (1958: 65–67), Najm (1963), and Moreh and Sadgrove (1996: 21–29).
22. Ben Halima (1974: 33) mentions the problem of nationalism among Tunisian Jews, citing the October 18, 1907, issue of the newspaper *al-Ṣawāb*.
23. Ben Halima (1974: 72).
24. Schirmann (1980: 179n9) mentions a booklet titled *Khlāʿat purim* (Tunis, n.d.) containing a Judeo-Arabic text in verse known as *Teʾatro*. He estimates that the booklet was printed in the nineteenth century.
25. See Davidson (1907).
26. See later discussion in this chapter on the attitude to theater in Judeo-Arabic literature in Tunisia. We note that in Makhlūf Najjār's bibliography and in book lists of the Tunisian Jewish publishers (*tajrīdas*), more booklets in Judeo-Arabic are mentioned under the heading *Teʾatro*. We intend soon to devote a special article to the place of theater in Judeo-Arabic literature in Tunisia in the first half of the twentieth century.
27. We did not have the booklets described here before us. *Ḥasīn* and *māya* are names of musical modes in the musical tradition of Tunisia, and they are generally indicated together with other modes in the many songbooks printed by the Jews of Tunisia. Incidentally, what is written here corroborates what

was said earlier about the great influence of the Egyptian world of entertainment on that of Tunisia.

28. On Sulaymān Qardāḥī, see Ben Halima (1974: 205, s.v. Qardāḥī).
29. For a *malzūma* on this hospital, see Chapter 3.
30. Ben Halima (1974: 39–44) relates the incident in the chapter on Qardāḥī. Qardāḥī was surprised at the behavior of the members of the Muslim Circle, who were known for their liberal religious outlook, and raised the possibility that they adopted their stance on nationalistic, anti-Jewish grounds or that perhaps certain members of the Jewish hospital board had taken out French citizenship (Ben Halima, 1974: 111n1).
31. Ben Halima (1974: 88).
32. On al-Kāhina, see Slouschz (1933).
33. Ben Halima (1974: 111n1). *La Kahena* is mentioned by Attal (1993: 336, no. 5560). On three other plays in French about al-Kāhina, one by Jean Hilaire (1922), one by Emile Roudie (1922?), and one by Jacob Guiramand (1977), see Attal (1993: 336, no. 5560; 314, no. 5156; and 315, no. 5176).
34. Moreh and Sadgrove (1996: 36), according to Idrīs (1993: 36n134). Kiki Guetta is mentioned in the booklet *Afkār al-ʿushshāq dāʾim al-ʿayn al-ḥabāra bi-al-ʿarabī wa-bi-al-fransīs, al-ʿadad al-sādisī*, printed by Jacob Guez (Tunis, n.d.). The title-page states that the poems (*ghnāyāt*) are "min famm kīkī" (of Kiki's mouth).
35. Ben Halima (1974: 34, 73, 82, 154).
36. Ben Halima (1974: 87n1).
37. See Taïeb (1989: 393–94). The records of Raoul Journo were popular in Tunisia, and recently many of his audiocassettes have been sold among former Tunisian Jews in Israel and France (copies of his records and of other Jewish singers from Tunisia, from the collection of the late Mennāna Ḥirārī, Nahariyya, are kept in the Phonoteca section at the National Library of Israel in Jerusalem at the initiative of Tsivia Tobi). In 1993 in Paris, a compact disc series was produced titled *Musique Judéo-Arabe* (vol. 2 in the series), with ten songs by Jewish male and female vocalists from Tunisia (at the end of the CD are five more songs by non-Jewish singers). The Jewish performers and the dates of the original performance are as follows: The Chemama Sisters (*banāt*), 1908 (two songs); Malouf, 1908; Laylā Sfez (aunt and teacher of Ḥabiba Messica in playing and singing), 1926 (two songs); Louisa al-Tūnsiyya (popular in Tunisia and among former Tunisian Muslims and Jews to the present day), 1945; Shaykh al-ʿIfrīt, 1932; and Raoul Journo, 1955.
38. Ben Halima (1974: 85).
39. On the Jews of Tunisia under Nazi occupation, see Avrahami (1989: 440–43). A most important source on this subject, in Judeo-Arabic, is the book by Guez (1943).
40. The use of the vernacular was common in Arab theaters in Tunisia. The first production in this dialect was as early as 1913 at al-ʾĀdāb theater. See Ben Halima (1974: 59n2); Ben Halima (1974: 112) also notes that beginning in 1939 the joint theater (formed in 1936 and functioning until 1949)

devoted itself to Tunisian folklore and that in fact all its presentations were of plays written in the popular language based on Eastern folktales. The Arabic literature of the Tunisian Jews during that period was all published in their vernacular. On the different languages in use in the Jewish theater and on how fluent Tunisian Jews were in literary Arabic and their ability to relate to dramatic literature in this language, as distinct from their spoken Arabic, see Moreh and Sadgrove (1996: 40).

41. See Ben Halima (1974: 158).
42. Ben Halima (1974: 85–86).
43. Ben Halima (1974: 140).
44. For details of the activity of Najjār's theater, see Moreh and Sadgrove (1996: 30–37).
45. This booklet is extremely rare and of immense importance. The yearbook's title page states *'Am awwal—première année*, no doubt indicating the intention of making the yearbook a regular publication. But Najjār did not publish any more volumes. The quoted passage is given almost literally, obviously in the language of the original, by Daniel Ḥagège (see Chapter 9).
46. On the *ḥikāyāt* genre, see Chapter 8.
47. Makhlūf Najjār, *Tajrīda* (Sousse, 1936: [22] [the pages are not marked in the original booklet]). The booklet *Charlotte* was printed by Najjār (Sousse, n.d.).
48. Ben Halima (1974: 161–62). A chapter on Ḥabiba appears in Būdhīna (1992: 163–65). See also Y. Tobi (2010c).
49. Hence Ḥabiba Messica's education was not in Arabic but purely in French.
50. *Adwār* (sing. *dawr*) and *ṭaqāṭiq* (sing. *ṭiqṭiqa*) are genres of light songs.
51. Many Egyptian actors and singers went to Tunisia and greatly influenced artistic life there. Most noteworthy is the singer and actor Ḥasan Bannān, who went to Tunisia and never left; he became a pioneer of local theater (Ben Halima, 1974: 38).
52. Ḥabiba Messica wanted to build a hospital in Ariana for poor Jews and Muslims (noted by Ben Halima [1974], citing the journal *al-Nahda*, February 7, 1930).
53. "An unusual change in customs regarding the dead," writes Raoul Darmon, who was surprised at the great honor given to "a local singer, a courtisane" (Ben Halima, 1974: 162n2).
54. Rabbi Jacob Abūqāra (1843–1941), the chief rabbi of the Grāna community in Tunisia (1914–1941). In his eulogy the rabbi responded to the criticism voiced against those who seemed to shower excessive honor on the singer, who had unabashedly flouted the precepts of Judaism. He said that, just as according to the tradition fire purifies any contaminated vessel, so was Ḥabiba purified of all her wrongdoing and transgressions against Judaism by being set afire and consumed alive. We can assume that the traditional religious leadership of Tunisian Jewry did not view favorably the participation of Jews in theater activity and entertainment generally. We intend to expand on this elsewhere; here we note that we know of express opposition

to the participation of Jews in theater in other communities, chiefly Egypt, as evinced by the rebuke by Mordekhai Shelomo Ha-Levi, the warden of the Jews' Synagogue in Alexandria. See his booklet *Bet sefer yehudi* (A Jewish School) (Alexandria, [1933]). From this one learns of the opposition of the rabbis and also that many young people in the community were in the habit of going to the theater.

55. See *al-Nahda*, February 23, 1930; *al-ʿĀlam al-Adabī*, March 1930; and *al-Nadīm*, March 15, 1930 (Ben Halima, 1974: 162n3).
56. Later Ben Halima gives several strophes translated into French of the original Judeo-Arabic dirge on the death of Ḥabiba: *Fī tūnis ṣārat ghrība*. For the translation of this dirge and of another in Judeo-Arabic, see Chapter 4.
57. See Ben Halima (1974: 59).
58. Ben Halima (1974: 71–72).
59. Muḥammad Bourguiba was the brother of Ḥabīb Bourguiba, who became leader of the national movement in Tunis and eventually the president of the state after it achieved independence from France in 1956. On Muḥammad Bourguiba, see Ben Halima (1974: 152–53).
60. On Ḥasan Bannān, see Ben Halima (1974: 154–55).
61. See Ben Halima (1974: 72–76); on Akūdī, see Ben Halima (1974: 153–54).
62. Ben Halima (1974: 167–68).
63. See the journal *Lisān al-shaʿb*, March 7, 1923 (according to Ben Halima, 1974: 80n5), and February 18, 1925 (Ben Halima, 1974: 88n3).
64. Ben Halima (1974: 45n1; 56n1). As is known, in conservative societies men played women's roles, such as in the classical Greek theater and in the play *Naḥat ru'aḥ*, which was performed before the Jewish community in Algiers at the end of the eighteenth century.
65. Ben Halima (1974: 137).
66. Ben Halima (1974: 93).
67. According to Le Théâtre arabe à Tunis (1932: 543). We have not seen the book itself.
68. Ben Halima (1974: 98).
69. On Faḍīla Khītmī, see Le Théâtre arabe à Tunis (1932: 543) and Ben Halima (1974: 82, 88, 94, 97–98, 113, 139).
70. Le Théâtre arabe à Tunis (1932: 542–43).
71. On the film and the portrayal of Ḥabiba Messica's feminine character in it and in Jewish folklore, see Chapter 4.

Chapter 8

1. Ha-Nagid (1966: 221).
2. Ha-Nagid (1966: 1).
3. Ibn Ezra (1975: 107).
4. Lewin (1934: 34–35).
5. Lewin (1934: 58–59).
6. Y. Tobi (2010a: 422–66); Fenton (1980).

7. Brann (1992).
8. Y. Tobi (2010a: 467–82).
9. Ibn Qayyim al-Jawziya (1991).
10. The *maqāma* is a special medieval literary genre written in rhymed prose that is popular in Arabic and Hebrew literature but also in some other Middle Eastern languages, such as Persian and Turkish.
11. Schirmann (1957: 594); see also Huss (1983; 1995).
12. Maḥberet is the medieval Hebrew translation for maqāma.
13. Immanuel (1957); Y. Frances (1969); I. Frances (1932).
14. Y. Tobi (1988).
15. ʿAntebi (1843: 119b–120a).
16. Cf. Chapter 1; Chetrit (1994: 48–54).
17. Translations of passages from this novel are given in Chapter 1.
18. See Nicholson (1969: 238).
19. In a conversation we had with Rabbi Asher Ḥaddād at his home in the town of Netivot in 1991 during Passover.
20. In the Hebrew and Judeo-Arabic of the Jews of southern Tunisia the word *siddur* means any holy book, not necessarily a compilation of prayers. In the dialect of the Jews of northern Tunisia it means a book of any kind.

Chapter 9

1. In the two appendixes we list the titles of all the printed works mentioned in Ḥagège's book with an English translation and the author's name.
2. *Intishār al-ktāyib al-yahūdiyya al-barbariyya al-tūnisiyya* was first published as installments in Makhlūf Najjār's weekly *al-Najma* in 1938. *Al-Barbariyya* refers to the vernacular dialect, which is different from the literary dialect. This distinction applies in Ḥagége's text throughout (translated in this chapter). Makhlūf Najjār's printing house in Sousse has been the sole and last printer in northern Tunisia since the 1930s. On Najjār, see later discussion in this chapter; on Najjār's Judeo-Arabic newspaper *al-Najma,* which lasted until 1962, see Y. Tobi (2013b). We extend our heartfelt thanks to the late Robert Attal, who was so kind as to give us a copy of Ḥagége's precious work as a gift. A generous man will be blessed.
3. Manuscript 6516, Ben-Zvi Institute, Jerusalem.
4. On that cultural trend, see Y. Tobi (2007; 2013a; 2013c).
5. The author surely does not mean the beginning of the use of Judeo-Arabic in Tunisia, but the beginning of Judeo-Arabic printing in that country.
6. But the "Tunisian Arabic-Berber language" was not spoken by all Jews in northern Tunisia; some of the educated circles in the 1930s and later spoke and wrote French only.
7. This is indeed a modern and liberal attitude toward a Jewish dialect of Arabic, which was not shared in contemporaneous Jewish educated circles in other Arabic-speaking countries, not to mention educated Muslim circles with regard to the local spoken Arabic dialects.

8. On Mordekhai Tapia, Bīshī Chemama, and Eliyahu Elmāleḥ, see Vassel (1904: 18–20); on Bīshī (Moshe) Chemama, an expert in classical Arabic, see also Y. Tobi (2007: 261).
9. We may mention, however, that the first Hebrew publication in Tunis was *Baqqashat ha-ḥayyim ve-ha-shalom*, blessings and poems in Hebrew and Arabic (in Arabic characters) in honor of Muḥammad al-Ṣādiq Bey, the Tunisian sovereign, printed in Tunis in 1860 by the Englishman Richard Holt.
10. *Ma'ase sha'ashu'im*, a compilation of Hebrew tales collected from rabbinic sources and translated into Judeo-Arabic, was not printed in Tunis but in Livorno; see Vassel (1904: 22–23). On Rabbi Eliyyahu Guez, see B. R. Cohen (1986: 141–42).
11. On the character of the storyteller in Tunisia—*fdāwī* or *fdāwjī* in the local vernacular--see Y. Tobi (2007: 17–18n17).
12. For a list of Ḥai Ṣarfati's compositions, see later in this chapter. We could not determine the interpretation of this nickname.
13. A tavern was a kind of coffeehouse, but it served alcoholic drinks in addition to coffee and tea.
14. At that time this tender was not current in Tunisia, and the intention is perhaps the *soldi*.
15. This is the era of the Ḥafṣid dynasty in Tunisia, during which Ibn Khaldūn, the great Tunisian scholar, lived.
16. Souriau-Hoebrechts (1969: 34) notes that it was dangerous to publish a newspaper under the Muslim Bey, so Abraham Ṭayyib had *al-'Amāla al-tūnisiyya* printed in Livorno; only three issues appeared.
17. Only thirty-five issues of the weekly *al-Shams* were printed, of which the first twenty were printed in both Arabic and Judeo-Arabic; the remaining issues were printed in Arabic and in French. By doing so, the paper's owners conveyed the trend of openness to Arabic culture and French culture; see Y. Tobi (2007). It is likely that *al-Shams* was printed in Paris because Muslims in Tunis did not tend to cooperate with the Jewish publishers.
18. On Ṣemaḥ Halevi, see later discussion in this chapter.
19. Shalom Flāḥ (1855–1936) was an enthusiastic supporter of the Hebrew language. He indefatigably worked to enhance its knowledge among the Jews of Tunisia. He was the only one among the Jewish writers of his time to compose a comprehensive Hebrew work, *Ṣedeq ve-shalom* (Tunis, 1897), dedicated to the separation of the Jewish community in Tunis into two groups: the Twānisa (the Arabic speakers of the local original community) and the Grāna (the immigrants from Livorno, who also spoke Italian). On Flāḥ, see later discussion in this chapter and also T. Tobi (2012b).
20. Yiṣḥaq Cattan is a forgotten Orientalist who published several papers in the important journal *Revue tunisienne*.
21. On Ya'aqov Chemla, see later discussion in this chapter.

22. Yosef Cohen Ganūna was one of the most important advocates in the field of Judeo-Arabic journalism in Tunisia; Ḥagège frequently referred to him, although Ganūna did not leave publications in Judeo-Arabic.
23. The first printing of this long Arabic romance, translated into Tunisian Judeo-Arabic by Shalom Flāḥ, was in Livorno (1885); at 1,642 pages, it was too daring an assignment to carry out in the newly founded Hebrew printing houses in Tunis.
24. The printing of this Arabic romance, in Tunis in 1887, was much more modest than *al-Azaliyya*, and it included only the first volume of it (255 pages), probably because of its size.
25. The semantics of the word *haggin* is not clear, but most likely it is the Hebrew word *ha-gin*, a corruption of *ha-qina* (the dirge). It notes the liturgy of 9 of Av.
26. The name of this journal, "Freedom" in translation, and of others, such as *Ittiḥād*, *al-Istiwā*, and *al-Ikhāwa*, all of them taken from the slogans of the French revolution (as the author himself remarks; see later discussion in this chapter), expresses the French modern ideas that fascinated the educated individuals of the Jewish community in Tunis at that time and their aspirations to better the social and cultural conditions of their coreligionists. On *al-Ḥurriyya* as an organ with the aim of protecting the rights of Tunisian Jews, see later discussion.
27. *Mariṣtān* (*Māristān*) means "hospital," especially a hospital for the mentally ill; *al-Mariṣtān* was a satirical journal.
28. On Mas'ūd M'ārek, see later discussion in this chapter.
29. *Les mystères de Paris* was written by Eugène Sue.
30. *Al-Muḥayyar* (The Perplexed) and *Nāṣir al-muḥayyarīn* (Supporter of the Perplexed) (discussed later) expressed the feeling of social and spiritual mission that filled the hearts of the educated men in Tunis.
31. *Al-bān* is the moringa or Ben tree, known from Arabic poetry and from Jewish poetry in Yemen. It is known for its fragrant oil.
32. On Ya'aqov Cohen, see later discussion in this chapter.
33. It is probable that the point was not financial but the wish of the French authorities to inspect the new media, in particular, the Muslim press.
34. *Nāzlat drayfūs* is another bit of evidence of the impact of French culture and politics on the Jews of Tunis. It should be kept in mind that in 1904 the supporters of Alfred Dreyfus appealed to the Supreme Court of Appeal to acquit him, and he was eventually acquitted, in 1906.
35. Namely, French or Italian, from which many words were borrowed by the Jews of Tunisia in their Judeo-Arabic vernacular. That comment emphasized not only Daniel Ḥagège's high estimation of Judeo-Arabic, but also his high esteem of most other Judeo-Arabic writers at that time, particularly Ya'aqov Cohen.
36. On all of these men, see later discussion.
37. On Abraham Ṣabbān, see later discussion.
38. Item 9 is missing in the original.
39. On Ya'aqov di Moshe Abrahami, see later discussion.

40. On Ḥai Bel'īsh, see later discussion.
41. See Saadoun (2005b: 177).
42. On the Zionist activities in Jewish communities of northern Tunisia, see Saadoun (2005b).
43. The name of this paper, *al-Waṭan* (Homeland, namely, Tunisia), reflects new trends among some of the Tunisian Jews after World War I that they could join the national Tunisian movement to combat the French government and establish an independent state.
44. Al-Sāḥel (the coast) is the name of the coastal area south of Tunis, down to Sfax, the capital of which was Sousse.
45. Mahdiyyah is a coastal town south of Tunis. In the Middle Ages it was an important port for commerce on the way from Spain to Egypt and the Far East; it had a significant Jewish community.
46. Al-Ḥakīm Ghabyūn was an important character in the romance *Sayf al-azal.*
47. *Al-Tijāra al-tūnisiyya* (the Tunisian Commerce), a further expression of the wish of some of the educated Jews in northern Tunisia to integrate in the general population.
48. The aim of the Society of Intishār al-ktā'ib al-yahūdiyya was to preserve the Judeo-Arabic legacy of the Tunisian Jewish community against the strengthening influence of French culture.
49. That is, irregularly.
50. *Al-Yahūdī* (The Jew) was an attempt to protect Jewish identity.
51. Compare what is said by one of the protagonists of the novel *Bayn ḥuyūt tūnis* (by Michel Uzan; Tunis, 1926) pertaining to the Jewish journals: "The buyer is one and the readers are a hundred." See Chapter 1 appendix. As noted earlier, Judeo-Arabic literature was popular among the Jews of Tunisia; the newspapers especially provided local and international information--Jewish and general--in the most comprehensible language for them.
52. It seems that the small number of subscribers or buyers of the journals, as opposed to the large number of readers, was a real problem for Ḥagège and other journalists.
53. In the original the list is arranged according to the Hebrew alphabet.
54. In the original, *sherka hālka.*
55. In the original: *lūkān al-sherka fīhā khīr la-kānū yitshārkū 'tnēn fī mar'a.*
56. In the original this popular short Arabic poem is transcribed in Hebrew characters. Here is the transliterated Latin characters: yaḥdath 'alā al-'abd sā'āt / shay' alladhī lā yu'ālim / banī adam yaqra' al-'āqibāt / tab'ad 'alayhi al-maẓālim / ḥakartu wa-wazantu bi-'ithbāt / lā ḥad min ḥad sālim. The poem was performed in public by singers, and it is described as an *'arūbi* performed in the mode (*maqām*) of *muḥayyar 'irāq*. See, for instance, www.ward2u.com (accessed April 11, 2010).
57. In the original: *yā mzeyyin min barra ēsh ḥālak min dākhel.*
58. Ḥagège ignores the estrangement of almost all the educated circles in the 1930s from Judeo-Arabic culture and their almost total immersion in French

culture. This was the generation of the great Jewish writers who wrote exclusively in French: the cousins Vehel (Jacques Victor) and Ryvel (Raphaël) Lévy and Vitalis Danon. Thus the theatrical group Les Escholiers, which was established in Tunis by young alumni of the school of Alliance in 1927 (many years later, in the early 1950s this group adopted the Hebrew name Ha-Qol [The Voice]), performed solely in French. See Y. Tobi (2013c).

59. We could not find any further information on Israel ʿArqī (Arki), save a short French article by him in *Le judaïsm tunisien* (1913: 119–20), signed Sir Elyachar; see Attal (1993: 189, no. 2976, s.v. Archi, Israël). Sebag (2002: 34) uses it as a family name, Archi, but incorrectly traces it from the Arabic word *ʿarsh*.
60. Ḥai Ṣarfati.
61. *The Duties of the Heart*, by Baḥya ibn Paqūda, translated from Ibn Tibbon's Hebrew translation of the original medieval Judeo-Arabic into Tunisian Judeo-Arabic.
62. By Daniel Defoe, translated into Tunisian Judeo-Arabic.
63. In the original: *jamʿiyyat ḥatan ve-khalla.*
64. The custom of the *douta* (the obligation imposed on the young girl or her parents to pay a significant sum of money for her appointed groom) produced indecent behavior of the young girls to get the money, which the author realistically depicts as "sink[ing] into wicked ways and degeneration." On the extreme negative results of that custom and how it was aggressively criticized in the Judeo-Arabic literature of all genres, see T. Tobi (2012b: 85–88).
65. The reference is to the Jews' naturalization as French citizens. The French government frequently put obstacles in the way of Jews seeking French citizenship.
66. The ancient name of this synagogue was *ṣlāt* (synagogue) *gueddīd* (no one can explain the meaning of that word). See Najjār (1919, pt. 3: 31); for pictures of that synagogue, see Bismuth-Jarrassé (2010: 237) (the explanation given there for *gueddīd* as meaning "new" is not correct).
67. Yosef Shabbetai Farḥi was born in Jerusalem in 1812, and he moved to Livorno in 1842, where he engaged in publishing popular literature in Hebrew, Judeo-Arabic, and Ladino, including translated tales from Arabic sources. He died in Livorno in 1884. His best known book is *ʿOse pele*, a compilation of a wide range of sources--medieval and later, Jewish and Arabic. On Farḥi, see Yasif (1982). Farḥi's literary work was, probably, a source of inspiration for Judeo-Arabic writers in Tunis.
68. We can assume that Ḥagège means *Le Garçon et l'aveugle* (The Boy and the Blind Man). This tale of a trickster tricked is an early comic French play, dating from the second half of the thirteenth century. It was first published in a scholarly periodical in 1865 and later in the public press in Paris in 1911 (2nd ed., 1921), edited by Mario Roques.
69. The Street of the Sudanese, known as Blacks' Alley.
70. In the original: *anā līk w-antī liyyā.*
71. A Jew of Livornese origin.
72. A metaphor, usually said of a young loved-one, such as a son or a pupil.

73. Bar Kokhba.
74. None of the Judeo-Arabic journals, save al-Najma, survived beyond the early 1930s.
75. *Mu'ārek* in Arabic means a fighter.
76. Translation of *Ahavat zion* by Abraham Mapu.
77. The city of Tunis is known for its marvelous manufacture of decorated and painted ceramic tiles.
78. In the original: *hādū al-khīrāt al-kull tfarratū wa-lām 'ād lhum wujūd bi-al-marra.*
79. In the original: *taṣlīḥāt fī al-dīn min ghīr mā ytemmim al-dīn.*
80. On the tension between modernists and the Jewish Orthodoxy in Tunis, see Saadoun (2005a: 80–81).
81. A town in northwestern Tunisia, not far from the Algerian border.
82. We could not find any trace of Khammūs Arīs's works in Judeo-Arabic or any other language or any other reference to him. In addition, he is not mentioned in Attal (2007).
83. Bar mitzvah anniversary.
84. A town in northwestern Tunisia, east of the capital, Tunis.
85. *Al-Ṣabāḥ* in Arabic means "the morning."
86. Asher Mizraḥi (1890–1967), a poet and composer. He was not an Egyptian but a Jerusalemite, who left the Holy Land in secret during World War I to avoid compulsory service in the Ottoman Army and settled in Tunis. In 1919 he returned to Jerusalem, but in 1929 he resettled in Tunis, where he shortly became the mentor of *payytanim* (performers of traditional liturgical poetry), introducing them to the Jerusalemite Sephardic liturgical music. In 1967 he left for France for medical treatment, but three months later he moved back to Jerusalem, where he died after short time. One of his best close friends in Tunisia was Makhlūf Najjār.
87. A special genre in Tunisian poetry. On it, see Chapter 3.
88. "The Quarrel Between the *f ma'lūf* and the Egyptian." The *ma'lūf* was the local musical style (which originated in Andalusia, Spain), whereas the Egyptian songs, brought to Tunis by singers (male and female), dominated musical performances in cafés and theaters.
89. Several of the Judeo-Arabic publications in Tunis and Sousse were first published as feuilletons in Judeo-Arabic journals; see Attal (2007: 174–80).
90. The Valensi family was one of the most eminent in the Grāna community of Tunis and produced many personalities. On Alfred Valensi, see Saadoun (2010). Théodore Valensi is the author of *Yasmina, roman arabe, parmi les encens du harem*, which was printed at least three times (Paris, 1922, 1926, 1927). *The Roman* was filmed in 1926 by the French producer Abdré Hugon (stills from this film were printed in the 1927 edition of the book).
91. We could not find any record of Rabbi Natan Halevi, perhaps because his name is given incorrectly here.
92. Yehuda Jarmon was an eminent rabbi in Tunis (1812–1912). On him, see B. R. Cohen (1986: 147–48).

93. In the original: *ʿānid wa-lā taḥsid.*
94. A special genre of Tunisian poetry. On it, see Chapter 4.
95. For *Riyāqat al-nufūs*, see Vassel (1904: 40) and Attal (2007: 152, no. 714). The *ghinā* and *ʿurūbiyyāt* are two highly popular genres of songs performed in cafes and theaters. The *ʿurūbiyyāt* are a local North African genre, whereas most of the *ghnāyāt* (pl. of *ghinā*) were imported from Egypt. On the *ghnāyāt*, see Chapter 5 and Attal (2007: 180–227).
96. His brother Victor Levi.
97. The style of Andalusian music in Tunisia. In the original the word *nawba* was used for "mode."
98. An ancient shore town on the Mediterranean, south of Sousse.
99. In the original: *bārak allah fīk.*
100. The number of pages of each publication, as noted in the original, is given in parentheses.
101. In the *maʾlūf* mode, the style of Andalusian music in Tunisia.
102. In the original: *sheikh al-yahūd.*
103. Namely, in the feuilleton in *al-Najma*, before the booklike publication.
104. In the original: *alladhī ʿindhū ḥajra yirmīhā fī bīr.* This saying means, "Anyone who doesn't like it can do as he pleases."

Bibliography

Abitbol, Michel. 1986. Tahalikhe modernizaṣia ve-ha-hitpatḥut ba-ʿet ha-ḥadasha. In Shmuel Ettinger (ed.), *Toledot ha-yehudim be-arṣot ha-islam*, 2: 363–465. Jerusalem: Merkaz Shazar.

Adādī, A. H. 1976. *Ha-shomer emet*, 2nd ed. Tel Aviv: Vaʿad Qehillot Luv.

Alkalay, Ben-Zion. 1884. *ʿAshir va-rash*. Jerusalem: Elḥanan Ben Avraham Yiṣḥaq (2nd ed., Jerusalem: Defus Yerushalayim, 1934). Translated into Judeo-Arabic as *al-ʿAshir wa-al-mazlūṭ* (Livorno: Eliyahu Ben Amozeg U-Banav, 1908).

Allali, Jean-Pierre. 1988. Habiba Msika: l'oiseau du feu. *Tribune Juive*, no. 1006 (January 29–February 4): 30–32.

———. 1989. *Les Juifs de Tunisie: Images et textes*. Paris: Editions du Scribe.

ʿAntebi, Avraham. 1843. *Ohel yesharim*. Livorno: Ottolenghi.

Attal, Robert. 1960. Aperçu sur la littérature des juifs tunisiens. In Ben Zvi Institute, *Studies and Reports*, 3: 50–54. Jerusalem: Ben-Zvi Institute.

———. 1973. Les missions protestantes anglicanes en Afrique du Nord et leur publications en judéo-arabe à l'intention des juifs. *Revue des Études Juives* 132: 95–118.

——— [Avraham Hattal]. 1975a. ʿAl reshito shel ha-defus ha-ʿivri bi-ṣfon-āfriqa. In Robert Attal (ed.), *La Haggadah d'Alger*, 5–9. Jerusalem.

——— 1975b. Les traductions en judéo-arabe tunisien des oeuvres d'Abraham Mapu. *Revue des Études Juives* 134: 137–44.

———. 1979. Littérature judéo-arabe. In Robert Attal and M. Sitbon, *Regards sur les Juifs de Tunisie*, 203–210. Paris: A. Michel.

———. 1980a. Evocation de la France dans la littérature judéo-arabe tunisie. In Michel Abitbol (ed.), *Judaïsme d'Afrique du nord aux XIXe–XXe siècles*, 114–24. Jerusalem: Makhon Ben Zvi.

———. 1980b. *Ha-ʿittonut ha-yehudit bi-sfon-africa*. Jerusalem: Makhon Ben Zvi.

———. 1980c. Sur quelques letters de Rachel. *Le Vieux Papiers* 276 (April): 54–56.

———. 1982. Autour de la dissension entre 'Touansa' et 'Grana' à Tunis. *Revue des Études Juives* 141: 223–35.

———. 1983. Ha-ʿitton ha-yehudi ha-rishon ba-maghreb *L'Israelite Algerien* (Adziri), 1870. *Peʿamim* 17: 88–95.

———. 1986. ʿAl germania ha-naṣit ba-shira ha-ʿamamit shel yehude tunisia. *Peaʿmim* 28: 126–30.

———. 1993. *Yahadut sfon-afriqa: Bibliographia*. Jerusalem: Makhon Ben Zvi.

———. 1996. *Kitve ʿet ve-ʿittonim yehudiyyim bi-sfon afriqa*. Tel Aviv: Tel Aviv University.

———. 2007. *Ha-Sifrut ha-ʿaravit ha-yehudit be-tunisia*. Jerusalem: Makhon Ben Zvi.

Attal, Robert, and Joseph Avivi. 1989. *Registres matrimoniaux de la communauté juive portugaise de Tunis aux XVIIIe et XIXe siècles*. Jerusalem: Makhon Ben Zvi.

Attal, Robert, and Meira Harosh. 1986/87. Ha-defus ha-ʿivri be-Aljir. *Kiryat Sefer* 61: 561–72.

Avishur, Yiṣḥaq. 1988. Ha-targumim la-tanakh ba-ʿaravit-yehudit ba-mizraḥ ba-ʿet ha-ḥadasha. In Mose Bar-Asher (ed.), *Meḥqarim bi-lshonot ha-yehudim*, 39–54. Jerusalem: Misgav Yerushalayim.

———. 1998. Targume tanakh rabbaniyyim ba-ʿaravit-yehudit ba-meʾot ha-12-15 veziqqatam le-targum r. seʿadia gaʾon. *Teʿuda* 14: 1–18.

———. 2003. *He-ḥakham ha-bavli mi-calcutta*, 2 vols. Tel Aviv: Pirsume Merkaz Archeologi.

Avrahami, Yiṣḥaq. 1980. ʿAdat ha-grāna be-tunis le-or pinqaseha: ha-maʾavaq ʿal ha-otonomia. In Michel Abitbol (ed.), *Yahadut sfon afriqa ba-meʾot 19–20*, 64–95. Jerusalem: Makhon Ben Zvi.

———. 1986. Tahalikhe demoqratizaṣia bi-qhillat yehude tunis: mi-qāʾid memunne le-moʿeṣa nivḥeret. *Shorashim Ba-Mizraḥ* 1: 37–80.

———. 1989. Yehude tunisia taḥat shilṭon vishi ve-ha-kibbush ha-germani, October 1940–May 1943, yaḥas ha-memshal ve-ha-seviva. *Shorashim Ba-Mizraḥ* 2: 440–43.

Bar-Asher, Moshe. 1986. Le Diminutif dans les dialectes judéo-arabes du Tāfilalt. *Massorot* 2 (French section): 1–14.

Bar-Ḥen, Eliyahu. 1988. *Penine ḥen: Sippurim ʿal yehude tunis*. Kefar Ḥabad, Israel (no publisher given).

Bar-Tiqva, Binyamin. 1988. *Piyyuṭe r. yaʿaqov ibn-ṣur*. Jerusalem: Misgav Yerushalayim.

Benayahu, Meir. 1959a. *Rabbi Ḥayyim Yosef Azulay*. Jerusalem: Mossad Harav Kook.

———. 1959b. *Sefer ha-ḥida: Qoveṣ maʾamarim u-meḥqarim*. Jerusalem: Mossad Harav Kook.

Ben Halima, Hamadi. 1974. *Un demi-siècle de théâtre arabe en Tunisie*. Tunis: Université de Tunis.

Bismuth-Jarrassé, Collete, and Dominique Jarrassé. 2010. *Synagogues de Tunisie: monuments d'une histoire et d'une identité*. Paris: Editions Esthétiques du Divers.

Blau, Yehoshua. 1981. *The Emergence and Background of Judeo-Arabic*. Jerusalem.

Bold, Alan. 1979. *The Ballad*. London: Methuen.

Brann, Ross. 1992. *The Compunctious Poet: Cultural Ambiguity and Hebrew Poetry in Muslim Spain*. Baltimore: Johns Hopkins University Press.

Brown, L. C. 1974. *The Tunisia of Ahmad Bey, 1837–1855*. Princeton, NJ: Princeton University Press.

Būdhīna, Muhammad. 1992. *Mashāhīr al-tūnisiyyīn*. al-Ḥamāmāt, Tunisia: Manshūrāt Būdhīna.

Cassuto, M. D. 1936. Mi-shire yosef ben shemuel ṣarfati: ha-qomedia ha-rishona be-ʿivrit. In *Salo Baron and Alexander Marx (eds.), Meḥqarim le-zikhron r. ʿamram qohut*: 121–28. New York: Ha-Mossad Le-Zikhron ʿAmram Qohut.

Cazès, David. 1888. *Sur l'histoire des Israëlites de Tunisie*. Paris: Duriacher.

———. 1893. *Notes bibliographiques sur la littérature juive tunisienne*. Tunis: Imprimerie Internationale.

Chanhaz. 1962. Chanteuse d'hier et d'aujourd'hui: Habiba M'sika. *Faiza* 27 (July–August): 45, 70.

Chetrit, Joseph. 1980a. Frēḥa bat yosef: meshoreret ʿivriyya be-maroqo ba-meʾa ha-18. *Peʿamim* 4: 84–93; reprinted in *Peʿamim* 55: 124–130 (1993) and in Chetrit, *Piyyuṭ veshira be-yahadut maroqo*. Jerusalem: Hebrew University, 1999. 147–68.

———. 1980b. L'Influence de Français dans les langues judéo-arabes d'Afrique du Nord. In Michel Abitbol (ed.), *Judaïsme d'Afrique du Nord aux XIXe–XXe siècles*, 125–59. Jerusalem.

———. 1981. Ha-shira ha-ʾishit ve-ha-ḥevratit ba-ʿaravit yehudit shel yehude maroqo. *Mi-Qedem U-Mi-Yam* 1: 185–230.

———. 1983. R. David Elqāim: meshorer ʿivri be-maroqo. *Appirion* 1: 96–102. Enlarged version appears in Chetrit, *Piyyuṭ ve-shira be-yahadut maroqo* (1999): 277–315.

———. 1986. Mudaʿut ḥadasha la-anomaliyut ve-la-lashon: niṣṣaneha shel tnuʿat haskala ʿivrit be-maroqo be-sof ha-meʾa ha-19. *Mi-Qedem U-Mi-Yam* 2: 129–68.

———. 1989. Yesodot ʿivriyyim ba-ʿaravit shel yehude maroqo: lesono shel shir muslemi bi-lvush yehudi. *Massorot* 3–4: 203–84.

———. 1990. Moderniyyut leummit ʿivrit mul moderniyyut ṣarfatit: ha-haskala ha-ʿivrit bi-ṣfon afriqa be-sof ha-meʾa ha-19. *Mi-Qedem U-Mi-Yam* 3: 11–76.

———. 1991. Tenuʿat ha-haskala ha-ʿivrit be-maroqo be-sof ha-meʾa ha-18 u-trumata le-hitʿorerut ha-ṣiyyonut. In Yissakhar Ben ʿAmi (ed.), *Meḥqarim be-tarbutam shel yehude sfon-afriqa*, 313–31. Jerusalem: Vaʿad ʿAdat Ha-Maʿaravim.

———. 1994. *Ha-shira ha-ʿaravit yehudit she-bi-khtav bi-sfon-afriqa: ʿiyyunim poʾeṭiyyim, leshoniyyim ve-tarbutiyyim*. Jerusalem: Misgav Yerushalayim.

———. 1999. *Piyyuṭ ve-shira be-yahadut maroqo: asufat meḥqarim ʿal shirim ve-ʿal meshorerim*. Jerusalem: Hebrew University.

Cohen, Binyamin Refa'el. 1986. *Malkhe tarshish*. Netivot, Israel: self-published.

Cohen, David. 1964/75. *Le Parler arabe des juifs de Tunis*, 2 vols. Paris–La Haye: Mouton.

Cohen Hadria, E. 1976. *Du Protectorat français à l'indépendance tunisienne*. Nice: Centre de la Méditerranée Moderne et Contemporaine.

Darmon, Raoul. 1951. Un presque siècle de théâtre à Tunis. *Bulletin Economique et Social de la Tunisie* 52 (May).

David, Yona. 1972. *Ha-mahazot shel moshe ḥayyim luzatto*. Jerusalem: ʿAkhshav.

Davidson, Israel. 1907. *Parody in Jewish Literature*. New York: Columbia University Press.

———. 1923. *Oṣar ha-shira ve-ha-piyyuṭ*. New York: Jewish Theological Seminary.

Elmāleḥ, Avraham. 1928. Mustaʿrabim u-portugezim be-tunisia (le-toldot ha-perud ben ʿadat ha-tunisim ve-ha-livornim be-tunis). *Mizraḥ U-Maʿarav* 2: 19–28, 120–27.

———. 1929. Me-ḥayye ha-yehudim bi-tripolitanya. *Mizraḥ U-Maʿarav* 3: 50–55, 124–35.

———. 1946. Serid meshorere sefarad be-aljiria ha-rav yiṣḥaq marʿeli. In Avraham Elmaleḥ (ed.), *Ḥemdat Yisrael: Qoveṣ le-zikhro shel R. Ḥ. Ḥ. Medini*, 43–85. Jerusalem: Bet Ḥolim Misgav La-Dakh.

Ettinger, Shmu'el (ed.). 1981/86. *Toledot ha-yehudim be-arṣot ha-islam*, 3 vols. Jerusalem: Merkaz Shazar.

Fenton, Yosef Yinnon. 1980. Teshuva le-r. shemuʾel ben ʿeli gaʾon mi-baghdād be-ʿinyan ha-musiqa. *Taṣlil* 11: 12–13.

Fleischer, H. L. 1864. Jüdische-arabische aus Maghreb. *Zeitschrift der Deutschen Morgenländischen Gesellschaft* 18: 329–40.

Fraenkel, J. 1982. *L'Imprimerie hébraïque à Djerba*. Diss., Université de Paris III.

Frances, Immanu'el. 1932. *Dīwān*, ed. Shimʿon Bernstein. Tel Aviv: Dvir.

Frances, Yaʿaqov. 1969. *Kol shire yaʿaqov frances*, ed. Penina Nave. Jerusalem: Mossad Bialik.

Friedberg, Ḥayyim Dov. 1952. *Bet ʿeqed sefarim*. Tel Aviv (no publisher given).

Friedman, A. B. 1961. *The Ballad Revival: Studies in the Influence of Popular on Sophisticated Poetry*. Chicago: University of Chicago Press.

———. 1982. *The Penguin Book of Folk Ballads of the English-Speaking World*. Harmondsworth, UK: Penguin.

Gamli'eli, N. B. 1979. *Ahavat teman: shirat ha-nashim be-teman, ha-shira ha-ʿamamit*. Tel Aviv: N. B. Gamli'eli U-Vanav.

Ganiage, J. 1968. *Les origines du protectorat français en Tunisie, 1861–1881*. Tunis: Maison tunisienne de l'édition.

Guez, Gaston. 1943. *Tadhkarat al-khaddāma al-yahūd taḥt ghill almānya fī tūnis* (*Nos Martyres sous la botte Allemande*). Tunis: Uzan.

Guiramand, Simone. 1977. *Kaeéna: drame historique en cinq actes*. Tunis: Maison Tunisienne de l'édition.

Ha-Cohen, Mordekhai. 1979. *Higgid mordekhai*, ed. Harvey Goldberg. Jerusalem: Makhon Ben Zvi.

Ḥadad, ʿAmos. 1965. Bourguiba ve-ha-yehudim be-arṣo. *Ha-Areṣ* 11 (Adar II): 14.

Ḥagège, Daniel. 1939. *Intishār al-ktāʾib al-yahūdiyya al-barbariyya al-tūnisiyya*. Sousse, Tunisia: Makhlūf Najjār.

Ḥakham, Shimʿon. 1906. *Sippure maʿasiyyot*. Jerusalem (no publisher given).

Halevi, Ṣemaḥ. n.d. *ʿAṭeret yeshuʿa*. Tunis: Uzan.

Ha-Nagid, Shemu'el. 1966. *Dīwān: ben tehillim*, ed. Dov Yarden. Jerusalem: D. Yarden.

Harosh, Meira. 1984. Ha-defus ha-ʿivri bi-tripoli she-be-luv. *Kiryat Sefer* 59: 625–34.

Hassine, Juliette. 2012. *Sūlīqa ha-ṣaddeqet harugat ha-malkhut*. Jerusalem: Mossad Bialik.

Ḥazan, Efraim, ed. 1976. *Shire frājī shawwāṭ*. Jerusalem: Makhon Ben Zvi.

———. 1984. Lashon ve-signon be-shirat r. david qāʾim. *Peʿamim* 17: 53–75.

———. 1987. Ha-reqaʿ ha-du leshoni li-ṣmiḥat shire maṭrūz (riqma) bi-ṣfon afriqa. *Peʿamim* 30: 23–40.

Ḥazan, Efraim, and Raḥel Ḥitin. 2012. *Mi kamokha: piyyuṭim ʿal nes ve-haṣṣala meqomiyyim bi-qhillot ṣefon afriqa*. Beersheva: Ben Gurion University.

Hillare, Jean. 1918. *Le Kahéna: drame historique en cinq actes, en vers*. Rouen: Henri Defontaines.

Hirschberg, H. Z. 1965. *Toledot ha-yehudim be-afriqa ha-ṣefonit*, 2 vols. Jerusalem: Mossad Bialik.

Hoummous, 1987. Habiba Messika. *Libération*, May 13: 50.

Huss, Matti. 1983. Sippur ʿagavim o mashal musari: meliṣat ʿefer ve-dina le-don vidal benbenest. *Meḥqere Yerushalayim Be-Sifrut ʿIvrit* 14: 113–53.

———. 1995. Allegoria u-vidion: sugiyot bi-qviʿat meʾafyenav shel ha-modus ha-allegori ba-sipporet ha-meḥorezet ha-ʿivrit bi-sfarad. In Reuven Tsur and Tova Rozen (eds.), *Sefer israel levin: qoveṣ meḥqarim ba-sifrut ha-ʿivrit le-doroteha*, 1: 95–126. Tel Aviv: Tel Aviv University.

Ibn ʿAbd Rabbihi al-Andalūsī. 1928. *al-ʿIqd al-farīd*, v. 2. Cairo: al-Azhāriyyah.

Ibn Ezra, Moshe. 1975. *Sefer ha-ʿiyyunim ve-ha-diyyunim*, ed. A. S. Halqin. Jerusalem: Meqitse Nirdamin.

Ibn Qayyim al-Jawziya. 1991. *Kashf al-ghaṭaʾ ʿan ḥukm samāʿ al-ghināʾ*, ed. Rabīʿ ibn Aḥmad al-Khalaf. Cairo: Dār al-jīl lil-ṭabʿ wa-al-nashr wa-al-tawzīʿ.

Idrīs, Muḥammad Masʿūd. 1993. *Dirāsāt fī taʾrīkh al-masraḥ al-tūnisī*. Tunis: Dār saḥr lil-nashr.

Ilan, Naḥem. 1993. Midrash ʿal avraham avinu be-haggada shel pesaḥ shel yehude Jerba. *Sefunot* 21: 167–96.

———. 1996. Drasha memaṣṣaʿat ba-haggada shel pesah: ʿiyyun be-dugmat haggada mi-tunis me-reshit ha-meʾa ha-20. In B. Z. Qedar (ed.), *Ha-tarbut ha-ʿamamit: qoveṣ meḥqarim*, 305–26. Jerusalem: Merkaz Shazar.

Immanuel, Ha-Romi. 1957. *Maḥbarot*, ed. Dov Yarden. Jerusalem.

Kapeliouq, Menaḥem. 1963. Me-ha-shira ha-ʿamamit shel teman. *Ha-Mizraḥ He-Ḥadash* 13: 324–28.

Karmi, Janine. 1986. Be-darkhe ha-emanṣipaṣia: soṣiyalist yehudi be-tunis be-reshit ha-meʾa: Albert Cattan (1875–1932). *Shorasim Ba-Mizraḥ* 1: 81–120.

Landau, Jacob M. 1958. *Studies in the Arab Theater and Cinema*. Philadelphia: University of Pennsylvania Press. Translated into French under the title *Etudes sur la théâtre et la cinéma arabes* (Paris, 1965).

Laskier, Michael M. 1991. The Jews of France and North African Jewry: The Alliance Israélite Universelle's Political Encounters with the French-Educated Elite of Tunisia, Morocco, and Algeria. In Issachar Ben-Ami (ed.), *Recherches sur la culture des Juifs d'Afrique du Nord*, lxxxiii–xcviii. Jerusalem: Communauté Israélite Nord-Africaine.

Levin, Israel. 1973. *'Al Mot: Ha-qina 'al ha-met be-shirat ha-ḥol ha-'ivrit bi-sfarad 'al reqa' ha-qina ba-shira ha-'aravit*. Tel Aviv: Tel Aviv University.

Lewin, B. M. 1934. Teshuvot rav haye ga'on le-qābes. *Ginze Qedem* 5: 33–35, 58–59.

Marçais, William, and Abderrahmān Guiga. 1960. *Textes arabes de Takroūna*, v. 2, *Glossaire*. Paris: P. Geuthner.

Marciano, Eliyahu. 1989. *Sefer bne melakhim ve-hu toledot ha-sefer ha-'ivri be-maroqo mi-shenat 1517 'ad shenat 1989*. Jerusalem: Makhon Ha-Rasham.

Marzūqī, Muḥammad al-. 1967. *al-Adab al-sha'bī fī tūnis*. Tunis: al-Dār al-tūnisī lil-nashr.

Maume, Jean-Louis. 1970. *Situation du Théâtre Tunisien*. Paris (no publisher given)

Melkman, Joseph. 1951. *David Franco Mendes*. Jerusalem: Massadah.

———. 1966. Ha-maḥaze 'yesod 'olam' le-rabbi moshe zakut. *Sefunot* 10: 299–333.

Mettrop, A. 1971. (No title given). *Institut des belles lettres arabes* 34: 194–95.

Mi-qartago li-yerushalayim: ha-qehilla ha-yehudit ba-'ir tunis. 1986. Tel Aviv: Bet Ha-Tefuṣot.

Moreh, Shmuel. 1974. *Ḥibbure yehudim ba-lashon ha-'aravit 1863–1973*. Jerusalem: Makhon Ben Zvi.

———. 1978. Ha-yeṣira ha-ruḥanit shel yehude 'iraq ba-safa ha-'aravit. *Meḥqarim Ba-'Aaravit U-Va-Islam* 2: 60–68.

———. 1987. The Shadow Play (*Khayāl al-ẓill*) in the Light of Arabic Literature. *Journal of Arabic Literature* 18: 46–61.

———. 1992. *Live Theater and Dramatic Literature in the Medieval Arab World*. New York: New York University Press.

Moreh, Shmuel, and Philip Sadgrove. 1996. *Jewish Contributions to Nineteenth-Century Arabic Theatre*. Oxford, UK: Oxford University Press.

Naḥum, A. S. 1925. *Shire ha-teḥiyya*. Baghdad: A. Shoḥeṭ.

Najjār, Makhlūf. 1919. *Kitāb snāwī*. Sousse, Tunisia: Makhlūf Najjār.

Najm, Yūsīf. 1963. *Ya'qūb Sanū'*. Beirut: Dār al-thaqāfah lil-ṭaba'ah wa-al-nashr wa-al-tawzī'.

Nicholson, Reynold A. 1969. *A Literary History of the Arabs*. Cambridge, UK: Cambridge University Press.

Preminger, Alex, and T. V. F. Brogan, eds. 1993. *The New Princeton Encyclopedia of Poetry and Poetics*. Princeton, NJ: Princeton University Press.

Pronier, Ernest. 1942. *Une vie au théâter: Sarah Bernhardt*. Geneva: A. Jullien.

Raccāḥ, Gabriel. 1945. *Reshima shel kitve yad rabbane ve-ḥakhme ṭripoloṭania*. Tripoli (no publisher given).

Raccāḥ, Ya'aqov. 1858. *Qeshurim le-ya'aqov*. Livorno: Ben Amozeg.

———. 1863. *Oraḥ mishor*. Livorno: Shlomo Belforti.

Ratzahbi, Yehuda. 1980. Maqāma 'aravit me-'eṭo shel alḥarizi. *Biqqoret U-Farshanut* 15: 5–51.

———. 1986. Shire qaṣīd temanyyim. *Yuval* 5: 169–91.

———. 1997. Shira ʿaravit be-fi yehudim be-andalusya. In Reuven Tsur and Tova Rozen (eds.), *Sefer israel levin: qoveṣ meḥqarim ba-sifrut ha-ʿivrit le-doroteha*, 1: 329–50. Tel Aviv: Tel Aviv University.

Rojas, Fernando de. 1963. *La Celestina*, trans. Yaʿaqov Israel Fink. Tel Aviv: Maḥbarot le-Sifrut.

———. 2009. *La Celestina*, trans. Peter Bush. New York: Penguin Classics.

Roudié, Emile. 1922. *Le Kahena: piece en quatre actes, en vers*. Paris: Libre théâtrale.

Saadoun, Haim. 2005a. Irgun ha-qhilla. In Haim Saadoun (ed.), *Tunisia*, 71–84. Jerusalem: Ma-khon Ben Zvi.

———. 2005b. Ha-ṣiyyonut. In Haim Saadoun (ed.), *Tunisia*, 171–83. Jerusalem: Makhon Ben Zvi.

———. 2010. Alfred Valensi. In Norman A. Stillman (ed.), *Encyclopedia of the Jews in the Islamic World*, 4: 590–591. Leiden: Brill.

Sadan, Joseph. 1996. Rabbi yehuda alḥarizi ke-ṣomet tarbuti: biografia ʿaravit shel yoṣer yehudi. *Peʿamim* 68: 16–67.

Saraf, Michal. 1979. Ha-sifrut ha-yehudit be-tunisya: mifʿal bibliography. *Peʿamim* 3: 90–93.

———. 1984. Frājī shawwāṭ hu refaʾel mallaḥ meshorer noded be-tunis. In Zvi Malachi (ed.), *Yad le-heman: qoveṣ maʾamarim le-zekher a. m. habermann*, 244–77. Lod, Israel: Makhon Habermann.

———. 1986. R. avraham khalfon: hisṭoryon ve-ish eshkolot bi-tripoli ba-meʾa ha-18-19. In Zvi Malachi (ed.), *Be-oraḥ maddaʿ: mehqarim be-torat israel muggashim le-aharon mirski*, 403–28. Lod, Israel: Makhon Habermann.

———. 1987. Daniel ḥagège ve-ḥibburo ʿal toeldot ha-sifrut ha-ʿaravit yehudit be-tunisia 1862–1939. *Peʿamim* 30: 41–59.

———. 1988. *Megillat hiṭler bi-ṣfon afriqa: sifrut yehudit be-maroqo u-v-tunisia ʿal mappelet ha-naṣim*. Lod, Israel: Makhon Habermann.

Schirmann, Ḥayyim. 1946. *Ha-maḥaze ha-ʿivri ha-rishon, ṣaḥut bediḥuta de-qiddushin: qomedya be-ḥamesh maʿarakhot me-et yehuda somo ish mantuba (1527–1592)*. Jerusalem: Tarshish.

———. 1957. *Ha-shira ha-ʿivrit bi-sfarad u-bi-provence*. Jerusalem: Mossad Bialik.

———. 1980. *Le-toledot ha-shira ve-ha-drama ha-ʿivrit: meḥqarim u-massot*, 2 vols. Jerusalem: Mossad Bialik.

Sebag, Paul. 2002. *Les noms de juifs de Tunisie: origines et significations*. Paris: Harmattan.

Sharabāni, Naʿīm. 1969. *Ha-sifrut ha-ʿaravit ha-yehudit shel yehude bavel*. Jerusalem.

Sharaf al-Dīn, al-Munṣif. 1997. *Min ruwwād al-masraḥ al-tūnisī wa-aʿlāmih*. Tunis: al-Maktabah al-ʿatīqah.

Shokeid, Moshe, and Shlomo Deshen. 1977. *Shinnuy ve-hemshekhiyyut be-ʿolamam shel yoṣʾe ṣefon-afriqa*. Jerusalem: Makhon Ben Zvi.

Slouschz, Nahum. 1918. Sifrut-ʿam bi-yehudit ʿaravit. *Luʾaḥ Aḥiʿever* 1: 73–89.

———. 1933. *Dahiyya al-kāhina malkat afriqa*. Tel Aviv: Omanut.

———. 1943. *Massaʿi be-ereṣ luv*, v. 1. Tel Aviv: Vaʿad Ha-Yovel.

Souriau-Hoebrechts, Christiane. 1969. *La Presse Maghrebine*. Paris: CNRS.

Stern, M. 1963. Arabic Poems by Spanish-Hebrew Poets. In Moshe Lazar (ed.), *Romanica et occidentalia: études dédiées à la mémoires de Hirma Peri*, 254–63. Jerusalem: Magnes.

Stillman, Norman. 1991. *Jews of Arab Lands in Modern Times*. Philadelphia: Jewish Publication Society.

Sukkari, Yaʿaqov. 1882. *Yoru mishpatekha le-yaʿaqov*. Calcutta: Eliyahu Moshe Dweik Ha-Cohen.

Taïeb, Jacques. 1989. Yehude tunis ben shte milḥamot ha-ʿolam. *Shorashim Ba-Misraḥ* 2: 369–401.

Le Théâtre arabe à Tunis. 1932. *Revue des Etudes Islamiques* 4: 537–44.

Tobi, Tsivia. 2012a. *From Bride to Mother-in-Law: The Women's World in the Jewish Communities of Southern Tunisia During the First Half of the 20th Century*. Diss., Hebrew University, Jerusalem.

———. 2012b. Ha-rav ha-maskil eliʿezer farḥi vi-yṣirotav ha-saṭiriyyot (Tunis 1851–1930). *Ben ʿEver La-ʿArav* 5: 127–44.

Tobi, Yosef. 1982. *Kitve ha-yad ha-temanyyim bi-mkhon ben-zvi*. Jerusalem.

———. 1986. *ʿIyyunim bi-mgillat teman*. Jerusalem: Merkaz Shazar.

———. 1988. Hashqafato shel r. yehoshuaʿ benbenest (Constantinople 1634) ʿal takhlita shel ha-shira. *Dappim Le-Meḥqar Be-Sifrut* 4: 19–34.

———. 1991. Targumim u-millonim ʿarviyyīm le-ʿmishne tora' la-rambam. *Sefunot* 20: 203–22.

———. 2007. L'ouverture de la littérature judéo-arabe tunisienne à la littérature arabo-musulmane. In Denis Tanouji-Cohen (ed.), *Entre Orient et Occident: Juifs et Mosulmans en Tunisie*, 255–75. Paris: Editions de l'Eclat.

———. 2008. Targumim ʿarviyyīm yehudiyyim li-tfillot ha-qevaʿ ve-la-piyyuṭim. *Masoret ha-Piyyut* 4: 169–203.

———. 2009. Ha-yaḥas la-safa ha-ʿivrit ve-limmuda be-tunisia be-shilhe ha-meʾa ha-teshaʿ esre u-va-meʾa ha-ʿesrim. In Efraim Ḥazan and Ḥaim Saadoun (eds.), *Tarshish: Meḥqarim Be-Yahadut Tunisia U-Morashta*, 269–310. Ramat Gan, Israel: Bar Ilan University.

———. 2010a. *Between Hebrew and Arabic Poetry: Studies in Spanish Medieval Hebrew Poetry*. Leiden: Brill.

———. 2010b. Literature, Judeo-Arabic. In Norman Stillman (ed.), *Encyclopedia of Jews in the Islamic World*, 3: 271–78. Leiden: Brill.

———. 2010c. Messika, Ḥabiba. In Norman A. Stillman (ed.), *Encyclopedia of the Jews in the Islamic World*, 3: 408. Leiden: Brill.

———. 2013a. Judeo-Arabic as Reflected in Jewish Theatrical Arts in Tunis During the 20th Century. *Quaderni di Semitistica* 28: 363–80.

———. 2013b. *al-Najma: ʿitton al-najma shel makhlūf najjār* (in press).

———. 2013c. *Ha-Qol: Ha-sofer ve-ha-meḥannekh refaʾel levi (ryvel) ve-teʾaṭron les escholiers (ha-qol) shel bogre bet ha-sefer ʿkol israel ḥaverim' be-tunis* (in press).

Tsur, Yaron. 1986. The Two Jewish Communities of Tunis (Touansa and Grana) on the Eve of the Colonial Period. *Proceedings of the Ninth World Congress of Jewish Studies*, Div. B, 3: 67–73.

———. 1988. *Ṣarfat vi-yehude tunisia: ha-mediniyyut ha-ṣarfatit klape yehude ha-medina u-fʿilut ha-ʿillitot ha-yehudiyyot ba-maʿavar mi-shilṭon muslemi ʿaṣmaʾi le-shilṭon qolonyali 1873–1888*. Diss., Hebrew University, Jerusalem.

———. 1990. Yahadut tunisia be-shilhe ha-tequfa ha-ṭrom-qolonyalit. *Mi-Qedem U-Mi-Yam* 3: 67–113.

———. 2010. ʿAhd al-Amān. In Norman A. Stillman (ed.), *Encyclopedia of the Jews in the Islamic World*, 1: 93–94. Leiden: Brill.

Turkī, Zubayr al-. 1967. *al-Aghānī al-tūnisiyya*. Tunis: al-Dār al-tunisiyya lil-nashr.

Vajda, Georges. 1978. Judaeo-Arabic Literature. In *Encyclopedia of Islam*, 4: 303–7. Leiden: Brill.

Vance, Sharon. 2011. *The Martyrdom of a Moroccan Jewish Saint*. Leiden: Brill.

Vassel, Eusèbe. 1904. *La littérature populaire des Israélites tunisiens*. Paris. (Addition published in 1907.)

———. 1908. *Satire judéo-tunisienne contre les Juifs de Djerba*. *Revue Tunisienne* 15: 121–34.

Verses, Shmuel. 1989. *Ha-Targumim le-yiddish shel 'ahavat ṣiyyon' le-avraham mapu.* Jerusalem: Akademon.

Ya'ari, Avraham. 1932. Avraham mapu ben yehude arṣot ha-mizraḥ. *Moznayim* 3.48: 10–12. Revised version: Mi-qovna 'ad teman: 'Ahavat Ṣiyyon' shel mapu ben niddeḥe israel be-arṣot ha-mizraḥ, *Ma'ariv*, April 8, 1955.

———. 1937/40. *Ha-defus ha-'ivri be-arṣot ha-mizraḥ*, 2 vols. Jerusalem.

Yaniv, Bracha. 1994. Hashpa'ot me-italia u-mi-ṣarfat 'al 'iṣṣuv tiqe sefer tora be-luv u-ve-tunisia. *Pe'amim* 57: 82–113.

Yaniv, Shlomo. 1986. *Ha-Balada ha-'ivrit: praqim be-hitpatḥutah*. Haifa: University of Haifa.

———. 1999. *Ha-Balada ha-'ivrit bat zemannenu: masoret ve-ḥiddush*. Haifa: University of Haifa.

Yasif, 'Eli. 1982. Terumato shel sefer ose pele la-sipporet ha-'amamait ha-yehudit. *Meḥqere Yerushlayim Be-Folklor Yehudi* 3: 47–66.

Zafrani, Haim. 1980. *Littératures dialectales et populaires juives en occident musulman: L'ecrit et l'oral*. Paris.

Zuareṣ, Frīja, Ammishddai Gwayṭa', and Ṣuri'el Shaqed (eds.). 1960. *Yahadut luv*. Tel Aviv: Va'ad Qehillot Luv.

Zuareṣ, Frīja, and Frīja Ṭayyar. 1972. *Se'u zimra*. Tel Aviv: Va'ad Qehillot Luv.

INDEX

Name Index

Subject Index

Place Index

Books Index

www.ingramcontent.com/pod-product-compliance
Lightning Source LLC
Chambersburg PA
CBHW060543310726
48982CB00009B/1359/J

* 9 7 8 0 8 1 4 3 2 8 7 1 2 *